LOCAL LABOUR AND

A study of cha...
politics and policy in Southwark
from 1919 to 1982

I should be happy if . . . social scientists would . . . see history as an exceptional means of discovery and research. Is not the present after all in large measure the prisoner of a past that obstinately survives, and the past with its rules, its differences and its similarities the indispensible key to any serious understanding of the present?

Braudel, *Civilisation and Capitalism 15th–18th Century*, vol. 3
The Perspective of the World, foreword.

LOCAL LABOUR
AND
LOCAL GOVERNMENT

A study of changing interests,
politics and policy in Southwark
from 1919 to 1982

SUE GOSS

EDINBURGH UNIVERSITY PRESS

© Sue Goss 1988
Edinburgh University Press
22 George Square, Edinburgh

Set in Linotron Times Roman
by Photoprint, Torquay, and
printed in Great Britain by
Redwood Burn Limited,
Trowbridge, Wilts

British Library Cataloguing
 in Publication Data
Goss, Sue
    Local Labour and local government : a study
    of changing interests, politics and policy
    in Southwark from 1919 to 1982.
    1. London. Southwark (London Borough)
    Local government. Role of Labour Party
    (Great Britain), 1919–1982.
    I. Title.
    352.0421′64

ISBN 0 85224 585 8
ISBN 0 85224 586 6 Pbk

Contents

Acknowledgements

This book originated with a PhD thesis at Sussex university. Thanks go to all my colleagues there, but the book owes most to the patient support of John Dearlove, who kept the project down to earth, and constantly advised me to 'keep it short' and 'get it finished'. I would like to thank the large number of Southwark councillors and activists who gave me hours of their time and especially those who gave me access to precious documents, including Fanny Stroud, Fred Francis, John O'Grady and Rod Robertson. Discussions with many friends proved invaluable, particularly discussions with Stewart Lansley, from which the concept of 'front-lash' originated. Jenny Shepherd and John Reynolds gave badly needed stylistic advice. I am especially grateful to Mark Leopold who not only typed the thesis with rare accuracy, but acted as discussant, advisor, spell-check programme and friend rolled into one. Finally thanks to Dick, who believed in me, even when the going got rough.

List of Abbreviations

AMA	Association of Metropolitan Authorities
AMC	Association of Metropolitan Councils
BSA	Building Societies Association
BSP	British Socialist Party
CCCS	Centre for Contemporary Cultural Studies
CDP	Community Development Project
CIPFA	Chartered Institute of Public Finance and Accountancy
CP	Communist Party
CRE	Commission for Racial Equality
CURS	Centre for Urban and Regional Studies
FWW	Federation of Women Workers
GLC	Greater London Council
GMC	General Management Committee
IEA	Institute of Economic Affairs
ILEA	Inner London Education Authority
ILP	Independent Labour Party
LCC	London County Council
LSE	London School of Economics
MHLG	Ministry of Housing and Local Government
MOH	Medical Officer of Health
MORI	Market and Opinion Research International
MP	Member of Parliament
NALGO	National Association of Local Government Officers
NEC	National Executive Committee (of the Labour Party)
NHS	National Health Service
NSCDG	North Southwark Community Development Group
NUR	National Union of Railwaymen
NUWM	National Unemployed Workers' Movement
PWLB	Public Works Loan Board
SAUS	School of Advanced Urban Studies
SCVS	Southwark Council for Voluntary Services
SDP	Social Democratic Party

SDF	Social Democratic Federation
SHAC	Shelter Housing Aid Centre
TB	Tuberculosis
TGWU	Transport and General Workers' Union
UGC	Unemployment Grants Committee
UNESCO	United Nations Educational, Scientific and Cultural Organisation

Introduction

THIS book examines community, Labour and local government in Southwark during the period 1919–82. It examines the nature of the local political culture that developed over this period, and how far it was represented both in the ideas of the local Labour party and in the policies of Labour in local government. In examining the changes that have taken place, a number of contemporary questions are raised in relation to the nature of class and other social cleavages, the nature of the Labour Party and its declining support, and the present crisis facing local government.

I was prompted to undertake this study because, as an active participant in local politics during the late 1970s and 1980s, it seemed to me that the available theories, in both the academic and the person-in-the-street sense of the word, did not adequately explain the events going on around me. Over the last five years local government has been a site of great political excitement. New radical initiatives in local government, the shifts towards both decentralised services and a decentralising philosophy in some Labour authorities, the increasing struggles between central and local government – these would all provide the raw material for interesting research. At the time when I began this study, 'new urban Left' councils were poised to take over in Southwark as well as Islington, Camden, Greenwich, Lewisham, Hackney and elsewhere. It would have seemed obvious, in some way, to concentrate on these new initiatives; comparing the performances of different local authorities, or contrasting the achievements of a 'new Left' local authority with its manifesto, and attempting to draw conclusions about the limits of local government; or exploring the struggles between one or more local authorities and the Thatcher government. But, as I thought myself into the subject further, these areas of study seemed to beg a series of important questions.

I questioned the formulation of the problem facing Labour in local government that the strategies of the new Left were designed to solve. Local activists on the Left saw the problem as that of an old, élitist, moribund party which had lost support by opposing local community campaigns, by failing to consult or involve local people, and by failing to follow socialist policies which would have won support, or to defend local services against cut-backs. Hence, it was argued, the local party and local population could be reanimated and reunified by new participatory structures, by vigorous socialist policies, and by a strong policy of confrontation with the government. But how adequate was this, either as an assessment or as a programme?

This question led, in its turn, to others. I felt an unhappiness, politically and intellectually, at the complete polarisation between the two 'sides' within the Labour Party locally. This polarisation created a climate within which events were 'explained' by putting total blame on 'the other side'. Hence, for the Left, the loss of Labour's support could be attributed to the misdeeds of the Right. Similarly, for the Right, any loss of support inevitably followed from the Left's preoccupation with confrontation, socialism, and support for dotty schemes and minority interests, instead of addressing itself to the pragmatic concerns of the working class. Both Left and Right seemed to refer back to a 'tradition betrayed', and the need to return to the status quo ante, a golden past. But had there been such a past? And, if there had, could both Left and Right possibly refer for inspiration to the same one?

Similarly, both Left and Right appealed to 'the working class' and working-class interests. These interests were introduced as a totem; they were known in advance – there was no effort to find out from local people what their interests were – and they were entirely circular. Thus, for example, the Left argued that, since the sale of council houses was known to be against working-class interests, to attempt to support the sale of council houses was to be, *de facto*, against the working class. They assumed a homogeneous working class to which interests could be attached, and which were *represented* by one faction or another. But what was the local working class? Did it have interests? And how far were they represented by Labour?

In all this there was a feeling that the major structural upheavals in the local economy and local community had not been translated into the language and ideas of the local Labour Party. Simple assumptions about the nature of the working class made it impossible to analyse the composition of the new community, or to understand divisions or conflicts within it. It seemed, dimly, that there was trouble ahead. Finally, the Bermondsey by-election fiasco, the defeat in Bermondsey at the 1983 general election and a series of council by-election defeats for Labour showed that we were not witnessing a temporary dip of support in a solid Labour area. In Bermondsey, the roof had fallen in on Labour. The question was why. Why had the area been solidly Labour before, and why was it no longer so?

All these questions pushed my attention further back in time. In order to understand what was happening to Labour in Southwark, it seemed important to examine what had gone before. At the same time it seemed impossible to examine just local government, or just the Labour Party, or just the local community. These areas seemed to overlap constantly.

The available academic theories did not provide a very useful framework for thinking about these problems. Firstly, there is no obvious body of literature that had built up and refined the study of Labour in local politics, and to which I could relate my study. What work there has been, and it has been excellent,[2] has addressed earlier periods, and has been firmly based in historiography. My concerns are, however, firmly rooted within political science, and I have therefore brought together literature from within several disciplines, relating to cultural studies, work on class, cleavages and interests, studies of Labour and labourism, local government studies and work on the state, in order to try and show the interrelations between areas of study traditionally treated in isolation.

Secondly the present 'state of the art' admits of no single fashionable theory within which empirical work in political science can be neatly fitted. For the moment, I believe that advances will be made through empirical analysis. That is not to suggest that theory and empirical work are in some way separable, or that empirical work is external to theory. But it is to make a point about the appropriate level of theorisation.

Considerable damage has been done, theoretically and practically, by a local state literature which hitched local politics to a structuralist analysis, in which events at local level could be explained by reference to the needs of capital and the structurally necessary functions of a unitary state, and with only a cursory and superficial reference to actual events. Structuralism has now lost much of its intellectual fashion, and has been subjected to a powerful and telling critique. In that context, an analysis of the detailed inadequacies of the 'local state' literature is less important, although I take issue with it on points of detail during Part 1 of my study. But, for a time, for both activists and academics involved in local politics, it blunted our intellectual tools, encouraged laziness of thought, and led to dangerously inadequate prescriptions. If the theoretical framework is pitched at too high a level of generality, it cannot be used to analyse events in a locality. Either the causal factors are located at the macro-level, in which case the politics of a local area are written out of such explanations – or it offers general laws or ideal type categories which can be claimed to have explanatory power at a 'higher level', despite the existence of contrary evidence within any single study. For an analysis at local level to have sufficient explanatory power, it must be both more concrete, and more complex. For it to inform political practice, it must deal, not with taxonomies or categorisations, but with the inter-relations of processes of change and their concrete effects.

This approach determined the shape of the book. It is in two parts. The first is a chronologically ordered account of Southwark between 1919 and 1982: the development of the local economy and community, the local Labour Parties and councils. My decision to study a single area came in part from a consciousness of the generality and superficiality of many comparative studies. However, the study is a comparative one, not geographically, but over time. I approach the historical evidence, however, as a political scientist, rather than as a historian. Indeed, my study covers a longer period of time than would be realistic in a piece of academic history. My primary concern has been to make sense of the present and, where data have been missing or recorded in ways that are not readily accessible, I have not been able to carry out the painstaking reconstruction of a historian. On the other hand, the rich detail that I have been able to reconstruct about particular events has, all too often, had to be pared down to a minimum in the interests of brevity.

I have used a number of different sources to build up a careful picture of the main factors at work. To research the Labour Party and local authorities in the early period, I relied on primary sources, including local documents, minutes and private papers and, in particular, local Labour papers and journals of the period, which conveyed a vivid impression of local party attitudes. During the later period, these sources were supplemented by interviews with local councillors, ex-councillors, local party activists and community campaigners. While this did not in any sense form a representative sample of local people, it did span a wide range of experience, views and political attitudes within the local community and labour movement. Attempts at a formal questionnaire were abandoned at an early stage, standard questions merely elicited banal and uninformative answers, and did nothing to tap the rich vein of experience and observation. The interviews were therefore unstructured, lasting for between one and five hours.

Interviews of this kind count almost as oral history, and thus present the problem identified by the Popular Memory Group, in a study of methodology, that 'oral history testimony . . . is profoundly influenced by discourses and experience of the present'.[1] Political activists have selective memories, and, while recorded facts can be checked, events from the past have been selected and interpreted by the interviewees with the benefit of hindsight. However, in my research, it was the very subjectivity of these interviews which gave them their value. Of crucial interest here was not 'what happened', but what people thought happened; their perceptions and interpretations and, indeed, how they had structured their experience. In addition, from 1979 onwards, I played the role of participant observer both within the local Labour Party and, from 1982, as a councillor. Data on the changing local economy and the structure of the population was gained from census reports, local authority papers, and local statistics.

Finally, and as an essential guide to detail, public attitudes and chronology, I read the twice-weekly local paper, the *South London Press*, for the whole period 1919–82, not least because the paper's sometimes dramatic changes of political line provided a useful barometer of the local political climate.

The second part of the study relates the subject matter of Part 1 to current debates at a theoretical level, in order to provide explanations and answers to the questions raised above. In Chapter 5, I attempt to relate the material changes that have taken place to changes in assumptions, traditions and institutions within the local community, and explore the importance of class and other forms of cleavage in creating lines of identity and division within the local population. In Chapter 6, I attempt to account for the growing support for Labour in the area from 1919 to 1952, and its decline thereafter. I examine other studies of the Labour party and suggest that they do not satisfactorily explain the growth of Labour's support in the early years, nor its present volatility in an inner-city heartland. I attempt to construct an explanation which related the material and cultural changes considered earlier to changes both in the structure and image of the Labour Party. Finally, in Chapter 7, I attempt to relate the foregoing discussion to what I describe as an emerging crisis for Labour in local government. In conclusion I point to the implications of these changes for the problems that now face the Labour Party.

The book is therefore not simply concerned with the study of Southwark, but with questions about Labour, and about Labour in local government, today. But by looking at a local area, tying together changes in the local economy, in the local community, in the Labour Party and in the scope and policies of the local authority, it is possible to approach these questions with greater clarity and sharper analysis.

I recognise that, having decided on this approach, caution is required, since it cannot be assumed that conclusions drawn from my study of Southwark necessarily have a higher level of applicability. Parallels can, however, be drawn between different areas, and I hope to have illustrated an approach which would throw light on the politics of other areas. There is no substitute, however, for similar studies elsewhere which would enable us to build up a deeper and broader picture of Labour in local politics.

NOTES AND REFERENCES

1. Popular Memory Group 'Theory, Politics, Method' in R. Johnson, G. McLennon, B. Schwartz and D. Sutton (eds.), *Making Histories: Studies in History-Writing and Politics* (London, Hutchinson, 1982), 205–53, 243.
2. See, for example, Bush, J., *Behind the Lines: East End Labour 1914–1919*; Thompson, P., *Socialists, Liberals and Labour: The Struggle for London 1885–1914*; Wyncoll, P., *The Nottingham Labour Movement 1880–1939*.

PART 1

One

1919–45: The Build-up

THIS is a study of a thin, spindly triangle of industrial south London. Beginning with the river, from Waterloo Bridge in the west to Rotherhithe in the east, it stretches down to the suburban oasis of Dulwich Village, encompassing Bermondsey, the Elephant and Castle, Walworth, Camberwell, Peckham and East Dulwich. The municipal reorganisation of 1899 replaced the numerous vestries and joint boards which made up the local administration of the area with three metropolitan boroughs: Southwark, Bermondsey and Camberwell. And it is with the politics of the inhabitants of these boroughs, the nature and policies of local Labour parties, and of the local Labour councils that this chapter is concerned.

1. Local Economy and Local Community

As my study begins this was pre-eminently an industrial area. The metropolitan borough of Bermondsey was dominated by the Surrey Commercial Docks at Rotherhithe and the wharves and factories stretching the length of the riverside along Tooley Street to London Bridge. Behind the river was a tangle of factories, warehouses and houses jostling for space. The Bermondsey riverside edge had been an industrial centre since the seventeenth century, at the centre of food importation, brewing and the leather industry. Originally a compact industrial area, Bermondsey grew rapidly with the opening of the London and Greenwich railway in 1835. The population grew from 46 281 in 1801 to 85 308 in 1851 and peaked at 136 600 in 1891.[1] The leather trade was in decline by the 1920s because of high overheads and lack of space, but Bermondsey remained its most important centre. The Surrey Docks, importing grains and timber, were not only the major employers in Rotherhithe, but spawned related industries: wood and furniture production, milling, corn factors and granary keepers. Other major industries included engineering and metal working, a declining textile sector, and brewing and food manufacture.[2]

Southwark, the old 'ward without' of the City of London, had also been an industrial area for as long as the City. J.E. Martin suggests that in London, during this period, 'probably the largest concentration of engineering shops, large and small, was in an area of the South Bank of the Thames bounded by London Bridge at one end and Vauxhall Bridge at the other.'[3] By the 1920s these were no longer concentrated on heavy engineering. With the death of the shipbuilding industry in London, the bulk of London's engineering was in smallish workshops; machine making, instrument making and repair. By the early 1920s the printing and paper industries based in Walworth constituted the second most important industry, specialising in the newspaper trade, printing, book binding and manufacture of cardboards and paper. Riverside industries were also important: there were ropemakers, anchorsmiths, lightermen, watermen, barge builders and boat repairers, although much of the boat building was slowly moving downstream to Deptford and Woolwich.

Camberwell, by contrast, was primarily a residential suburb, although it was for the most part a very poor one. Dyos tells us that, at the beginning of the nineteenth century, Camberwell was a semi-rural suburb occupied by representatives of the prosperous middle classes. The opening up of the railways with cheap workers' fares and the rapid build-up of cheap housing brought the working class to the suburbs of Nunhead, East Dulwich, Peckham and Camberwell. The population grew from 39 868 in 1841 to 259 339 in 1901, making Camberwell one of the largest metropolitan boroughs in terms of both acreage and population. As early as the 1880s Booth wrote that 'North of the Peckham Rd is a large district becoming steadily poorer as the fairly comfortable move south and immigrants from Walworth arrive.'[4] Dyos notes that rateable values per head in Camberwell by the early 1890s were the lowest in London.[5] By 1932, as the Medical Officer of Health reports, 'the inhabitants with few exceptions are of the working class, many of whom are unemployed and very poor.'[6] The area had, nevertheless, a significant industrial base of its own. The Medical Officer of Health's report went on:

> The chief industries in the borough are those associated with the manufacture of gas and its by-products, factory laundries, paper works, food preparation, timber trades, engineering and wearing apparel.[7]

Camberwell housed omnibus yards and railway goods sidings, tramways, timber yards, and a heterogeneous manufacturing sector.

Rapid industrial growth had stamped a particular identity on the whole area and the community, and brought with it overcrowding, poverty and squalor. Row upon row of grimy tenements and insanitary cottages were packed into Bermondsey and Southwark. Booth wrote in 1903:

> It will be found when the different parts of south London are compared with each other and other districts in London in respect of poverty, that St Saviours, Southwark, is the poorest of all.[8]

Certainly the area continued to feature dramatically in London statistics for overcrowding and child mortality, the traditional indices of poverty. Infant mortality, maternal mortality and deaths from tuberculosis, diptheria, scarlet fever and measles were very high compared with the rest of London. Overcrowding was considerable. Southwark and Bermondsey were some of the worst boroughs in London in relation to size of dwellings and number of persons per room.

The 1931 census shows Southwark to be the most densely populated borough in London with 151.7 persons per acre. In St John's ward, Southwark, this increased to 230.9 people per acre, second only to the notorious St George's in the east ward in Stepney. Southwark borough had almost no open space, with only 'one acre of park for every 14 200 people'.[9] Alfred Salter, MP for Bermondsey from 1922, describes graphically the effect of overcrowding on his constituents' lives:

> Bermondsey is not a nice place to live in. The air is thick and sooty. The smells are – well, they are. The streets are dingy and grey. The houses are small, poky and inconvenient. There are no noble buildings and no fine monuments. The people are herded together and huddled together – overcrowded per room, overcrowded per house, overcrowded per acre. They have no space to move, no room to store their clothes or their food and there is little chance of privacy and quiet.[10]

Successive reports of the Medical Officers of Health complained of overcrowding and its medical consequences. In Southwark the MOH commented in 1925

> the population is too large for the borough to accommodate, and still it increases. The houses are getting worn out in many parts of the area and are almost without exception let out to members of more than one family.[11]

In Camberwell, the Medical Officer of Health commented that 'a large number of these houses are more or less worn out',[12] while in the south many of the larger houses had become tenements let out by the room.

The area had long been one of chronic underemployment and casual labour centred on the docks. But by 1919 some areas of work were more permanent; the food and drink factories began to offer work all the year round instead of laying workers off out of season. Unemployment levels, though never as high as those in the 'distressed regions', were nevertheless high for the prosperous South-East where employment generally was expanding. Unemployment fell sharply locally after the First World War, but once economic constraints were dismantled in the belief that war dislocation was over, unemployment rose sharply.[13] Unemployment figures drawn from employment exchange returns were inevitably underestimates, because they related to the insured population only. The depression of the 1930s brought unemployment nationally up to 20 per cent. The 1931 census records male unemployment rates of 15 per cent in Bermondsey, 14.5 per cent in Southwark and 10.3 per cent in Camberwell.

An examination of the main occupational groups in the area during this period is complicated by the fact that the census data record occupation according to place of work in 1921, and according to place of residence in 1931. However, both censuses show surprisingly similar data, which indicate the extent to which people lived and worked in the same area. In 1921 'Transport and Communications' was the biggest single occupational group for men in all three boroughs. In Bermondsey this was concentrated on water transport, and dock labourers comprised the biggest single occupational group. In Southwark and Camberwell transport workers were concentrated in occupations related to road and railway transport. Other important occupations were metal work, leather and warehousing in Bermondsey, cardboard manufacture, printing, warehousing, personal services and clerical work in Southwark. In Camberwell the most significant occupational groups next to transport and communications were commerce and clerical work, metal workers, cardboard workers, printers and wood and furniture manufacturers.

All three boroughs had high economic-activity rates for women; in 1921, 36 per cent of women aged twelve or over were 'occupied' in Camberwell, 41 per cent in Southwark and 40 per cent in Bermondsey. In all three boroughs, personal services (charring, domestic service and laundering) were the major occupational categories, followed by textiles. Other important occupational groups included commercial and clerical work, cardboard manufacture, mental work, food, drink and tobacco (the jam and condiment factories and breweries of Bermondsey mainly employed women), warehousing and shopkeeping.

The vast majority of workers were manual or low-paid clerical workers. In all three boroughs in 1921 no more than 6 per cent were professionals, employers or self-employed. In 1921 in the docks, for example, of the 5 998 men employed, 3 589 were labourers, 1 822 were skilled pilots, bargemen, stevedores or seamen, 255 were foremen or trimmers, wharfingers or master stevedores and 38 were shop owners and officials.

The damp, smoke, overcrowding and squalor of the local area, the closeness of work and home, and the large concentrations of workers in huge factories bound the local community together, more obviously so in Bermondsey and Southwark than in the newer communities of Peckham and Camberwell. Neighbours were also comrades at work, shared the same landlords, met at the union meeting, queued at the same cinema, gossiped on the tenement stairs. This created an effective communications network; ideas and news of trouble, or of strikes, travelled fast.

The growth of trades-unionism also acted to bind the community together. In the nineteenth century the longstanding craft unions had constituted the main form of industrial organisation. These craft unions had strong links with radicalism and liberalism. H.R. Taylor, for example, controlled the Camberwell Liberal party from a trades-union base as Secretary of the Amalgamated Society of Operative Bricklayers. The docks and factories in the north of the borough had proved notoriously difficult to organise, and were characterised by casual and seasonal work, and chronic under-employment.

By the beginning of the twentieth century, however, trades-unionism had begun to spread to the unskilled and semi-skilled workers. The 1889 dock strike demonstrated the discipline and effectiveness of unskilled workers.[14] The men of the Surrey Docks organised into the South Side Labour Protection League, a general union, later to evolve into the Dockers' Union.[15] The docks strike of 1889 ended the completely casual nature of dock work and strengthened the hand of the dockers. Although levels of unionisation and union membership in the docks continued to fluctuate, it was to remain the most powerful local union until it was finally absorbed into the Transport and General Workers' Union.

In 1911 there were a series of major local strikes. A walkout of dockers and carmen in 1911 spread through Bermondsey and 'without any organisation, without any lead, thousands of workers employed in Bermondsey, men, women and girls came out on strike'.[16] Women workers in the jam, food and mineral water factories were organised by the Federation of Women Workers, and in August 1911 14 000 women from 22 factories struck, finally winning increases of up to 4 shillings a week and setting up two new FWW branches. Bagwell stresses the importance of the 1889 and 1911 strikes for the growth of the NUR. The first national rail stoppage in 1911 marked the growth of strength and membership in the Railwaymen's Union.[17]

The new unionism continued to grow, spreading from the docks to the railways, engineering workers, construction workers and haulage. By 1914 the skilled trades unions on the Camberwell and Southwark Trades Councils had been joined by the Amalgamated Society of Engineers, the National Union of Railwaymen, the National Transport Workers' Federation, the Dockers' Union, the National Union of Gasworkers, the National Amalgamated Union of Labour and the United Organisation of General Labour in London. Trades-unionism had become a way of life in south-east London.

The importance of the growth of new unionism in an area traditionally dominated by casual and unskilled workers must not be underestimated. Slowly, during the period from the turn of the century to the First World War, one can see the transformation of the local community through the growth of industrial unionism and the development of the labour movement. During this period it is possible to trace the evolution of a new political culture – by which I mean a new set of institutions, ideas and assumptions which structured and made sense of the lives and experiences of local people. A process was taking place which Wyncoll identifies as the 'restructuring of working-class institutions',[18] from those described by Stedman Jones as 'the pub, the sporting paper, the race-course and the music hall'[19], to include the trades-union branch, the 'divi' card and the Labour Party dance. The emergence of the new political culture has been attributed to the growth of the new, unskilled unionism,[20] and to the fierce industrial struggles of 1889, 1911 and 1912, which 'helped forge class attitudes'.[21] Stedman Jones noticed the beginnings of these changes, but dismissed them as a 'vague predisposition towards collectivism or the defence of trades union rights', and in any case occurring, not in old radical London, but in the 'outlying working class areas'.[22] He fails to recognise the importance of both the new level of organisation and the shift of political initiative away from the old skilled artisan centres of radical activity, towards the new centres of unskilled trades-unionism, such as Poplar, Woolwich and Bermondsey. Local community cannot be separated from the development of working-class strength, confidence and political control.

This is not to suggest a sophistication of political affiliation or of socialist ideology. Drucker has suggested the development of a common ethos based on solidarity and fraternity, perhaps especially so in an unskilled, predominantly casual community where iron discipline was essential for successful industrial action. Drucker suggests that class solidarity acted as an 'organisational glue' arising out of a 'shared past, from a series of folk memories, or shared expression of exploitation, common struggle and gradually increasing power'.[23]

At the same time, the political culture reflected the nature of the local community. Here divisions did not emerge between a labour aristocracy and the unskilled – after all, the entire area had been characterised by middle-class London in the nineteenth century as inhabited by the 'dangerous class' and 'the residuum'.[24] However, in the restructuring of working-class institutions that took place, a clear distinction does seem to have been drawn between the decent and the criminal, between the feckless and the hard-working, the deserving and the undeserving. It was from the criminal and immoral elements, notorious in Rotherhithe and the Elephant and Castle, that local labour-movement activists and trades-unionists distinguished themselves. It was, at base, a culture based on the respectable manual labourer and his family, employed in back-breaking work by day and expecting to be waited on at home, generous to comrades and courageous in struggles, but with narrow standards of behaviour, distrust of 'outsiders' and hostility to those who broke the social rules.

Finally, there is the question of the significance of the Church locally. Stedman Jones and Thompson have described the culture of east and south-east London in the nineteenth century as secular,[25] and certainly the local population was not keen on church-going, or on the interference of the temperance movement. Key social leaders such as Scott Lidgett and Alfred Salter were devout Nonconformists and saw the transformation of the area as a religious crusade. But they made political rather than religious converts. However, local people have insisted that the Catholic Church can be seen as a powerful influence on the local communities of Bermondsey and Rotherhithe, where a large Irish Catholic population had built up around the docks. As we shall see, the Catholic Church has had an impact on the local Labour parties, and, perhaps more importantly, had the effect of binding more closely together the dockside communities of Bermondsey and Rotherhithe.

2. The Growth of Labour's Support

In the early years of the twentieth century Labour was not the only party appealing for the support of working people. As early as

1869, a trades-unionist, George Odger, had stood with the support of F.W. Souter's Radical Club 'in the working men's interest',[26] opposed by Liberals as well as Conservatives, and was only narrowly beaten. The Radicals subsequently joined forces with the Liberals to form a Lib-Lab group, with strong links with the craft unions, especially the print workers. In Southwark and Camberwell in particular, this group attracted the majority of working men's votes until 1918.

The SDF, and later the British Socialist Party, although occasionally active locally,[27] had never built up any significant support. By the 1920s, however, the Communist Party developed a high profile of local agitation, and the National Unemployed Workers' Movement, organised by the Communist Party, was successful in politicising the issues of unemployment and poor relief, with a dramatic campaign of meetings, marches, pickets and some spectacular battles fought over the eviction of unemployed tenants.[28] The NUWM gained considerable support over a number of years, and drew in Labour activists at times; but support for the NUWM does not seem to have been extended to the Communist Party. Some local Communists were well respected and seen as effective comrades in the trades-union movement, but they remained numerically small and politically isolated, failing utterly to construct a base of popular support, or to gain significant numbers of votes in elections.

Labour's support and strength, by contrast, grew steadily throughout this period. 1918 was, in many ways, a turning point. Several factors may be significant, including the dramatic decline in the fortunes of the Liberal Party, the reform of the franchise[29] and the growth of the new unions, which strengthened the Trades and Labour Councils. These had been set up locally in all three boroughs in 1903. After the Labour Representation Committee was set up nationally in 1906, the Trades and Labour Councils became local federations of all trades unions and socialist parties; including the ILP branches, the Women's Co-operative Guilds, and, at times, the BSP branches.[30] As the Camberwell Trades and Labour Council proclaimed in 1914:

> This Council is the meeting place of the organised workers of the borough. Here are discussed policies of mutual advancement, here the affiliated societies can cooperate for social betterment and the attainment of a higher standard of civilised life. Camberwell, though largely a working class borough, has no labour representative on any of its administrative councils at the task before the Council is the building

up of a workers' party to promote and safeguard the interests of the working class.[31]

The 1914–18 war played an important part in radicalising the young Trades Councils. They became actively involved in agitation against profiteering, the high cost of living and unemployment, monitoring local conditions of distress and at times producing handbills advising the unemployed not to worry about paying their rent. Trades Councils were given places on war-time committees set up by the government, which brought them closer than before to the levers of power.[32]

The Trades and Labour Councils formed the 'nucleus of the political organisation of Labour in the constituencies'.[33] Despite the fact that, in 1918, a new constitution established for the first time individual membership and constituency parties, McKibbon points out that, by 1922, only 16 out of 61 divisions in London had Divisional Labour parties, 'it was much more likely that the great majority of them were glorified trades councils and that the majority of them also had no significant individual membership'.[34] Individual membership began to build up rapidly in the 1920s, but it was not until the mid-1930s that this began to outweigh the influence of the trades unions at local level. The Councils helped to strengthen the links between the different arms of the labour movement. Comrades involved in industrial struggles came to the Party for support. In the dock strike of 1924 the Labour Party headquarters was placed at the disposal of the strikers until the arbitration of the Labour government led to a settlement. When the General Strike was called in 1926 the headquarters of all three local Trades and Labour Councils became strike bases; strike bulletins were produced on Labour presses and the labour movement locally was wholly absorbed in strike work.

During this period there is evidence of considerable electoral volatility, particularly in general elections, as local people struggled to come to terms with the changes that were taking place, and were torn between the old and familiar, and the new strident confidence of the labour movement. Of the nine new constituencies created in 1918 – four in Camberwell, two in Bermondsey and three in Southwark – only one was won for Labour in the 1918 general election. By 1922 Labour had won two seats, by 1923, three, and by 1924, seven. By 1929, only Dulwich remained in Tory hands. The effects of the collapse of the second Labour government in 1931 were dramatic, Labour lost all but one local parliamentary seat in the general election that followed, with Alfred Salter saved by the 'almost perfect electoral machine in

West Bermondsey'.[35] Recovery was rapid, however; in the general election of 1935, Camberwell North, Southwark Central, Southwark South-East and Rotherhithe returned Labour candidates. The extent of Labour's defeat in 1931 can in part be attributed to the fact that both opposition parties joined forces.

However, in London, the young Labour Party achieved its first successes in local rather than national elections. This reflects the organisation and determination in the London Labour parties, and, in particular, the stress on municipal socialism – a belief that real changes could be made at a local as well as at the national level. The local parties worked as hard for the LCC and local-borough and Board of Guardians elections as they did for the general elections. In 1919 Labour did well in the LCC and Guardians elections, and, for the first time, swept into power in the municipal elections, 'giving Boodle and Bumble their marching orders'.[36] Labour made sweeping gains in Liverpool and in Manchester, but it was in London that Labour's successes were the greatest; winning Battersea, Camberwell, Deptford, Greenwich, Shoreditch, West Ham, Woolwich, Bethnal Green, Fulham, Hackney, Islington, Poplar, St Pancras, Shoreditch, Southwark and Stepney. 'London Labour' said Morrison 'has come out of the wilderness and has entered into the domain of responsible power.'[37]

Labour's victories were short-lived, however. In Southwark and Camberwell, by 1922, the opposition had formed an 'anti-socialist' coalition capable of defeating Labour. Similar coalitions were formed elsewhere.[38] During this period, the Municipal Reform and Progressive parties, backed by ratepayers and independents and, in particular, by the local paper the *South London Press*, fought a fierce 'battle of ideas' to prevent the area from falling into Labour's hands. Much of the rhetoric, looking back from the 1980s, is surprisingly familiar. Plans for new housing were 'spendthrift', and the new houses were 'peopled by socialist and Communist friends of socialist councillors'.[39] The Labour councils, said the *South London Press*, had carried out 'a screaming farce of "how best to waste the peoples' money"'.[40] A vote for Labour was a vote 'for a Communist in disguise',[41] while a stark proposition was put to the voters of Camberwell:

> Will you do your duty to save Camberwell from Bolshevism, Bankruptcy and to reduce the terribly high rates?[42]

In Bermondsey, however, despite a combined opposition, Labour won convincingly in 1922. By 1925, Labour controlled the Bermondsey Board of Guardians and both LCC seats, and continued to increase its majority on the council. By 1934,

Bermondsey council was 100 per cent Labour. Labour's early success in Bermondsey can perhaps be accounted for by its roots in the powerful and imaginative ILP branch, and its strong industrial and trades-union base.

However, by 1925, Labour had begun to beat the local anti-socialist coalition, making gains in Southwark and Camberwell in the LCC elections and the Boards of Guardians elections, taking half the seats on Southwark Board of Guardians and enough seats in Camberwell to give two Progressives the balance of power between Labour and the Municipal Reformers. Local-election results were surprisingly unaffected by the 1931 fiasco, with only a slight dip in support at the municipal elections. In 1934 the prize of the London County Council finally fell to Labour, with only Dulwich, of the local LCC constituencies, returning Municipal Reform candidates. And at last Southwark and Camberwell Borough Councils were won for Labour. From 1934 onwards, Labour held the majority of parliamentary seats, all three borough councils and all but one LCC division.

I have pointed out that individual Labour Party membership did not become significant until the 1920s. The first membership figures available date from 1925, and, although records have been scrappy and inconsistent ever since, one can see that party membership increased steadily from this date.[43] Between 1925 and 1930 membership increased in Bermondsey from 180 to 800, in Rotherhithe from 180 to 1 000, in Camberwell North from 300 to 1 203, in Dulwich from 360 to 433, in Southwark Central from 120 to 452, in Southwark South-East from 360 to 400 and in Southwark North from 120 to 300.

Party membership fell everywhere after the MacDonald defection in 1931; falling in Bermondsey by 500 and in Peckham and Camberwell by about 200. It held in Southwark, according to the returns, but this may well indicate that Southwark was affiliating in standard membership numbers throughout this period. However, in the aftermath of 1931, the London Labour Party ran a determined membership drive, and membership began to increase again, rapidly. The east and south-east London Labour parties consistently had the highest membership figures. The London Labour Party created a membership trophy for the constituency which increased its membership the fastest, which was won in the first year by West Bermondsey, recruiting 354 members in two weeks – 2.5 per cent of the Labour vote. West Bermondsey came third in the second year, with one new member for every twenty electors; and in 1933 Rotherhithe was runner-up with one new member for every 24 electors. By 1938 West Bermondsey's membership was 3 156. *London Labour News* pointed out that here 'nearly ten per cent of the electors and nearly twenty five per cent of the Labour voters are party members'.[44] Rotherhithe party was also increasing membership fast, with over 3 000 members in 1938.

The Camberwell parties also quickly re-established significant membership figures: the combined membership for all four constituencies was just under 4 000 in 1938 and just over 4 000 in 1939. Southwark South-East constituency ran a very successful Labour journal, the *Walworth News*, with a claimed circulation of 10 000. In Southwark, however, membership grew slowly after 1931, if at all. *London Labour News* commented in September 1936 that, in Southwark South-East, 'in a constituency where electoral success came relatively easily before mass membership was a feature of party organisation, it is naturally difficult to impress the need for a large membership'.[45] Nevertheless, the Southwark parties, as early as the 1930s, were a fairly close-knit group of dedicated party activists, unwilling to recruit members on a large scale.

An examination of the local Labour parties reveals a high level of activity, both political and social. The local parties do not seem to have been significantly to the Left of the Party at national level. Bermondsey was a highly organised, active party, but supremely pragmatic in its politics; and, while powerful propagandists for socialism, they backed the Party leadership in internal disputes. Bermondsey ILP, which dominated the local party, refused to disaffiliate in 1932, unlike the ILP nationally. Bermondsey's radicalism consisted in a commitment to getting results, and a powerful pacifist and republican strain. The Camberwell parties were the closest to being 'Left' parties. The presence of respected Communist Party members on the Trades and Labour Councils meant that the Trades and Labour Council opposed the 1925 ban on Communists; and, by 1936, the local party supported the united front. By contrast, the Southwark parties were to the Right of the national leadership. Few resolutions from any of the local parties to national conference were in opposition to the national leadership; they concentrated on local problems such as housing, direct labour, nursing and midwifery services, Public Assistance Committees and the Means Test, although by the late 1930s peace, fascism and Spain had become important issues locally, and were reflected in resolutions.[46] What is perhaps remarkable is how seldom local parties bothered to send resolutions at all.

Local campaigning was, however, an important part of party life. In Camberwell and Southwark, the Trades and Labour

Councils campaigned actively over unemployment, levels of relief, and policies such as the use of labour colonies for the unemployed. After 1931 the campaign swung in Camberwell to the issue of housing, with conferences, deputations, a special manifesto to ratepayers and an emergency resolution to Conference. In Southwark the party campaigned over the means test, the dole cuts and the new Public Assistance Committees. In Bermondsey, where Labour had controlled the Council since 1922, much of the party's activity was involved with Council work, and in defending and publicising Council policies. Links with local people were well organised. Bermondsey, Rotherhithe and Walworth parties ran regular mass distribution journals delivered door to door. Bermondsey had a system of street stewards, responsible for distributing the journal and collecting subscriptions. Forester has argued that the idea of high levels of local Labour activity forms part of a myth of a 'golden past', and has rejected accounts of high levels of organisation in the 1930s and 1950s as expressing 'what *should* be the case, an ideal rather than a reality'.[47] And yet, evidence from Bermondsey and Rotherhithe indicates that such a high level of organisation did indeed exist, probably until the mid-1950s.

The party was a centre of social and political life. Rallies with big-name speakers were held constantly, and were well attended. Public meetings were held in the assembly halls attached to the Public Baths, with speakers such as Lansbury, Salter, MacDonald, Brockway, Saklatvala and Maxton. Open-air meetings were held on the Rye, and street-corner meetings wherever men gathered in the evenings. The Co-operative movement held meetings and lectures. The Womens' Sections met, sometimes twice weekly, and in Bermondsey had a full-time organiser. West Bermondsey had a social club, a swimming club, a youth club and a football club. The Labour Party organised socials, outings and dances, taking the children to the seaside and the old folk to the cinema. Surgeries and advice sessions were run from party headquarters, and in Bermondsey the Labour Institute put on weekly lectures.

Finally, it is important to note the extent to which the local Labour party grew out of the community. The attitudes of the Labour party closely mirrored attitudes held by local people. As one party veteran put it:

> The Salter Labour Party was the exact expression of the community – immense self-help, immense self-reliance, knowledge of everybody . . . systems of helping the genuinely disadvantaged – the codes were there rigidly.[48]

The party reflected local peoples' ideas of respectability, and their

clear views about who did or did not belong. The party saw itself as
representing the respectable unskilled and skilled working families.
For example, when the Communist Party attempted at one stage
to mobilise some of the 'less respectable' elements, *Bermondsey
Labour Magazine* referred to them as 'some of the worst rogues,
thieves, jail-birds, scroungers and hooligans ever collected together
in the borough' and insisted that 'they must purge themselves of
the crooks and parasites who at present encumber their ranks if
they are to win the respect of decent people.'[49]

The sanctity of home and hearth, and the importance of family
and family life were common themes. Despite a high level of organisation of women members through the Co-operative Womens'
Guild and the women's trades unions, women were addressed less
and less during this period as workers in their own right. By the
1930s, Labour addressed women almost solely as housewives and
mothers.

The Catholic Church can also be seen as an important influence
in Bermondsey. It threw its weight behind the struggles of local
people to overcome poverty and squalor, and eventually behind
the Labour Party, but acted deliberately as a moderating influence.

Inevitably, much of Labour's support came from the local trades
unions, and an important part of Labour's programme was based
on trades-union rights and trades-union rates. Councillor Craigie,
chairman of the Railwaymen, and a Bermondsey Councillor,
made it clear when he stood for election in 1921 that 'as a
representative of the Labour Party he stood first and foremost for
trades union conditions for all employees of Borough Councils'.[50]
Foster describes the 'growth of a breed of municipal socialism
which placed prime emphasis on direct labour and the use of
municipalisation to campaign for unionisation and union rates'.[51]
Foster, however, associates this with the old Labour aristocracy,
whereas in south-east London it was associated with the new
general unions.

But the ideology of the local Labour party was not merely trades
unionist. It reflected the nature of the local party as a federal
structure, at local, as well as national level in the early years. It
was a curious mixture of pragmatism, revolutionary fervour,
visionary Christianity and class solidarity. In the years immediately
after the First World War, a Towns Meeting held by Camberwell
Labour Party and Trades Council in 1922 resolved 'to work
unceasingly for the overthrow of capitalism and the establishment
of a workers' republic',[52] while Labour's manifesto in the 1919
municipal elections proclaimed that:
    The Labour movement will not rest until it has eliminated

from the world the parasitism of the rich and the poverty of the masses and has substituted for capitalism and profiteering that human brotherhood which can only be secured by the establishment of a co-operative commonwealth.[53]

The editor of *Bermondsey Labour Magazine* looked forward to the

final triumph when the workers of Bermondsey together with the workers of the world shall march into a new order of society in which slums and starvation, low wages and high prices, disease and bad conditions shall find no place.[54]

As the revolutionary fervour of the First World war subsided, Labour's message became less apocalyptic. Labour never promised less than a complete transformation of society, but, beneath the utopian rhetoric, Labour's revolution was a practical and limited one. As Bermondsey MP Ben Smith put it

It is an axiom of socialist philosophy that all things that are commonly used should be commonly owned.[55]

Alfred Salter was committed to achieving Labour's ideals in one borough, to turning the Bermondsey he loved into a

New Jerusalem, whose citizens shall have reason to feel pride in their common possessions, in their civil patriotism, in their public spirit, in the joint sharing of burdens, and their collective efforts to make happier the lot of every single dweller in their midst.[56]

Labour presented concrete programmes to improve the lives of working people – decent housing, health care, education, open space. Socialism was about 'social justice and a living wage'.[57] Fundamentally, the programme around which support was built locally can be summed up as planned social provision to replace the squalid tenements and ugliness around them, and to meet the needs that the private sector could not and would not meet. Municipal provision for need and not profit was a demonstration of socialism in action. The programme was based very much around the experience and demands of local people – municipal rather than national in its scope.

3. Labour in Local Government

When Labour first took power in the early 1920s in local government in London, it was in very different institutions to the ones that exist today. Firstly, local-government structures consisted of both the Metropolitan Borough Councils and the directly elected Boards of Guardians, responsible for poor relief. This section deals primarily with the Municipal Councils, and secondarily with the Boards of Guardians, since, during this period, poor relief constituted the biggest single rate-borne expenditure.

The Metropolitan Borough Councils. The Borough Councils, created in 1899 as a second tier below the LCC, had fewer and more limited powers than the present London Boroughs. The LCC had major powers in housing and planning, education and social services. Local boroughs were responsible for street-lighting and cleansing, refuse collection, libraries and galleries, baths and wash-houses, parks, maternity and child welfare and public health-services except hospitals. In Southwark and Bermondsey the local authorities were responsible for statutory undertakings, e.g. gas or electricity. Local Borough Councils were poor relations to the County Councils in terms of power and resources; but the marginal nature of government grant-aid also gave them the freedom to extend service provision without recourse to central government, if local ratepayers would accept the financial burden. Poplar's struggles had led to some rate equalisation, but only in relation to poor relief. In 1922 about four-fifths of local authority income came from rates. Subsidy consisted of specific grants and some assigned revenues, until 1929 when they were replaced by a general exchequer contribution.

Labour, as it gained control of local authorities, saw its task as improving services for local people to demonstrate 'municipal socialism' in action. But how effectively were these policies implemented – and what were the obstacles? Inevitably, in this early period, any analysis of Labour-controlled authorities in this area must concentrate on Bermondsey. Bermondsey was Labour-controlled for seventeen years out of the twenty covered in this chapter, while Southwark and Camberwell were each Labour-controlled for eight years in total.

In Bermondsey the achievements of the new Labour administration were important in building up Labour's base locally, and setting the stage for the political developments of the future. The Council was seen as an extension of the work of the labour movement, as a tool to be used in the service of local working people. The new Council made much of political gestures: including erecting a red flag over the Town Hall, and refusing to take part in armistice celebrations, organising instead 'No More War' rallies and demonstrations. In 1935, Bermondsey Council, out of republican sentiments, refused to receive the King – arguing that the cost could not be justified!

The commitment of the local party to trades-union values and solidarity was also reflected by the council. During the dock strike and the General Strike, council facilities were placed at the disposal of the strikers; indeed, in 1926, the Borough Council suspended itself and delegated powers to an emergency committee in order to concentrate energies on organising for the strike. A direct-labour organisation was established as an early priority, and wage rates that were, by and large, higher than trades-union rates established. Staff were given the day off with pay on May Day to join the rallies and demonstrations. Bermondsey was committed to providing relief work for the unemployed and continually borrowed money for construction projects, despite obstruction and delay from both the LCC and the UGC.

However, the councillors' demonstrations of socialist commitment were not limited to gestures of this kind. They took practical steps to demonstrate the principles of collective provision. The first area of concern was health. Salter had a doctor's dream of reducing the high death and infant-mortality rates. The greatest killer was tuberculosis. Bermondsey had a tuberculosis dispensary, but Salter was determined to experiment with the new sunlight treatment, first by sending tuberculosis patients to Switzerland, and then by building a solarium in Bermondsey itself. Fairby Grange, a country house that Salter had bought in 1917, was turned into a convalescent home for mothers after confinement. A propaganda campaign was begun to promote preventative care, with films, leaflets, electric signs, town-halls lectures and open-air demonstrations. Health services were expanded, with a new health centre in Grange Road, with maternity, tuberculosis and dental clinics, a solarium and a foot clinic. Municipal welfare centres and under-fives' centres were set up, free insulin distributed to diabetics, and free milk, eggs and fresh food to 'necessitous mothers'. Other services were expanded. Bermondsey Council opened new and luxurious baths in Grange Road in 1927, a public laundry was established, new lecture halls were built, a municipal choir and orchestra was set up. The municipal electricity enterprise kept electricity prices low, gave free lightbulbs and hired out or sold new electrical appliances. The new Council set up a Beautification Committee which, under Ada Salter, set out to plant trees, encouraging garden competitions and horticultural glories in the grim backyards.[58]

Finally, the Council was committed to sweep away Bermondsey's slums. Its idea was to 'demolish two thirds of the borough and rebuild it as a garden city',[59] and it was at this point that it came into confrontation with central government. The strategy was never more than begun; based upon a dramatic thinning-out of the population, it was rejected as unworkable by central government and the LCC, who insisted that the Council build tenements, rather than cottages, in order to rehouse an equal number of people to those displaced. Faced with such opposition, the Council held Towns Meetings in Bermondsey and Rotherhithe town halls to rally support, to which all citizens were invited, attended by representatives of the trades unions, chapels, churches, settlements, parents' unions, ratepayers, the British Legion and every organisation that could be traced. They unanimously instructed the Council to proceed with the policy of building cottages. The Council battled on, and permission was eventually granted by Wheatley when Labour formed the government in 1924, but was withdrawn again by the Conservatives. Eventually the Council completed the Salisbury Street scheme, the first and last part of the garden city. To this day, an island of cottages with big, rambling gardens stands in the midst of the riverside flats.

Many of these initiatives remained small scale, limited as they were by lack of powers and lack of money. However, several policies were dramatic in their effects, particularly the new health provision. The Council was committed to high levels of service-spending despite the low rate base and the poverty of local people. In September 1926 Bermondsey's rate was 9s 7d in the pound, compared with 6s 2d in Camberwell, and 6s 11d in Southwark. By 1938 Bermondsey's rates were 17s 6d in the pound compared to 12s 7d in Camberwell and 13s 8d in Southwark.[60] Only the other East-End boroughs, Poplar and Stepney had comparable rates. Rates were very volatile throughout the 1920s and 1930s, and the absolute level was far more dependent on the general level of prices, wages, unemployment and levels of central government grant than on the programmes of individual authorities. But Bermondsey was always a relatively high-spending borough and was positive about the value for money obtained by spending on the rates. By 1931, for example, Bermondsey was spending £24 000 annually on housing and £35 000 on public health, while Southwark and Camberwell respectively spent £37 404 and £30 232 on the two services combined. Bermondsey spent £19 730 on maternity and child welfare, compared with £11 818 for Camberwell and £12 069 for Southwark. Bermondsey spent £36 877 on baths and wash-houses, while Southwark spent £13 020 (Camberwell's spending on baths was included in a total of £17 870 covering all public services). In addition Bermondsey spent £12 948 on 'beautification'.[61] Indeed, Bermondsey spent more in absolute terms on many services than did authorities with a far higher penny-rate product.

The borough borrowed whatever it could whenever it could to

finance capital schemes. By 1938, the *South London Press* reported that Bermondsey 'owes one third of South London's nine million debt!'[62] Bermondsey had total debts of just over £3 million, compared to £623 562 for Camberwell and £509 917 for Southwark, despite Municipal Reform protests about waste and extravagance.[63] But even the *South London Press*, usually virulently anti-socialist but panicked by the effects of mass unemployment and, perhaps, swayed commercially by growing Labour support in the area, wrote in a leader in 1930:

> Because Bermondsey's rate is nearly double that of Wandsworth we are not going to say that it is too high. The justification of a rate depends entirely on what the rate-payers get in return for their money, and Bermondsey, suffering from all kinds of disadvantage, is rapidly becoming one of the best government boroughs in South London . . . So great have been the improvements that many parts are unrecognisable as the slum areas of years ago, and so long as the ratepayers are prepared to pay for these improvements they can have no grievance against the Council.[64]

None of this is to argue that the Council was free to act as it pleased. Service expansion must have been limited by what the rate-payers would bear. Central government intervened directly, by withholding loan approval for housing schemes, as illustrated above, and by putting upward pressure on local-authority rents. Construction schemes depended on loans and could be obstructed or blocked at both government and LCC level, especially those schemes dependent on Unemployment Grants Committee support. In a sense, throughout this period, Labour local authorities were testing their strength, and the early years especially were characterised by important struggles between Labour authorities and the government – testing the limits of local authorities' powers. The best known of these were those waged by Poplar between 1919 and 1924, primarily over the issue of poor relief, and then over the issue of wage rates. Poplar gained some important victories in relation to poor relief, notably the partial equalisation of the rate burden between London authorities. They had been less successful over the issue of a local authority's right to determine wage rates. The right of the District Auditor to surcharge councils for paying 'excessive' wages had been established in the Lords in *Roberts* v. *Hopwood* in 1925. By 1926, Bermondsey faced a similar confrontation. The Council had reduced wages in 1922 as prices began to fall, but by 1926 the District Auditor was asking for further reductions. At first the councillors remained defiant:

> The Labour Party in Bermondsey has unanimously decided to

resist to the very end those encroachments of the bureaucracy in the sphere of local autonomy. Arrangements are being made for a united front on the part of all the Labour boroughs and Mr Neville Chamberlain may be faced with the dilemma of putting over 200 men and women, including many of the responsible and respected public representatives and administrators in London, in prison for refusing to obey his orders to reduce labourers' wages below the living rate.[65]

However, the Labour boroughs appeared weaker now than they had been several years earlier. Chamberlain introduced the 1927 Audit (Local Authorities) Act, which provided that all those surcharged for sums of more than £500 would be automatically disqualified from holding office for five years. By July 1927, Salter was telling his comrades

> I think that further resistance to the Auditor's demands is useless . . . it would be an irreparable disaster to Bermondsey if some fifty men and women including the very pick and cream of our citizens are to be eliminated from the municipal life of the borough.[66]

On June 30 1927 a meeting of all employees were held – about 800 trades unionists gathered in Bermondsey Town Hall. A motion 'expressing confidence in the Council, accepting the situation and recognising that the wage reduction had been forced on the Council by the Tory government' was carried unanimously.[67]

Camberwell, in its brief years of Labour control 1919–22, concentrated on building council housing. The original intention had been to build over 2 000 homes under the generous Addison Acts, whereby the government met housing costs over a penny rate. The Acts were, however, repealed, and the borough was forced to revise its plans. Eventually, 450 homes were built, which was still a substantial policy innovation at a time when few councils were building housing. Other initiatives included the reorganisation of the public health-services, the establishment of three infant welfare centres and the up-dating of baths, wash-houses and lavatories. A closed shop was introduced within the Council's work-force, and wages were raised. However, during this period rates rose steeply, forced up by steep price increases and the increasing precepts of the Board of Guardians as unemployment and relief also increased. As has been described earlier, there was a substantial protest movement generated by the opposition parties, 'rate-payer' groups and the local press, and in 1922 Labour lost control to an anti-socialist coalition.

In the years following their defeat, the Labour Party complained that:

not a single house has been built, rents have been raised, tenants harshly treated, plans for clearing away slums have been shelved, public health neglected . . . no provision of work has been made for the unemployed.[68]

Labour gained power again in 1934, at the same time as the new Labour LCC determined to increase the precept to finance a massive housing programme. Camberwell's Medical Officer of Health records that:

The year 1934 will be remembered as the year during which the Council in collaboration with the LCC started a campaign of slum clearance in Camberwell and this campaign is still being vigorously pursued.[69]

Three clearance areas were declared in the first year, council rents were reduced and the exterior of flats were repainted by the new, direct-labour force. Camberwell also began to emulate Bermondsey's health propaganda and provision – leaflets, free insulin, a new diphtheria immunisation clinic, extended midwifery services, home-helps and free meals and milk to expectant and nursing mothers. The voluntary welfare centres that were closing were taken over by the borough and new premises found. A convalescent service was begun, new dental treatment and sunlight treatment introduced and a new health centre opened in 1938, with a solarium, general dental scheme, foot clinics, an X-ray department, gynaecological clinic and breast-feeding and child-guidance clinic.

Southwark Council in the years 1919–22 increased spending on roads, cleaning depots and maternity and child welfare, and set up a municipal store in the borough to supply milk, medicine and drugs to expectant mothers at cheap rates. Labour lost control of Southwark in 1922, confronted by the same problems of rising prices and high rates, and a similar vicious campaign from both opposition parties and the *South London Press*. Under Municipal Reform control from 1922, service provision was run down, and much of the health and social-welfare work was left to voluntary organisations. Despite numerous reports from the Medical Officer of Health that 'overcrowding is universal and the position is acute',[70] housing provision was left to be undertaken, if at all, by the LCC.

After 1934, when Labour took control, the main progress in the new administration was in public health, maternity and child welfare schemes were enlarged, convalescent services for mothers were extended, maternity nurses and home nursing for children with infectious diseases begun. Health propaganda was distributed in libraries and baths and a new health centre was built in Larcom

Street; the TB dispensary was enlarged and the inevitable sunlight treatment promoted. Council house-building began slowly. Southwark Council was able to rehouse 99 families by 1938, while the LCC rehoused 436.[71] Although heralded as the 'first fruits' of a Labour administration, these changes fell short of the dramatic changes achieved in Bermondsey.

In an examination of local-service provision in all three local boroughs during this period, several factors stand out. Firstly, the difference in service provision and style between the authorities. Secondly, the question of who benefits varied considerably from service to service. The new health services, the baths and the parks benefited almost everyone, but only a small proportion of local people benefited from council housing, which was in short supply. In some areas housing provision was barely started, and, while the majority of local people aspired to new council homes, only a minority had access to them. Council housing was of better quality than privately rented housing, but it was also relatively expensive compared to rents for privately rented rooms.[72] Tenants were therefore primarily drawn from the better-off working class, often the politically organised, or council employees.

Thirdly, it is important to recognise the considerable power over the day-to-day policies and practices of the local authorities that was exerted by individual councillors and their political parties. The authorities were small, and the officers performed clerical and administrative tasks, rather than management or policy development tasks. Most council officers were local people and had worked their way up the council ranks. There was neither a clear career structure, nor a level of professional organisation or training which could develop a professional view of policy formation. All decisions, large or small, were, it seems, made in the committee meetings, or in Labour groups. The political direction of local-authority policy was clearly apparent. A failure to achieve real changes, for instance in Southwark and Camberwell, can be attributed, not to bureaucratic inertia, but to external constraints, the short life of Labour administrations in these areas, and to lack of political imagination.

The Boards of Guardians. It would be wrong to end a discussion of Labour in local government during this period without referring to the Boards of Guardians. While they remained in existence only until 1929, they were an important site of political struggle during this period, because of the importance of the issue of unemployment, and the hardship caused by inadequate poor relief. The National Unemployed Workers' Movement was active in the area throughout this period, although its effects, in terms of achieving higher relief and more sympathetic treatment, seem to have been far less important than the relative success of Labour in controlling the local Guardians. Here there are clear parallels with the situation in the local councils.

From 1922 Bermondsey's Board of Guardians was controlled by Labour and the Progressives; from 1925 Labour held sole control. By 1924 the Minister of Health had picked out Poplar and Bermondsey as the highest spenders. In 1923 the average cost of outdoor relief for the able-bodied was 3s 9½d nationally; but in Poplar it was 52s 10¼d, and in Bermondsey 27s 11d.[73] By 1928, of a population of 119 452, 15 303 able-bodied men were relieved in Bermondsey. The *South London Press* commented that 'Poplar and Bermondsey put a premium on pauperism'.[74]

When Bermondsey and Poplar were giving generous relief, Southwark and Camberwell, controlled by anti-socialist coalitions, were attempting to keep the precepts, and thus the rates, low. Cuts were made in relief rates in 1923; Camberwell introduced a work test as a condition of outdoor relief for able-bodied men, while Southwark sent single and married men to the labour colonies of Bellmont and Wellesley Bay. The local unemployed groups protested constantly, with demonstrations, bands and banners, to the Guardians about scales of relief and conditions for the unemployed. The deputations to Southwark and Camberwell were, as often as not, refused. In Bermondsey, the NUWM was less active and less well supported, presumably because of the strong hold Labour had on the area. Nevertheless, here, despite the conflicts between the Labour Party and the NUWM, the deputations were received and concessions made.

In Southwark, the Municipal Reformers and Labour were evenly represented after the 1925 elections, but in April 1927 Labour took the chairmanship and began to increase provision slightly. Southwark's ratepayers began to organise protests against the extra expenditure, while the NUWM continued to campaign against the low levels of relief! By 1928, despite a clear Labour majority, the Guardians felt helplessly trapped between a desire to keep rates low and a desire to relieve the misery of unemployment. Southwark's Labour Guardians were never as unambiguously committed to a policy of high relief as their comrades in Bermondsey.

The *South London Press* campaigned vociferously against high poor relief, writing 'it is tolerably certain that until it becomes impossible to bribe voters with rate payers' money, lavish outlay on poor relief may be expected',[75] and recommending the disenfranchisement of paupers. As early as 1926 the District

Auditor began to investigate Bermondsey and Southwark, and to disallow cases of relief he considered over-generous. The 1926 Board of Guardians (Default) Act gave the government powers to appoint commissioners to replace over-zealous Boards, and was a powerful deterrent. The new inspectorate under the 1926 Act did not take long to reach Bermondsey. By October 1927 the Guardians were under attack for making it possible 'for a lazy fellow to maintain and increase his family in the most undesirable conditions',[76] and warned not to exceed the maximum scale of relief and not to pay so large a proportion in cash. By November it was clear that the Bermondsey Guardians faced the prospect of reducing relief or facing a surcharge. The Boards in West Ham, Bedwelty and Chester-Le-Street had already been removed under the 1926 Act.

The Guardians met in November with two simultaneous public meetings in Rotherhithe and Bermondsey Town Halls, to ask approval for a decision to reduce the scales of relief. Salter argued powerfully that 'the guardians had no right to take a spectacular course'. If they defied the Minister, they followed the course adopted by West Ham, and 'they all knew the result'.[77] Despite bitter Communist-led resistance, the Guardians agreed to reduce the scales of relief, with the backing of the Trades and Labour Council.

Now that the Labour authorities were in retreat, however, the government was determined to regain control. Despite protests, the 1929 Local Government Act finally abolished the Guardians and transferred responsibility for poor relief to the Public Assistance Committees appointed by the County Councils. An arena of local government where working people had been able to gain at least limited control of the distribution of resources had been brought to an end.

4. Summary

Any trend drawn from a study of twenty years of complex local history will inevitably involve over-simplification. This was a period of experiments and set-backs. However, I think we can identify a change in the nature of working-class institutions and practices leading up to this period, and the construction of a new local political culture, drawing strength from the spread of trades-unionism to unskilled workers. The young Labour Party both contributed to and reflected this local culture. It grew from a loose federal structure organised through the Trades and Labour Councils to one which, while retaining a firm base in the Trades and Labour Councils, had a considerable individual membership, and which reached into the social and political life of the community. From a party which, at the beginning of this period, had achieved little electoral success, it had become one almost assured of electoral victory at local and general elections.

While much of the party's activity was aimed at gaining parliamentary power, this was in no way the limit of its activities, and local campaigning work and efforts to gain municipal power were taken as seriously as efforts to gain power nationally. Indeed, the gaining of power locally, before Labour gained power nationally, had significant effects on the evolution of the party.

At the same time, the ideas which won Labour support crystallised around the class solidarities and trades-unionism developed in the industrial struggles of the years 1880–1920, and around a programme of public provision to meet local needs. Labour fought on a local platform committed to the sweeping away of slum housing, the development of health care, the relief of poverty caused by unemployment. It was a practical programme of amelioration which reflected the common sense of local people. The ideas of the local party reflected and evolved from those generated within the local community. During this period, Labour councils were far from unconstrained; they were severely limited in their powers, and central government intervened directly whenever it felt strong enough. This was, however, a period of a testing of strength between central and local government, and, while there were times when central government was prepared to remove powers from local level to prevent the undermining of policy objectives, there were equally others when local authorities were able to make a significant impact on the local area, through a policy of high rates to fund collective service provision.

NOTES AND REFERENCES

1. Unless otherwise stated, statistical information in this chapter concerning population, community health and occupation is drawn from the census figures for 1921 and 1931, and from LCC *Statistical Abstracts* for the period 1919–37. For further details, see the Bibliography of Primary Sources.
2. Clarke, E.T., *Bermondsey* (London, Elliot Stock, 1900), 237.
3. See Wilson, C.H., and Reader, W., *Men and Machines: A History of D. Napier and Son* (1958), quoted in J.E. Martin, *Greater London: An Industrial Geography* (London, G. Bell and Sons, 1966), 15.
4. Booth, C., quoted in H.J. Dyos, *Victorian Suburb: A Study of the Growth of Camberwell* (Leicester, Leicester University Press, 1973), 59.

5.   op. cit., 192.
6.   Metropolitan Borough of Camberwell: MOH Report, 1932, 5.
7.   Ibid.
8.   Booth, C., *Life and Labour of the People in London*, vol. i. *East, Central and South London* (London, Macmillan, 1892), 265.
9.   Offord, J.E. (ed.), *The Book of Walworth* (London, Browning Hall, 1925), 34.
10. Salter, A., in *Bermondsey Labour Magazine*, April 1920, 1.
11. Metropolitan Borough of Southwark, MOH Report, 1925, 50.
12. Metropolitan Borough of Camberwell, MOH Report,. 1930, 36.
13. *South London Press*, 6 January 1922, 15.
14. Oram, R.B., *The Dockers' Tragedy* (Hutchinson, London, 1970), 42.
15. See Lovell, J., *Stevedores and Dockers: A Study of Trades Unions in the Port of London 1870–1914* (New York, Augustus M. Kelly, 1969), ch. 4; and Torr, D., *Tom Mann and his Times* vol. 1. (London, Lawrence and Wishart, 1956), 293.
16. Brockway, F., *Bermondsey Story: The Life of Alfred Salter* (London, Allen and Unwin, 1949), 46.
17. Bagwell, P.S., *The Railwaymen* (London, Allen and Unwin, 1963), 129, 290.
18. Wyncoll, P., *The Nottingham Labour Movement 1880–1939*, 91.
19. Stedman Jones, G., 'Working Class Culture and Working Class Politics' in *Languages of Class: Studies in English Working Class History 1832–1982*, 207.
20. On this development in working-class culture, see Bush, *Behind the Lines: East London Labour, 1914–1919*; Hinton, *Labour and Socialism*; and Wyncoll, op. cit.
21. Bush, op. cit., 12; see also Hinton, and the local history recorded by F. Brockway and by J. Lovell, op. cit.
22. Stedman Jones op. cit., 210.
23. *Doctrine and Ethos in the Labour Party*, 31.
24. Stedman Jones, G., *Outcast London* (Oxford, Oxford University Press, 1971), 11.
25. Stedman Jones, 'Working Class Culture and Working Class Politics', 196; and Thompson, P., *Socialists, Liberals and Labour: The Struggle for London 1885–1914*, 17.
26. Souter, F.W., *Recollections of a Labour Pioneer* (London, Fisher Unwin, 1923), 28–51.
27. Thompson, op. cit., 113–36.
28. See the Wal Hannington Papers in the Marx Memorial Library.
29. Cook, C., *The Age of Alignment: Electoral Politics in Britain 1922–1929* (London, Macmillan, 1975), 1–4, 341–343.
30. Camberwell Trades and Labour Council, *Annual Report: 1914* (Affiliated Societies).
31. Ibid, 1–2.
32. Similar activity in East London is described in Bush, op. cit., 83–4, 53–5.
33. Speech by chairman of the Eleventh Annual Conference of Trades

Councils, reported in Southwark Trades and Labour Council, *Annual Report: 1935*, 50.

34. McKibbon, R., *The Evolution of the Labour Party 1910–1924*, 138–139.

35. *London Labour News* no. 86, December 1931, 2. Results from general and local elections for the period discussed in this chapter have been taken from contemporary reports in the *South London Press*.

36. *Daily Herald*, 3 November 1919, 1.

37. *Daily Herald*, 19 November 1919, 1.

38. See Cook, C., 'Liberals, Labour and Local Elections' in G. Peele and C. Cook, *The Politics of Reappraisal 1918–1939* (London, Macmillan, 1975) 166–88.

39. *Vote for the Progressive Candidate: Camberwell Borough Council Elections 1922* (London, Baker and Co. (TU), 1922).

40. *South London Press*, 22 September 1922, 13.

41. *The Labour-Socialists and the Communists: London Borough Council Elections Leaflet No. 2.* (London, London Municipal Reform Society and National Union Of Ratepayers Associations, 1922).

42. *Support Municipal and Ratepayers Associations Candidates* (London, Keyse and Owen (TU), 1922).

43. Data on membership have been taken from Annual Reports of the London Labour Party, and from *London Labour News*, the journal of the London Labour Party. Not all figures are available, but no other source could be found. Figures recorded are those on which local parties affiliated, and therefore, in some cases, may only be approximate.

44. *London Labour News* no. 167, September 1938, 8.

45. *London Labour News* no. 143, September 1936, 8.

46. For example, Bermondsey CLP in 1939 sent a resolution opposing conscription. See *Labour Party Resolutions For The 38th Annual Conference.* (London, Labour Party, 1939).

47. Forester, T., *The Labour Party and the Working Class* (London, Heinneman, 1976) 73, 93–5.

48. Interview with Anne Ward.

49. *Bermondsey Labour Magazine* no. 89, November 1931, 6–7.

50. Councillor Craigie, quoted in *Southwark and Bermondsey Recorder and South London Gazette*, 31 October 1919, 3.

51. Foster, J., 'How Imperial London preserved its Slums' in *International Journal of Urban and Regional Research*, vol. 3. 1. (March 1979), 93–114.

52. *South London Press*, 6 October 1922, 10.

53. Labour's Manifesto in the 1919 Municipal Elections, quoted in *South London Press*, 17 October, 8.

54. *Bermondsey Labour Magazine*, no. 1, April 1920, 1.

55. Smith, B., writing in *Rotherhithe Labour Magazine*, October 1935, 3.

56. Salter, A., writing in *Bermondsey Labour Magazine*, no. 22, October 1925, 1.

57. Interview with Fanny Stroud.
58. Bermondsey Borough Council Election Manifestos: *Six Years of Labour Rule 1922–1928*; *12 Years of Labour Rule on the Bermondsey Borough Council 1922–34 'Labour's Magnificent Record'.*
59. Interview with Jack Murphy.
60. Levels of rates have been taken from contemporary reports in the *South London Press.*
61. See 'Annual Estimates to Year Ending 1932' for the Metropolitan Boroughs of Southwark, Camberwell and Bermondsey.
62. *South London Press*, 8 April 1938, 24.
63. See, for example, Councillor Sullivan, a Municipal Reformer, quoted in *South London Press*, 8 July 1930, 20.
64. *South London Press*, leader, quoted in *Bermondsey Labour Magazine*, no. 73, May 1930, 5.
65. *Bermondsey Labour Magazine*, no. 34 November 1926, 15.
66. *Bermondsey Labour Magazine*, no. 42 July 1927, 6.
67. *Bermondsey Labour Magazine*, no. 43 September 1927, 6.
68. Statement of Labour Party Policy in the *Camberwell Gazette* (journal of Camberwell Labour Party), November 1925.
69. Metropolitan Borough of Camberwell, MOH Report, 1934, 1.
70. Metropolitan Borough of Southwark, MOH Report, 1926, 50.
71. Metropolitan Borough of Southwark, MOH Report, 1938, 66.
72. Minutes of Bermondsey Housing Committee, 23 July 1924.
73. *South London Press*, 29 August 1923, 1.
74. *South London Press*, 29 August 1924, 1.
75. *South London Press*, 29 January 1926, 2.
76. *South London Press*, 21 October 1927, 9.
77. *South London Press*, 4 November 1927, 16.

Two

1945–64: Consolidation?

THIS chapter is concerned with a twenty-year period, one that takes us from the upheaval of the Second World War, to that of local government reorganisation and the social changes in the 1960s and the 1970s. I have not dwelt on the period of the war itself, partly because this could command a book in itself (James Stewart has written an interesting account of war-time Bermondsey[1]), but partly because the war represented a period of dislocation. Population declined rapidly, through the call-up, evacuation and death. The area sustained some of the worse damage of the war, situated as it was at the apex of the south London railway network and the docks. Local Labour party activity inevitably dwindled, and the local authorities, concerned with air-raid precautions and repairing bomb damage, turned over many of their activities to emergency committees. Nevertheless, the war was to have considerable effects, particularly on government policy, and these will be referred to where relevant. In this chapter, then, I re-examine the areas covered in the previous chapter: local economy, local community and political culture, and then the local Labour parties and the policies of Labour in local government.

1. Local Economy and Local Community

The local economy seemed little changed in the years following the war. It remained dominated by manufacturing industry and the docks, indeed the docks increased in importance during this period. While the majority of factories were medium sized, a small number of very large factories employed a large proportion of the total work-force. Overall, in Southwark, while only 12 per cent of factories employed over 50 workers, they accounted for 66 per cent of the work-force. In Camberwell, only 12 per cent of factories were classified as large, but they employed 69 per cent of the work-force: in Bermondsey, 15 per cent of factories accounted for 76 per cent of the work-force.[2] By 1951, London's industry had begun to move from the areas of riverside in Southwark, in Bermondsey, Lambeth, Deptford and Poplar, downstream to Woolwich, West to Wembley and Willesden and South to Croydon. The importance of the river as an industrial centre was slowly being superseded by road and rail links. Warnes estimates that industry declined by 15 per cent in Bermondsey from 1921 to 1951,[3] but this was during a period when total population also decreased sharply.[4] Avery traces the changes in occupational categories within manufacturing industry in Bermondsey and Southwark, and concludes that there was a marked increase in employment in printing and engineering, wood and cork manufacture and a predominance of food industries, while clothing and footwear, textiles and instrument making declined in importance.[5]

The occupational spread in the area had not significantly changed and, by 1951, was still dominated by engineering, transport, building, printing, leather and paper and wood manufacture, as well as personal services, clerical and commercial work. The census shows that, of the total adult male population, only 0.8 per cent in Bermondsey, 2.2 per cent in Camberwell, and 0.7 per cent in Southwark were classed as professional. Intermediate workers accounted for 8 per cent of the workforce in Bermondsey, 11.3 per cent in Camberwell and 6.1 per cent in Southwark, while 91.2 per cent in Bermondsey, 86.5 per cent in Camberwell and 93.2 per cent in Southwark were manual workers. About half the manual workers in all three boroughs were skilled and half semi-skilled or unskilled. By 1961, some changes are apparent. The classifications changed slightly, and therefore comparisons are approximate, but professional workers increased to 5.3 per cent, 9.7 per cent and 5.1 per cent respectively, while the proportion of other non-manual workers doubled. Skilled workers fell dramatically as a proportion, by 10 per cent in Bermondsey, 20 per cent in Camberwell and 15 per cent in Southwark, while unskilled workers fell as a proportion by 10 per cent, 5 per cent and 10 per cent respectively.

By the early 1960s there were noticeable increases in commercial activity and office work. The Southwark Medical Officer of Health reported in 1960, in relation to office accommodation in the northern part of the borough, 'the momentum of development has . . . of late rapidly increased'.[6] These changes seem, however, to have been concentrated in Camberwell and the Borough area of Southwark.

In some ways, the political culture described in the previous chapter reached its greatest strength and confidence during this period. Local people were better off than they had ever been, although they were still poor by national standards, and there was now virtual full employment. Trades-unionism was perhaps at its strongest locally, and this was a period of continual unofficial stoppages, especially in the docks. The Transport and General Workers' Union, which had absorbed the Dockers' Union, was immensely strengthened by the decasualisation of the docks and the introduction of the National Dock Labour Scheme, which created a guaranteed minimum wage paid by the Dock Labour Boards if dockers could not find any other employment. This was a period of immense strength and confidence for the dockers. A retired docker told me:

> When you saw a mass walk-out at the dock gates, there was always a cry 'Well, we don't know what we're going out for – but we're not going back until we get it!' There was always this blind loyalty . . . I remember we came out for a week for the Courage girls – 'cos we were so powerful then. . . . London was the port of the world, there was always full employment then.[7]

They remained, however, a particularly close-knit group. As one docker's son put it:

> The dockers all used particular pubs where they'd all talk about the jobs – they more or less stayed in a group . . . Rotherhithe Labour Club would be well patronised . . . people hung more together . . . and the dockers hung together, they were a community.[8]

The local communities were close-knit and stable. Turner reports, for example, that:

> Bermondsey represents a traditional, working class community, whose inhabitants are overwhelmingly engaged in manual labor . . . less than four per cent of the inhabitants had moved to Bermondsey from other places . . . Most of the adult Bermondsians have lived in the community for long periods of time . . . Bermondsey's isolated position on the riverside, the homogeneity of its social structure, the strong family linkages and the shared experience of hardship during the depression and the bombing have combined to weld it into a tightly knit community with a distinctive character.[9]

Conditions in the local area had improved significantly by the close of the Second World War, but were still relatively poor. The vast majority of local people rented from private landlords and many households lacked basic amenities. There was considerable over-crowding, and a severe housing shortage. Conditions in the tenements of Walworth and the Elephant and Castle were especially poor. Larger houses in Peckham and Camberwell had become multi-occupied, and deteriorated rapidly. Local health had improved, partly due to the new health services, to improved sanitation and public health, and to war-time measures. But the incidence of serious diseases, such as tuberculosis and diphtheria, remained high.[10]

The population was slowly ageing; between 1931 and 1951 the proportion of over-sixties had doubled to ¢over 10 per cent, while those aged five to fourteen and fifteen to twenty had decreased, as younger skilled workers moved out to the newer industrial areas. The old ways were changing:

> in pre-war days, if you married a girl more than five streets away from you, you were marrying a foreigner – you got married and got rooms within a street or two – you only got a room 'cos your mother knew, or your father knew, someone with rooms to let . . . the war began to change all that . . .[11]

Slowly, also, newcomers were joining the community. Some of the West Indian arrivals on the 'Empire Windrush' in 1948 settled in south-east London. At first they were billeted in old air-raid shelters, and common lodging houses, often facing considerable hostility. In Deptford, angry whites beseiged Carrington House where black workers were staying.[12] The majority of black people settled in neighbouring New Cross and Brixton – which did nothing to stop the growth of anti-black feeling in Bermondsey and Southwark. Only Peckham and Camberwell developed a significant black community; the proportion of residents born in the Commonwealth or colonies in 1951 was very low: 0.3 per cent in Bermondsey, 1.3 per cent in Camberwell and 0.75 per cent in Southwark.

Black people faced a colour bar in pubs and dance halls. There was also a colour bar operated by many landlords; local black people were forced into the worst and most overcrowded lodgings, while local tenants strenuously opposed the granting of tenancies to any black families.[13] The LCC withdrew its first offer of a tenancy to a black family because of the strength of local pressure.[14]

By the late 1950s, immigration had become a major issue in the area – fuelled by scares about health and housing. The Camberwell Medical Officer of Health produced reports in 1958 and 1963 suggesting that immigrants produced special health problems. The 1958 report was headlined in the local paper 'Immigration Brings Friction and Spreads TB', and reported that, for immigrants, 'there is a tendency to live in overcrowded and unsatisfactory housing conditions and with frequent changes in employment and movement from place to place, with opportunities of infecting others and being infected'.[15] These stories were made the most of by local fascist groups.

The development of racist feeling in the 1950s and 1960s, and its expression via fears about 'immigration' have been well documented by Miles and Phizacklea and others.[16] The development of racist feeling locally was part of an expression of antagonism to 'outsiders', developed within a close-knit community. Such divisions were to widen in the next two decades.

2. The Local Labour Party

Support both for the labour movement and the Labour Party was a matter of tradition, of local identity, of community solidarities and loyalties. It reflected a general feeling that Labour represented working people, rather than a burning commitment to socialist ideals. But there was support for Labour's national and local programme – at least at first.

> I had it drummed into me when I was a kid that the only salvation for the working class was the Labour Party. . . . The Labour Party was just an opposition to the Tories. Most working people knew that the Labour Party was for them and the Tories were against them. They didn't go into politics or philosophy – they knew the Labour Party would change things.[17]

During this period, this area of south-east London became indisputably a Labour area: indeed, places like Southwark and Bermondsey became impregnable Labour fortresses. For a period, there was scarcely any opposition. In a significant number of wards during this period the Conservatives and Liberals declined to put up candidates at all, and several councillors were elected unopposed.[18] Indeed, the only serious opposition to Labour in Southwark came from the Communist Party – which was able to win up to 1 000 votes in council-ward elections, pushing the Conservatives into third place. In Camberwell the Communist Party was less successful, although able to make a respectable showing in ward by-elections, and in Bermondsey it had little support.[19] With the exception of the Communist Party, and the few short-lived and unstable tenants' associations organised in private tenements, there were no other community organisations, tenants' organisations, amenity groups or pressure groups outside the Labour Party. The wide range of interest groups and pressure groups that we have become accustomed to in recent years did not exist during this period. Political pressure was, by and large, organised through the Labour Party structures, or not at all.

The dramatic reduction in population in the aftermath of the war led to local, constituency-boundary changes, which were fiercely opposed locally. The 1950 general election was the first to be fought on the new boundaries, with Rotherhithe and West Bermondsey merged to form a single constituency, the three Southwark constituencies merged into one, and the constituencies of Camberwell North and Camberwell North West absorbed into Peckham and Dulwich. Party membership, which had disintegrated during the war, increased rapidly in the immediate post-war years. By 1950, membership figures in most local constituencies had reached and overtaken the highest figures of the pre-war years. Bermondsey's membership was often the highest in London. Party membership for all constituencies reached a peak in the early 1950s: in 1952, recorded affiliated membership for Bermondsey was 4 689, for Peckham 3 028, Dulwich 3 136 and Southwark 1 481.[20] By 1955, membership in Bermondsey still represented nearly 20 per cent of all Labour voters in the 1951 election.[21] Nevertheless, membership was now beginning to fall. By 1959, the London Labour Party had stopped publishing individual constituency membership figures, although the Annual Report expressed the hope that 'membership recruitment in the constituencies will result in the downward trend being reversed'.[22]

Electorally, Labour seemed invincible. In the municipal elections of 1945, Labour won control of the whole of south London; in the LCC elections of 1946 it dropped only six seats in south London. All three boroughs were Labour-controlled throughout the period 1945–64 and, apart from a brief reappearance of three Conservative Councillors in Bermondsey from 1945–9, both Southwark and Bermondsey had 100 per cent Labour representation.

General Election successes were even more marked. Bob Mellish, a young ex-army captain who worked for the Transport and General Workers' Union, had won a by-election in Rotherhithe in 1946 and, when the two constituencies merged, secured, with TGWU support, the new Bermondsey seat. Together with George Isaacs in Southwark, and Freda Corbett in Peckham, he was to clock up some of the largest majorities in the country. In 1950 Mellish in Bermondsey, Corbett in Peckham, and Isaacs in Southwark clocked up majorities of 18 000 or more; and achieved similar majorities in 1951 and 1955. Dulwich, won from the Tories in 1936, was lost again in 1951 and only regained in 1964. It was only in Dulwich that either the Conservatives or the Liberals were able to implement any realistic election machine.

The percentage poll, having dipped in 1945 because of the outdated electoral register, was by 1950 and 1951 higher than ever before. In the 1951 General Eelection the poll was 76 per cent in Peckham, 84 per cent in Dulwich, 72 per cent in Southwark and 78 per cent in Bermondsey. By 1964, however, although Mellish was still recording the biggest majority in London, with a majority of 59 per cent over the Conservatives, victories were based on falling polls. By 1964, the poll in Peckham had fallen to 58 per cent, in Dulwich to 74 per cent, in Southwark to 55 per cent and in Bermondsey to 63 per cent. Labour's majorities were therefore falling. We can measure Labour's support by a combination of party membership, Labour votes and percentage polls, and one thing is very striking; all three variables reached a peak around 1952. However, the size of Labour's majorities and the strength of Labour control in the area masked the fact that, from the mid-1950s, Labour's support had begun steadily to decline.

The parties also began to change. The Trades and Labour Councils, which had formed the base of the Labour Party in the years 1914–39, were dismantled, which dislocated the political and industrial wings of the labour movement. In Camberwell, the Trades and Labour Council had been broken up before the war by the TUC, after the industrial section had insisted on claiming autonomy on political questions under Communist Party leadership. By 1948–9 the TUC had a clear policy of insisting on separation, and the Southwark and Bermondsey Trades and Labour Councils were split into separate political and industrial organisations.[24] Battles within the new Trades Councils continued over 'Communist infiltration'. In Bermondsey, attempts at a Communist take-over failed dramatically. In Southwark and Camberwell there were continual ructions, and the Trades Councils chose to risk disaffiliation over work with the local Communists or front organisations, inviting Communist speakers and voting money for the proscribed local Southwark Peace Council.[25] In 1951 Vic Feather was expressing concern over Southwark Trades Council: 'the few resolutions that they submit to the TUC appear to originate "left of centre"'.[26] Southwark Trades Council was among twenty-four disaffiliated in 1952 for refusing to abandon the London Trades Council in favour of the TUC substitute, the 'Federation of Trades Councils'. The TUC established an official Southwark Trades Council, and the rebel body was finally wound up in 1954, advising branches to re-affiliate to the official body.[27]

The division between the Labour parties and Trades Councils weakened both. The trades unions were less involved in the Labour Party than before, although they retained control when necessary – the Transport and General Workers' Union was capable of packing Bermondsey GMC if they needed to. The Labour Party lost its direct links into the trades-union movement. Even the Communist Party was unhappy, despite their frequent

domination of the new Trades Councils. One Communist veteran
wrote that:

> Nobody benefitted. The trades council meetings were reduced
> to a handful of delegates and lost the small influence they
> had in the local trades union branches. There was a paucity
> of trades or industrial issues on the agenda, as indeed there
> are today, and, cut off from the political wing, Camber-
> well Trades Council lapsed into an insignificant coterie of
> activists.[28]

At the same time, the local constituency parties, which had been
politically very active in the immediate post-war years, were, by
the mid-1950s, settling down to a less challenging role. Levels of
activity varied from constituency to constituency. In Bermondsey,
the party had re-established pre-war activities; MP's surgeries,
socials, meetings, lectures, tennis clubs and darts matches and
strong womens' and youth sections. Party members were encouraged to join local organisations to improve Labour's image.[29] The
full-time agent, John Thomas, organised membership drives: 'On
appointed days, the workers would swarm through a neighbourhood while the MP would work from the sound truck'.[30] Turner
reports that levels of organisation were high; by the 1960s all six
wards held regular meetings and regularly scheduled speakers, and
one ward had 900 paid-up members in 1961. Nevertheless, he
reports that attendance was highly variable and that, of the 3 000
members, only about 100 or so were active, at best.[31] This description is corroborated by interviews with local party-members.[32]
The local party was a part of the community, organising events and
socials, as well as, or perhaps instead of, political events:

> It was part of the community, it saw itself as part of it . . . it
> wasn't just the local councillors or GMC members that
> organised things . . . in our ward, although it was relatively
> small, we had outings throughout the year, not just for
> Labour Party members . . . sports days and childrens'
> outings.[33]

> The old ethos of the Bermondsey party was to become and be
> seen as part of the community itself, and not as a purely
> political party.[34]

> [The wards] . . . were very good at talking about social events
> and they were very good at involving themselves in the local
> community, whether it was taking the elderly out on a trip or
> taking local kids out or sports things . . . They acted like, sort
> of, social workers, they were only concerned with the local

activities of social groups . . . the vulnerable . . . there was no political discussion.[35]
In Southwark, on the other hand, the party was increasingly dominated by a small, almost dynastic group, the 'four families', who held power tightly in their hands, froze out newcomers, and indeed discouraged membership!

The tiny membership policy is known to be the idea of the 'old guard' of the party leaders who believe in an easily controlled nucleus of experienced labour workers which can be expanded for elections but kept within bounds the rest of the time.[36]

We never bothered about mass membership – membership wasn't big – we always worked on the basis that if someone joins and is interested they're a much better member than if you knock on the door and talk them into joining.[37]

There were periodic attempts to challenge this concentration of power from younger members, but with little success.

A similar trend of less active membership, and of increasingly social, rather than political, organisation was also reported in Camberwell. As one Camberwell member put it:

The Labour Party was seen as a kind of social worker thing . . . politics didn't come into it much, . . . it wasn't ideology or anything like that . . . if people had domestic problems then the Labour Party would sort them out . . . . At the ward meeting . . . the kind of things we used to talk about . . . they could talk solid about paving stones for two hours . . . very parochial things, really . . . we'd have a discussion for two hours about Mrs Brown who'd been ill, or talk about neighbours – but, as for politics, they were non-existent.[38]

The Peckham and Dulwich parties continued to send motions to Conference, however, during a period when it was rare for Bermondsey and almost unheard-of for Southwark to do so. Resolutions covered nationalisation, family allowances, the cost of living, housing and pensions, and seldom took sides in the conflicts that were dividing the party nationally: indeed, it is very hard to judge party activity in the terms of 'Right' and 'Left' that dominate such discussions in the 1980s. As one party member put it,

'Left wing? They weren't terms that were used. If you was in the party you were automatically Left wing'.[39]

On two occasions the debates that split the party nationally *did* impinge on local politics. The Camberwell parties sent a resolution to Conference in 1951 opposing optical and dental charges and a resolution on disarmament in 1952, which, however, stopped short of a Bevanite position.[40] In 1960 Bermondsey Labour Party voted to support unilateral disarmament. However, the decision was taken at a meeting when several prominent members were absent; it did not take Bob Mellish long to round up the 'big guns' and reverse the vote by 48 to 6.[41] Bermondsey agent John Thomas summed up their position at Labour Party Conference in 1953, when he said during a speech,

> My party in Bermondsey do not tread to the left and do not tread to the right; they tread resolutely down the road in the middle to the ultimate goal of socialism.[42]

The Peckham party was perhaps still seen as being the most 'Left' party locally, while the Southwark party, said the *South London Press*, 'is regarded by most vocal labourites as right wing and reactionary'.[43]

The local parties, by and large, shared the priorities of their Members of Parliament. The local MPs, Bob Mellish, Freda Corbett and George Isaacs wielded considerable local influence, and saw themselves first and foremost as representing their local communities. Bob Mellish spoke constantly in the House about the problems of the docks, and identified himself as the 'dockers' MP'. The *South London Press* commented that 'few other South London MPs have ever aligned themselves so much with the lives of the people they represent'.[44] This representation took the form of a vast network of personal contacts, an impressively detailed knowledge of the area, and seeing to it that 'their people' got a good deal.

The party was unlikely to find itself in conflict with the local councils. In many cases the party hierarchy and the Labour group on the council were interchangeable. By the mid-1960s, the sixty councillors in Bermondsey and Southwark probably constituted a significant proportion of the active membership.

> When you have a 100 per cent Labour council, there is more of the party *in* the council . . . sixty members of the Labour Party all directly involved in a small area – they were the bulk of the General Management Committee – they *were* the party.[45]

The party's role was far more likely to be one of support for the local councils, explaining to local people the problems the council was facing and defending their policies.

The outlook of the local Labour party changed. The 1945–51 Labour government had introduced many of the social programmes that the party had been fighting for, in relation to schools, hospitals and housing. The local parties supported these new services although, as the projects of central government, they were far from the 'municipal socialism' originally proposed. Labour's role locally seemed to have shrunk to that of electing a Labour government, and even that presented little challenge when the votes of local people could be taken for granted. It was suggested in the last chapter that Labour stood for both a utopian view of a community serving itself as a sort of socialist commonwealth, and for a fairly limited practical programme of reforms. When the latter was achieved, then at least there was time to draw breath and contemplate the achievements of a decade:

> The local Labour Party slowly got much more pragmatic and down to earth. So many of the earlier ideas were achieved. We improved housing beyond knowledge – it's only a few people who can remember what it was like before . . . youngsters used to go to school without shoes and stockings.[46]

> It was bread and butter politics – no airy fairy stuff – there wasn't the fervour in politics that there is now.[47]

The local parties were parochial, interested in immediate issues affecting their own lives first and foremost – housing, health, education – and in trades-union issues. The majority of party members were local working class people, older, perhaps, than the rest of the population. In social-policy terms, they were deeply conservative. In 1961 Bermondsey Labour party submitted a conference resolution which responded to local 'moral panics' about contagious diseases spread by immigrants:

> This conference deplores the fact that all immigrants to this country are allowed entrance without first ensuring that they have a clean bill of health, and urges that the Parliamentary Labour Party insist that strict medical examinations are made of intending immigrants before they are allowed to take up residence.[48]

At the same conference Peckham constituency submitted a resolution on 'unchecked immigration' calling for

> legislation to regulate and control this immigration, in view of the fact that Britain is already badly overcrowded and that the present position results in much squalor and consequent hardship to those who are allowed to come into Britain without restraint.[49]

Local MPs campaigned to clear local lodging houses of 'vagrants', to restrict immigration, and to protect the area from queue-jumpers and 'outsiders'.[50] The party was also traditionalist, patriarchal, and a firm supporter of the family and 'moral values'. The Catholic influence remained strong in these areas. There was clearly a correct, a respectable, order of things.

The principles of our socialism are based on the integrity of the family. We believe that the family is the all-important unit of our country – that the wage earner shall have a job that has good wages and decent conditions and that he shall have an adequate pension when he retires. That the mother of his children shall have a decent home, and in sickness and adversity shall have the best possible education and be insured from birth to death. These principles are in accord with the British way of life.[51]

3. *Labour in Local Government*

During this period the role of local government was to change substantially because of shifts in the financing of local programmes, the division of powers between central and local government, and the degree of central direction and planning. In London, as in many major cities, the scale of the Blitz made reconstruction a first priority. There was a powerful determination not to return to the conditions that existed in 1939. Throughout the war, Labour activists had been developing ideas about the future: Lewis Silkin wrote about the remaking of London with 'tree lined thoroughfares as beautiful as Paris or other continental cities'.[52] The 1942 *London Labour News* claimed that

> The central problem. is to eliminate the defective, the outworn, the inefficient, to preserve what is good and worthy of London as judged by modern standards.[53]

The professionals were also busy planning for the future. The Greater London (Abercrombie) Plan, published in 1944, was to form the basis of London's redevelopment, proposing a stabilisation of population at one million below 1939 levels, with overspill provided for by new towns outside a tightly-protected green belt.

When Labour won the general election in 1945, it seemed to the local labour movement that all these plans were finally to be realised. For a solidly Labour area like south-east London, a Labour government meant that services to working people, pioneered by Labour councils, could now be spread to the whole country. At the same time, it signalled that national resources would be available for local reconstruction. The 1945 Labour Manifesto spelt out Labour's project, in similar terms to the project described at local level:

> The nation wants food, work and homes. It wants more than that – it wants good food in plenty, useful work for all, and comfortable labour saving homes that take full advantage of the resources of modern science and productive industry. It wants a high and rising standard of living, security against a

rainy day, an education system that will give every boy and girl a chance to develop the best that is in them.[54] But, by 1945, that project had switched decisively to the central state. The experience of war-time planning and the construction of a machinery of government capable of administering vast national services meant that the incoming Labour government's attention was on policies implemented at national rather than municipal level.

The funding of local authorities changed considerably. During hostilities, the pre-war system of local government finance had broken down under the combined pressures of growing demands on local authorities, and the decimation of the rate base through bomb damage and evacuation. Central government had bailed out local councils with a series of loans which, by the end of the war, had to be translated into grants and interest-free loans. A new system of finance was introduced in Bevan's 1947 Local Government Act. This replaced the general exchequer contribution with an Exchequer Equalisation Grant aimed at redistributing resources towards the poorer boroughs, while at the same time increasing the proportion of local government spending met by central resources.

Bermondsey and Southwark were net gainers from the changes, but were sharply critical of the failure of the new Act to compensate for losses suffered as a result of industrial de-rating in 1929.[55] Camberwell's financial position remained largely unchanged. The Local Government Act established for the first time a system of substantial grant equalisation based around the idea of minimum levels of provision and performance. At the same time, local authorities were given extra powers to publish information, organise lectures, etc. and – a uniquely Bevan touch – to levy up to a 6d rate to provide entertainment, theatres, dance-halls and orchestras. The effect was both to relieve the rate burden in poor local authorities, and to reduce the autonomy of local authorities to determine priorities or levels of spending. If central government was to pay the piper, then it was also likely to call some of the tunes. This process was accelerated by the stress on minimum levels of provision (which inevitably became maximal) and on central control. The *South London Press* had by this time undergone a Pauline conversion to Labour, no doubt induced by the need to maintain sales in a solidly Labour area. It commented:

> The process of centralisation . . . is the result of people's demands for economy. Grouping of piecemeal services like housing is part of the drive to economic efficiency. Less than half the borough services are now charged to the local rate

. . . the rates are the best buy in your household budget. They have gone up since the war but they haven't doubled like other costs of living. The average rate-payer gets all his municipal services, from roads, schools, and police to swimming baths, libraries and dustbins emptying for about 4s a week. Less than you pay for half a pint of wallop a night.[56]

Several key services were shifted out of local-government control. Most important, locally, was the loss of health functions, which had been built up, particularly after the loss of poor relief in 1929, as the major local government service. Local reaction was ambivalent. The *South London Press* recorded:

> a mild revolt of many metropolitan councils against the loss of most council run health services . . . torn between allegiance to the Labour government and the health minister Bevan and defending their local health centres and services which have been built up over so many years at considerable cost, most of which they will now have to forfeit.[57]

The Labour Councils and Labour parties expressed support for the new National Health Service, realising that this would mean minimum standards of health over the rest of the country. But this was combined with bitterness, especially in Bermondsey, when it became clear that the new national provision meant a deterioration of standards locally. By 1956 the Bermondsey Medical Officer of Health was writing angrily about the fate of the Bermondsey Health Centre:

> The building still functions in a sort of way, though the heat has gone out of it. The MOH was still retained as a Hon. Medical Superintendent but shorn of all control, and instead of one authority there were three or four all of which had some say in the management of the centre, with much resultant confusion and lack of coordination . . . . The disappointment among the members of the Borough Council has naturally been intense, not so much, perhaps, at the transfer of function from their control, as at the slow demise of a living organism which they themselves had originated and which they saw slowly dying before their eyes simply through lack of knowledge and lack of interest on the part of 'the powers that be'.[58]

Even the Fairby Grange convalescent home, it seemed, could not be incorporated into NHS plans and, although maintained by Bermondsey council via a trust fund for several years, it was forced to close in 1952. Maternity and child welfare services were transferred to the LCC despite protests from the boroughs.

At the same time, the municipal utilities, gas and electricity, were transferred to regional, and less accountable, structures. After years of cheap electricity under municipal control, the people of Bermondsey and Southwark found themselves faced with increased charges and a marked change of attitude from the new authorities. When local people, councillors and MPs protested against the sharply increasing charges, they were told 'there is no question of asking your approval. Until a consultative council is appointed we shall tell you what we intend'.[59]

The third change in the role of local councils stemmed from growing central government commitment to infrastructural planning and to increased housing production. South-east London featured prominently in the development plans of the new Labour government. It had been severely affected by the Blitz; it had some of the worst housing conditions in the country; and, it must be noted, it had a disproportionate number of Ministers in the new Labour government anxious to see changes for 'their people'. Lewis Silkin, MP for Camberwell, having built up long experience at the LCC, was made the first Minister of Town and Country Planning. Ben Smith and George Isaacs were both in the cabinet. South-east London was singled out for early redevelopment. Of the 'areas of comprehensive redevelopment' designated between 1945 and 1960, six were in south-east London, including the South Bank, the Elephant and Castle and Bermondsey. Half of the 300 acres of open space planned by the LCC as the 'lungs of the new London' were in Bermondsey, Deptford, Lambeth, Southwark and Camberwell.[60] The new London Plan proposed to sweep away the 'tangle of derelict warves, warehouses, narrow streets and tumbledown houses'[61] along the southern riverfront, to build a complex with two theatres, a great concert hall, swimming pool, bandstand and cafés, with gardens and parks stretching to Southwark Cathedral.

These plans were no longer merely local, they were London-wide and national. Indeed, it was the Labour government, committed to national planning, that on several occasions insisted that national proposals should prevail over local plans. Local plans for Bankside were overridden after a long struggle with the Minister, in favour of plans for a new power station needed for national energy policy – although Bermondsey had repeatedly offered an 'equivalent' stretch of riverfront in Rotherhithe for the power station.[62] Plans by Southwark Council for the South Bank were subsumed into the development plans for the 1951 festival at Waterloo, and a massive complex of theatres, concert halls and bars substituted for the planned entertainment and leisure facilities for local people. Other plans for comprehensive redevelopment were shelved as a result of cuts in the national capital programme in 1947, including the proposed 'Piccadilly' at the Elephant and Castle, which was to have included new wide roads, homes, theatres and, perhaps, a university.[63] After 1951, the scale of redevelopment plans was reduced and emphasis switched from public planning to private development, although the structures and mechanisms remained.

Housing, while still a local authority responsibility, was, in the post-war years, a major area of central-government intervention. Housing numbers were now a measure of government's political success. Bevan, determined to 'plan with plannable instruments'[64] had rested responsibility for the new government's building programme with local authorities rather than the private sector. Private speculative builders had to apply to local authorities for licences to build. In Labour areas, such as Bermondsey, where the local authority needed skilled workers and materials for their own programmes, these were seldom granted. In place of obstacles and financial disincentives, there were now centrally set targets, which were carefully monitored. The housing cuts introduced in 1947 created serious damage, because they came just as local program-mes began finally to take off. There was a stream of protests to government from local councillors and MPs, as they attempted to salvage the programmes they had been encouraged to embark on.[65] A policy of public housing expansion to meet needs was further weakened, although not formally attacked, by changes in policy and subsidy introduced by subsequent Tory governments. The Conservatives switched the emphasis from the public to the private sector, reducing the role of the PWLB, raising interest rates and, by 1956, reducing subsidies for general-needs building. The emphasis on public-sector housing was switched towards slum clearance. But, in areas like Southwark and Camberwell, it was precisely the slum clearance programme which created a massive expansion in public-sector housing.

Housing was to become the most significant council service, and the central issue in local government, during this period, taking the place that poor relief and health provision had previously occupied. Local authorities now had sufficient resources to make a significant impact on local housing problems. Central-government power over local programmes increased accordingly, and cuts in central-government financial support now made a major impact on local authorities. However, direct central-government control was probably less significant than the powerful political consensus which existed between local authorities, central government, and the professionals; and therefore the points where policy options were constrained by central government become very blurred. A recent report has argued, for example, that central government circulars in the 1950s extolling the virtues of non-traditional building, and promising that 'anything the authority may do now in that direction will be taken fully into account when increases in programmes are being considered', amounted to 'little less than bribing the local authority to accept non-traditional houses as part of their programmes'.[66] However, Dunleavy has demonstrated the complex interrelation of central government, the role of the construction industry, professional fashions and prevailing social assumptions in the development of high-rise building.[67] In any case, 'bribery' is limited in its effectiveness in controlling local authorities. In Southwark, Camberwell and Bermondsey there was little interest in the new methods. Before 1964, as we shall see, even at the height of redevelopment the local authorities relied as much on traditional methods as on new systems and, for example, built very few tower blocks.

During this period the Labour administrations of Bermondsey, Southwark and Camberwell settled down to a less romantic role than that which they had hoped to play in the earlier period. Much of Labour's municipal programme had been translated into national policies. Much of it seemed to have been achieved. Councils saw their role as that of maintaining service provision, and innovating a little here or there, but always within frameworks laid down by government. Differences between authorities were nevertheless considerable, and local autonomy was jealously guarded. Despite the fact that all three authorities covered by this survey were now Labour-controlled, there were policy differences, and differences in the way they went about doing things.

Bermondsey during this period continued to be a high spender on services such as housing, health and public baths. Bermondsey was one of the few boroughs to continue building during the war, and had repaired its target of 8 200 homes by 1945.[68] In the early post-war years Bermondsey expanded its building programme rapidly, and consistently jostled with Deptford at the top of the 'Housing League Table' published in the local paper.[69]

Local Labour parties had expressed strong opposition to the use of temporary housing, arguing, for example, that

It is the desire of the Rotherhithe and West Bermondsey Labour parties to provide permanent homes with all the latest labour saving devices that modern science can provide.[70]

Although Bermondsey did use prefabs in the immediate post-war years, the Council concentrated on building permanent homes, always spending the maximum possible under the changing subsidy systems. By 1961, Bermondsey had erected 2 000 new homes and had another 400 under construction.[71] By 1963 the Bermondsey *Official Guide* boasted that council housing accounted for one-third of all the residential accommodation in the borough.

> Comprehensive redevelopment has . . . given the borough, once one of London's most notorious slums, standards of housing and civic enterprise undreamed of by previous generations.[72]

Shorn of its mainstream health responsibilities, the borough council created a vigorous public health service and launched a health programme campaign. Mobile 'cine-cars' toured the estates, showing films and giving lectures and demonstrations. New services developed during this period include meals-on-wheels services and municipal clubs for the elderly, with meeting rooms, socials and workshops.[73] John Turner argues that council services were highly popular among local people during the early 1960s:

> The new council estates are a source of pride for Bermondsey's citizens who spend a lot of time arranging their flats or sprucing up their homes . . . they are visibly pleased with their borough – its municipal housing, the public baths and the libraries, the schools and hospitals and the recreation program.[74]

As one informant put it, 'the main problem after the war was housing and the council did very well'.[75] Councillors in the neighbouring boroughs of Southwark and Camberwell also felt that Bermondsey Council continued to deserve its reputation as a pioneer:

> Bermondsey was one of the foremost Labour councils in the whole of Britain, with a housing record second to none.[76]

The borough had a reputation for providing efficient, locally responsive services. Many of the pre-war policies continued: the closed shop, the policy of low rents and the requirement that Council workers had to live in the borough. It is important to bear in mind the small geographical area and the shrinking population covered by the Council.

By 1961, the borough had a population of 51 860. The Council was small enough for members and officers to know each other, and to know the area they served. The Housing Department, for example, served an area equivalent to one of six present district offices within the new authority. Similarly, *four* committees responsible for libraries, baths, beautification and entertainments covered areas of service provision now covered by one committee. Councillors were able to concern themselves with the detail of policy; they could decide on the layout of flats, the location of a

library, and the colour of curtains in an old folks home. In a 100
per cent Labour council, the centre of decision-making was the
Labour Group. To the Bermondsey Group meetings came every
case of eviction for rent arrears, every post to be refilled or
regraded; items such as the floodlighting of a playground, or a
dangerous pothole, were discussed.[77] Housing was still allocated
on the basis of individual applications decided by councillors.[78]
The political machinery seems to have been able to exercise
control over the detail of policy.

Links between council, work-force and community were
inevitably formed by the requirement that council workers had to
live in the borough. Links with the community were made through
the local Labour party rather than through any attempt at formal
representation, but in 1950, for example, Labour Party membership represented nearly one in ten of the population. To the
outside world, the Labour Council and Labour party presented an
exterior of disciplined unity. Opposition to council policies was
rare. The Communist Party failed to make a significant impact in
Bermondsey. There were few, if any, voluntary organisations or
tenants' groups.

Southwark was also, during this period, represented entirely by
Labour Councillors. But, partly because the local Labour party
was so much smaller, the informal mechanisms for participation
that existed in Bermondsey did not seem to exist here, and the
Council was seen as closed and cliquey. Committee meetings were
held in secret; the Council meetings were little more than a
formality:

> To outsiders they presented an utterly disciplined, united
> exterior . . . council meetings could last as little as seven
> minutes – they'd take about five items on the nod . . . it was
> an old patronage structure . . . dissent was not tolerated . . .
> you had to keep in with the ruling clique.[79]

Nor was the scale of local authority provision as great. Southwark
began to build housing quite rapidly in the early post-war years,
but soon developed a reputation among neighbouring boroughs
for keeping rents low by neglecting their duties and leaving
housing development to the LCC. Rents in Southwark were indeed
low, in 1961 they were the lowest in London.[80]

Southwark, soon after the war, introduced the innovation of a
housing points-scheme, but allocation was still carried out by
councillors, 'bearing in mind the criteria of the points scheme'.[81]
Despite pressure from the local Trades Council, Southwark never
developed their own direct labour department. Southwark Council
was, however, influential in persuading the LCC to increase the

densities in the Greater London Development Plan for the area. Local evidence supports the suggestion made by Dunleavy, Merrett and others that one of the pressures for high-rise and high-density housing – though by no means the most powerful – came from the local Labour councils.[82] Under the headline 'Sardine Styles Can Pack Them In', the *South London Press* reported a deputation from Southwark Council to the LCC in March 1952 to persuade them to increase densities for housing from 136 people per acre to 200. Len Styles, Council Leader, said

> Thousands live in the closely packed area between the Elephant and Castle and Camberwell who cannot afford more fares if they are moved out. We believe that these people could be happy and well housed if we are allowed to build upwards and increase the density of population.[83]

Unlike Bermondsey, Southwark faced some opposition, partly due to the strength of the local Communist Party. Joe Bent, tireless Regional Organiser for the CP, and candidate in almost every election for twenty years, fought a powerful campaign over the borough's housing policy. He was able to build considerable support through a technique which Phil Piratin refers to as being used in Poplar,[84] canvassing an estate, finding out the problems, taking up a few cases, and then forming a tenants' association. A few tenants would join the Party, and, after a while, the association would fold. However, considerable activity was created among tenants of the Walworth tenement blocks, deputations were led to the Council demanding action to pull down the slums and redevelop. The Council stonewalled. There were a series of conflicts during council meetings throughout the 1950s and 1960s; the public gallery would be packed, the tenants would stamp and shout, and the police would be called.

> You would never get a response . . . You'd get 180 signatures out of 200 or so and when you presented the petition, the answer was just no. There may have been some councillors who secretly thought we'd got a point, but by the time it reached the council, the view was always no.[85]

Ironically, considering later community campaigns, the CP-led tenants were demanding more and faster redevelopment, and were great supporters of new building techniques, of industrial building and of high-rise:

> We in the Southwark party were great enthusiasts of 'to hell with the density – build', and if you have to build high, to do it – build high! . . . In the Southwark party I produced a grandiose scheme of building everything on top of the Bricklayers' Arms – like Corbusier.[86]

Southwark continued to provide greater than average levels of public health services, baths etc.; but there was little innovation in any of these areas. By the early 1960s, however, the Council had begun to develop new and dramatic schemes. By 1963, plans had been drawn up for the complete redevelopment of the Elephant and Castle into one of the first British covered shopping centres, with office blocks, a massive traffic roundabout system, underpasses and tower blocks. At the same time, proposals for slum clearance on a large scale were put forward, including the redevelopment of a 10-acre 'new town' in the centre of Walworth.[87]

Camberwell was, in many ways, different from the two northern boroughs. Although it was Labour-controlled throughout this period, there was always a significant Conservative opposition, which at least created a level of public debate. Camberwell was considerably larger than Bermondsey or Southwark, both in size and population. By 1950, it was the fourth largest London borough in geographical area, with a population of 178 000.[88] The suburban south and the residential character of much of the Borough meant that Councillors were more likely to be middle class or professional people.

Camberwell Council, in the years after the war, concentrated on repairing and rebuilding on in-fill sites, and on requisitioning property, and came under serious attack from the local papers and central government for its poor housing record. During this period it built up a direct-labour force and began work on several, major, housing estates. Camberwell prided itself on providing 'furnished homes', with spin-dryers, fridges etc, for tenants. It provided a good range of other services, although never quite on the same scale as Bermondsey. Housing allocation followed similar procedures in Camberwell to those in Southwark, with stress being laid on the fact that:

> whatever their need [applicants] should be of a type who could be expected to look after their property in a proper manner and meet their weekly commitments regularly.[89]

By the time Camberwell had embarked on a substantial housing programme, interest rates had been increased sharply and in 1956, Camberwell, with fewer traditions of opposition to the means test, introduced rent rebates along with steep rent rises to finance the programme.[90] This led to perhaps the most serious upheaval in the party throughout this period. Seventeen members of the Labour group voted against the rent increases. The rebels were expelled and, although the three Dulwich councillors were, after NEC intervention, accepted back into the group, the fourteen Peckham Councillors were not.[91] Several Labour Party members resigned, the party was badly shaken, but the rent increases and the means test remained. By 1965, Camberwell rents were far higher than those in Bermondsey or Southwark.

Again, opposition from outside the Labour party itself was considered suspect. A few tenants' associations began to emerge by the mid-1950s but were, for a while, ignored. The Dogkennel Hill Estate Tenants' Association wrote complaining about repairs and received a reply confirming 'the Council's policy of not recognising formally that any association represents the tenants on any particular estate'.[92] By 1954, however, Camberwell Council had altered their position a little, setting up their own tenants' association, to which they tried to persuade local associations to affiliate.[93]

4. Summary

This was a period of stability and of industrial prosperity. It marked perhaps the high point of the political culture which was built up during the previous three decades, and was a period of confidence and self assurance among the local trades-unionists and a close-knit local community. This was also a period of consolidation of Labour's support, one in which huge majorities were recorded at general elections, and one in which Labour held all the seats on Bermondsey and Southwark councils, while keeping comfortable control in Camberwell. The local authorities also seemed confident, successful and popular, providing services that the majority of the population wanted and depended upon. There was considerable support for the programmes of house building and slum clearance. The local Labour parties and councils were no longer seen as the van of socialist advance, they were pragmatic and cautious, but they reflected in many ways the close-knit, somewhat insular communities they represented, conservative in social policy, but with strongly held views on the loyalty and natural affiliations of the working man.

At the same time, there was a series of changes taking place, almost imperceptibly, changes which were to sow the seeds of future developments. Firstly, the slow decline in the importance of the area as an industrial centre, and a decline in population. Secondly, changes in the composition of the local population, a slight shift from manual to non-manual workers, and the beginnings of immigration. There were also, inevitably, changes consequent on the increase in local-authority housing. Although, for most of this period, Labour remained the only real source of local political organisation or pressure, local tenants' associations were beginning to form on the new estates. Thirdly, the apparent solidity of Labour's support masked a decline, from the high point of the mid-1950s, in membership and support. Links between the Labour Party and the trades unions were weakened by the dismantling of the Trades and Labour Councils. The Party itself was moving away from political agitation towards social and community functions.

Finally, the role of local government had changed considerably. A centralising Labour government had focused on national, rather than local, plans. Health services and the utilities were removed from local-government control and, while local councils had greater resources at their disposal than ever, central government increasingly controlled the purse strings. However, as I make clear in chapter seven, local authorities retained more autonomy and more power than they were aware. To the extent that central control was effective, it was due, not to the exercise of formal control, but to the existence of common policy-assumptions at both levels of government, and to a consensus that the role of local government had changed. Local councils did, however, pursue independent policies in several areas, and protest about the 'stop-start' approach of central government. All three local boroughs differed in style and in results. Indeed, there is little indication that the change to Conservative control at national level throughout much of this period was perceived as changing or redirecting policy to a significant extent, although subsidy policy was a persistent cause for complaint. There was, after all, a continuing consensus about the need for local services, and particularly local housing-provision, to expand to meet new needs.

NOTES AND REFERENCES

1. Stewart, J., 'Bermondsey in War 1939–45', unpublished.
2. Avery, M.D., 'Industry in South East London (Bermondsey and Southwark)', MA Thesis 1963, 321, 336.
3. Warnes, A.M., 'Employment Decentralisation in English Cities' in A. Evans and D. Eversley (eds), *The Inner City: Employment and Industry* (London, Heinemann, 1980), 25–45.
4. Unless otherwise stated, statistical information in this chapter concerning population, housing and occupation is drawn from the census figures for 1951 and 1961. For further details, see the Bibliography of Primary Sources.
5. op. cit., 243.
6. Metropolitan Borough of Southwark, MOH Report, 1960, 1.
7. Interview with ex-Southwark Councillor.
8. Interview with local resident.
9. Turner, J.E., *Labour's Doorstep Politics in London*, 96.

10. MOH Reports for the Metropolitan Boroughs of Southwark, Bermondsey, Camberwell, 1946–51.
11. Interview with Southwark Councillor.
12. *South London Press*, 22 July 1949, 3.
13. See *South London Press*, 7 November 1952, 7; 12 September 1958, 1; and 28 February 1969, 3.
14. *South London Press*, 2 October 1964, 1.
15. *South London Press*, 12 September 1958, 1.
16. For wider discussion see Miles, R., and Phizacklea, A., *White Man's Country: Racism in British Politics*. See also Hall, S., et al., *Policing the Crisis*; and Solomos, J., Findlay, B., Jones, S., and Gilroy, P., *The Empire Strikes Back* (London, Hutchinson, 1982). For a specific discussion about the Labour Party and racism see Joshi, S., and Carter, B., 'The Role of Labour in the Creation of a Racist Britain' *Race and Class*, 15 Winter 1984, 53–71.
17. Interview with Southwark Councillor.
18. For example, in the council elections in May 1954, Labour stood unopposed in seven wards. See *South London Press*, 15 May 1954, 1.
19. See *South London Press*, 12 May 1964, 5; and see London Borough of Southwark, *Records of Election Results*, 9 May 1968.
20. Executive Committee of the London Labour Party, Agenda 50 for meeting 4 March 1954. Membership of Constituency Parties 1952, 1953 and targets for 1951.
21. The London Labour Party was by this stage introducing a set of targets for membership as a proportion of Labour votes. See *Annual Report*, 1955: supplement dealing with individual membership.
22. See *London Labour Party Annual Report*, 1959, 19.
23. Elections results for this period are taken from contemporary reports in the *South London Press*.
24. Russell, D., *Southwark Trades Council 1903–1978: A Short History* (London, Southwark Trades Council, 1978) 41, 47.
25. *South London Press*, 21 February 1951, 1; 15 August 1951, 2; and 21 November 1951, 1.
26. Camberwell Trades Council correspondence, letter from Vic Feather, 2 March, 1952.
27. Russell, op. cit. 48.
28. Letter from Wally McFarlane, 7 July 1977, in the Dave Russell Collection, Bermondsey Local Studies Library.
29. See *Bermondsey Labour Magazine* 1946–51.
30. Turner, op. cit., 158.
31. Ibid., 126–7, 159.
32. Interviews with Southwark Councillor and local Labour Party member.
33. Interview with Southwark Councillor.
34. Interview with ex-Southwark Councillor.
35. Interview with Southwark Councillor.
36. *South London Press*, 26 March 1954, 1.
37. Interview with ex-Southwark Councillor.
38. Interview with Southwark Councillor.
39. Interview with local Labour party member.
40. Resolutions for the 50th Annual Conference of the Labour Party

(London, Labour Party, 1951), Resolution 13, 26; and Resolutions for the 51st Annual Conference of the Labour Party (London, Labour Party, 1952), Resolution 26, 43.

41. *South London Press*, 25 October 1960, 1.
42. Speech by J.H. Thomas seconding a composite amendment on Nationalisation, *Report of the Fifty Second Annual Conference of the Labour Party 1953* (London, Labour Party, 1953), 100.
43. *South London Press*, 15 January 1954, 1.
44. *South London Press*, 19 October 1951, 5.
45. Interview with Southwark Councillor.
46. Interview with ex-Southwark Councillor.
47. Interview with ex-Southwark Councillor.
48. Resolutions for the 60th Annual Conference of the Labour Party (London, Labour Party, 1961), resolution 395, 54.
49. Ibid., resolution 394.
50. See, for example, *South London Press*, 10 November 1961, 1; 15 October 1965, 1; and see Hansard, speech by Harry Lamborn, 3 March 1976, cols 906–1412; and Bob Mellish, 24 May 1976, cols 45–6.
51. Mellish, B., 'The Challenge of 1949' *Bermondsey Labour Magazine* no. 1, 1949, 1.
52. Quoted in *South London Press*, 11 April 1941.
53. *London Labour News*, June 1942, 208.
54. Labour Party Manifesto 1945 *Let Us Face The Future: A Declaration of Labour Policy for the Consideration of the Nation* (London, Labour Party, 1945) 3.
55. See *South London Press*, 31 October 1947, 1.
56. *South London Press*, 29 April 1949, 2.
57. *South London Press*, 25 June 1946, 1.
58. Metropolitan Borough of Bermondsey, MOH Report 1956, 10.
59. *South London Press*, 14 May 1948.
60. See *South London Press*, 29 July 1947, 1.
61. *South London Press*, 20 July 1945, 1.
62. See *South London Press*, 17 January 1947, 2; 21 January 1947, 1.
63. *South London Press*, 18 November 1947, 1.
64. *South London Press*, 10 October 1947, 1.
65. See Foot, M., *Aneurin Bevan, 1945–60*, vol. 2, 71.
66. AMA, *Defects in Housing 1938*. part I: *'Non-Traditional' Dwellings of the 1940s and 1950s* (London, AMA, July 1983), 8.
67. Dunleavy, P., *The Politics of Mass Housing in Britain 1945–75: A Study of Corporate Power And Professional Influence in the Welfare State.*
68. *South London Press*, 12 January 1945, 1.
69. See, for example, *South London Press*, 9 April 1947, 1.
70. *South London Press*, 26 February 1945, 5.
71. *South London Press*, 15 August 1961, 2.
72. Bermondsey, *Official Guide 1963* (London, London Borough of Bermondsey, 1963), 29.
73. See Metropolitan Borough of Bermondsey, MOH Reports, 1957–63.
74. op. cit., 97.

75. Interview with local Labour Party member.
76. Interview with Southwark Councillor.
77. Minutes of Bermondsey Labour Group 1956–64, in the private possession of John O'Grady.
78. Minutes of Southwark Housing Management Sub-Committee, 5th February 1947.
79. Interview with local Communist Party member.
80. *South London Press* 15 August 1961, 2.
81. Southwark Housing Management Sub-Committee, 5 February 1947.
82. See Dunleavy, P., *The Politics of Mass Housing in Britain 1945–75*; Merrett, S., *State Housing in Britain*, 128.
83. *South London Press*, 28 March 1952, 1.
84. Piratin, P., *Our Flag Stays Red* (London, Thames Publications, 1948).
85. Interview with local Communist Party member.
86. ıbid.
87. *South London Press*, 8 January 1963, 1.
88. Metropolitan Borough of Camberwell, MOH Report 1950, 1.
89. Metropolitan Borough of Camberwell, minutes of Housing Committee, 21 June 1947.
90. *South London Press*, 3 January 1956, 1.
91. *South London Press*, 24 April 1956, 1.
92. *South London Press*, 10 April 1953, 1.
93. *South London Press*, 28 May 1954, 1.

Three

1964–69: Reorganisation

1. The Reasons for Reorganising London Government

THERE had been occasional attempts to reorganise London government almost since the London County Council and the London Metropolitan Boroughs were set up in 1889 and 1899 – and a controversy in the early years about the weakening of the LCC by setting up boroughs beneath it. Since then, the LCC had been seen as an effective level of government and, under Labour control from 1934 onwards, had built up services that were the envy of other cities. A series of government commissions and investigations, such as the Ullswater Committee in 1921, the Boundary Commission set up in 1945–9 and the Abercrombie Plan had produced no proposals for major changes. However, strong pressure from academics such as Robson, who argued tirelessly for a larger London authority,[1] and the growing problems caused by the demands from big authorities, such as Ealing, for county-borough status, led to the setting up in 1957 of the Royal Commission on London Government under Sir Edwin Herbert.

The Commission was remarkable in that there was no one directly involved in local government, or in London, on the committee. It was seen as independent of the 'parochial' concerns of Londoners and local government officials. It saw its remit as examining a number of 'problems'; the growth of population, urban sprawl, the pressures of the green belt, the problem of bulging towns in the surrounding counties demanding county-borough status, and pressures for larger planning and traffic authorities. However, the evidence received indicated little support for change, with the exception of the Conservative Party organisations and some Conservative-controlled groups, who proposed a Greater London Council, and the LSE, which presented mountains of evidence, background papers, and three possible proposals for reform.

The response to the lack of enthusiasm for reform was interesting because, far from accepting this as evidence for the

strength of the existing system, the weight of evidence, said the
Commission,

> convinced us . . . that notwithstanding the many virtues of
> local government today the parochial outlook that has been
> one of the greatest obstacles to any serious reform of London
> is still very much alive.[2]

Arguments defending the existing structure on the basis of
'community' and 'local interest' and 'personal' services were
dismissed: 'They are so highly charged with emotion that they are
relevant to our enquiry only after the most careful analysis'.[3] No
attempts to research or to test notions of community, or to interview the public were made. Instead, equally untested arguments
were accepted about the minimum size of authority necessary to
provide services efficiently, the need to control local authorities'
powers which 'may go far in the restriction of individual freedom'
and the need to improve councillor calibre.[4]

The powerful evidence from the LSE Greater London Group
also stressed the need to re-establish a political balance in London.

> One of the things that has gone very wrong with local
> government in this country has been the exodus of the middle
> class from the big urban areas. . . . I think this is very bad for
> local democracy. One of the bad effects is a certain tendency
> to permanent majorities on some city and urban councils and
> somewhat weaker oppositions. Another, I think is possibly a
> certain bias . . . in the functions which authorities discharge.
> For example cities in Britain today are very clean and often
> there are good schemes of social reform in the spheres of
> housing, welfare, open spaces . . . but when it comes to large
> schemes of civic improvement, to coping with the motor age
> . . . dealing with the redevelopment of the central area, I feel
> that cities suffer often from the limited social, and in some
> ways political composition of their electorate.[5]

So the 'problem' to be solved by reorganisation was the tendency
of Labour authorities to intervene on behalf of local, working-class
communities, and not to provide the necessary infrastructure and
redevelopment to forward the interests of business and commerce.

The argument for larger-size boroughs is put very clearly:

> [In] the whole east and north-east of the County of London
> [is] what might be called solidly working class housing . . .
> which has a very similar character and social composition.
> Therefore if you get your administrative units too small, you
> get a lot of very homogeneous little units which I think is
> unsatisfactory and often leads to the permanent predomi-
> nance of one political party on the council.[6]

Increasing the size of the boroughs was a way to break down homogeneous working-class communities.

Such arguments have been analysed by Dearlove in *The Reorganisation of British Local Government*, in an examination of the reasons for reorganisation in 1972. He points out that while local government was reorganised because of an 'orthodoxy' about the need for streamlined, larger units, these arguments were unsupported and untested. There was never, for example, any real evidence that small-scale local government was more inefficient that larger scale units, nor that services were necessarily better provided in larger administrative areas, nor was it ever demonstrated that larger authorities would increase 'councillor calibre' by which it was meant replace local 'amateurs' with businessmen and professionals. The important question, Dearlove says, is why 'certain people should be so acutely worried about the calibre of councillors and officials at certain moments'. He concludes that these supposed neutral arguments had a hidden agenda, 'an overt strategy to place the control of government in particular hands'. The moves towards reorganisation represent a 'highly class conscious' attempt to break down working-class communities, to bring in businessmen and professionals, to centralise services and increase efficiency in order to control spending and to remove 'politics' (and the implication is Labourist or socialist politics) from the local-government arena.[7] Most importantly, Dearlove stresses that the movement for local government reform did not arise just from political parties or direct pressure, but was inscribed into the orthodoxy of the academic and official view of local government.

The Herbert Commission accepted the majority of the LSE arguments and proposed a Greater London Council to replace the LCC, together with fewer, but larger, bottom-tier authorities. However, in its report, it proposed authorities smaller than those proposed in either of the two LSE schemes. The powerful orthodoxy about the need for larger local authorities, which was to dominate the local government debate in the 1970s, had not yet found its voice.

The Conservative government's 1961 White Paper accepted much of the Commission's report, but with several major changes. Firstly, the total area included in Greater London was considerably smaller, secondly, the boroughs were to be fewer in number and larger, thirdly, education, instead of being shared, was to be transferred to the boroughs. At this stage the proposals became very clearly 'party political'. Smallwood, in his account of the conflict, asks 'Why should a seemingly pallid programme of structural reform spark off a protest drive to secure half a million signatures?'[8] The surface answer must be that it was seen as a direct attack on the LCC. By 1961, the LCC 'stood alone as an island of socialism in a sea of Conservative suburbia'. The LCC, the London Labour Party, the Metropolitan Boroughs Joint Standing Committee, the Labour-controlled Metropolitan Boroughs and the Labour MPs began to campaign against the government's proposals. A 'Committee for London Government' was set up; the LCC produced pamphlets. The proposals were seen as 'a clear, doctrinaire determination to destroy the LCC'.[9] Even the *South London Press* was moved to comment:

> By bringing the affluent parts of the Home Counties into London, [reorganisation] gives the Tories an automatic majority in the capital . . . it does look suspicious that a Labour enclave is to be sabotaged after an unsuccessful seige of twenty-eight years.[10]

In relation to education, the campaigning force of parents and the London Teachers' Association was sufficient to ensure that, when the London Government Bill was published, the LCC education area (later the ILEA) remained intact. There was also a considerable battle over proposals to transfer the childrens' and welfare services to the boroughs.[11]

Labour MPs mounted a vigorous opposition in Parliament. Reorganisation was seen as a Tory attempt 'to get rid of the insult of a Labour and socialist majority on the great municipality of the capital city'.[12] Opposition was also based on the fact that the government had considerably weakened the new, top-tier authority, the Greater London Council, so that it had insufficient powers in planning, housing or transport to make an equivalent impact to the LCC. Reorganisation was seen as a way of destroying a powerful central authority which could co-ordinate London-wide policies and replacing it by an authority which could not compel co-operation from the boroughs. Robson was to complain of 'a failure to confer sufficient power on the GLC and an excessive insistence on the independence of the London boroughs'.[13] No wonder Michael Stewart taunted the Greater London Group with their plans for greater co-ordination and more powerful London government:

> The Greater London Group which started out with such hopes, is looking in bewildered dismay at its offspring. But that is the kind of offspring which is produced, when academic knowledge, that simple maiden, sallies forth from the London School of Economics and is seduced by the gigolo from Tory Central Office.[14]

Throughout the battle over the 1963 Act, the labour movement in London was confident that with an incoming Labour government the Bill would fall. Clear promises had been made. Michael Stewart said at the third reading:

> If the change of government occurs this year we shall repeal the Bill. If the change occurs after the new boroughs are elected, we shall halt the transfer of functions and the break-up of the social services which the Bill seeks to effect.[15]

Several Labour boroughs and the LCC refused even to prepare for reorganisation, so confident were they that it would never happen.

Much to the delight and astonishment of Labour supporters, 1964 saw not only a Labour government in Westminster, but a Labour majority in the new GLC. Almost immediately after the election, Bob Mellish told Labour representatives of GLC and borough Labour groups that:

> Had a Labour government been returned a year earlier we should have repealed the local government act . . . the problem now was what changes, if any, should we make before April 1st.[16]

There was general agreement that the administration of children's facilities should be shared between the GLC and London boroughs rather than given up to the boroughs entirely.

However, it soon became clear that, despite the clear promises made before the election, the new government had no intention of amending the Act. In November Crossman comments in his diary, 'My God, the LCC pressure group is a formidable thing in a Labour Cabinet . . . at least we kept them at bay'.[17] By February, Crossman was answering a question in the Commons from Arthur Lewis MP by saying 'We must allow the transfer of functions to take place without amendment'.[18] It is thus interesting to ask why, given the ferocity of the opposition, no greater effort was made to amend or repeal the Act after 1964? A partial explanation must be the Labour majority on the GLC in 1964. But opposition to the GLC was based on more than the fear of an inbuilt Tory majority. It is important also to look at the changing ideas within the Labour movement.

The powerful London lobby was based on a defence of self-governing communities with emphasis on welfare provision in working-class areas. The metropolitan boroughs were locked into, and saw themselves as serving, working-class, urban communities, providing the housing, welfare and amenities that their local population demanded. But, by 1963–4, Labour's ideological commitment to local democracy was fading. In the run-up to the 1964 election, attention was focused clearly on the national state,

and on 'using local authorities as one of its instruments, restructured and enlarged where necessary to achieve greater efficiency'.[19]
It seems preparations were already being made for the restructuring of local government. Wilson commented:

> Many of our institutions and our processes, governmental and local government, for decision making are clumsy, amateurish, ineffective and out of date.[20]

In housing and planning he saw the need for:

> a big break in government organisation . . . it is becoming clear that the major decisions of land allocations and town and country planning will have to be taken by the government'.[21]

The new Labour ideology was based on what Dunleavy calls the 'technological fix',[22] a view that social and economic problems could be solved by technology and 'the scientific revolution'.[23] Part of both the attempt to move from a sectional appeal and the new scientism was a changing approach to traditional working-class communities, and, indeed, an attempt to break down these communities and replace them by socially integrated new communities without poverty or bad living conditions. By the 1970s, Labour was as willing to reform local government, in line with orthodoxies about efficiency and the need for large units, as the Conservatives.

Let us now return to examine the response to these proposals at local level. Opposition was fierce, and nowhere more so than in Southwark, Bermondsey and Camberwell. And yet this was one of the areas where Labour had no fear of losing control. Opposition to reorganisation was based, not on fears of Conservative takeover, but on a defence of the neighbourhood dimension of the metropolitan boroughs. South London in general, and Bermondsey, Southwark and Camberwell in particular, campaigned against the proposed reorganisation from the beginning. Bob Mellish felt that it 'would mean the death of South London as we have known it'.[24] Opposition came from a combination of pride and politics. Bermondsey's leader, Reg Goodwin, told a special meeting:

> Bermondsey Council has needed no prodding from government or other sources to remind it of the duties imposed on it . . . Bermondsey can claim to have been from time to time in the forefront of leading and progressive London Councils.[25]

Other arguments centred on the need for local councils that related to the people. 'Where are people going to pop in with their problems if the Town Hall is ten miles away?'[26] There was also a spirited defence of the LCC. 'The Council should remain totally opposed to the abolition of the LCC because its work for the people of Southwark is of outstanding quality'.[27]

Opposition within Labour's ranks was universal. Only the Conservative opposition in Camberwell supported the proposals for reorganisation. As many councillors told me:

I do not think anyone was favourably disposed to reorganisation.[28]

We felt absolute horror and opposition, the response of what one might call parochial councils to loss of identity.[29]

The councils refused to co-operate with the government over reorganisation, as the Standing Joint Committee of Metropolitan Boroughs and the LCC had asked. Camberwell resigned from the AMC because of their views on reorganisation, and petitioned the Queen in December 1962. Bermondsey recorded in September 1962 a resolution that 'the Council do continue to pursue their strongest opposition to the Government's proposals for the reorganisation of local government in Greater London . . .',[30] and produced 7 000 copies of a pamphlet putting the borough's case. Southwark provided facilities for displaying LCC posters and leaflets. The campaign was fought alongside teachers and parents in local schools, publicising letters and petitions received, organising marches and public meetings.

Southwark carried on fighting after the other boroughs had given up. Soon after the 1964 Labour victory the Labour Group of Southwark wrote to the NEC, stressing their serious concern 'to learn that endeavours are being made to perpetuate the GLC and to limit amendments to the London Government Act'.[31] But slowly, as other boroughs bowed to the inevitable, Southwark became isolated, and had to admit defeat. In response to a questionnaire organised by the Greater London Co-ordinating Committee asking Labour boroughs whether the Act should be allowed to work for a period before amendments were undertaken, only Southwark said no.[32]

The local councillors saw themselves as defending the successful traditions of public provision within the GLC and the metropolitan boroughs, although the fierceness of the opposition also stemmed from pride in their local councils, and a healthy concern for their personal power in a new structure. The old councils had been parochial – cliquey, fussy, sometimes old-fashioned – but, especially the small boroughs like Bermondsey and Southwark, had established rituals and traditions which reflected both the character and assumptions of the dominant working-class community. The increase in size and scale of the new authority was to lead to changes with more far-reaching implications, that merely increasing the electoral chances of the Tories.

At the same time, the debate within the Labour Party was significant. It is important not to overestimate the extent to which issues about government structures animate or mobilise local, working people. The struggles over London government were almost entirely 'party' struggles, with little interest from the wider labour movement. Nevertheless, within the Labour Party, a struggle for ideas took place in the 1950s and 1960s, with the eventual victory of the 'technological fix' over municipal socialism. The LCC and metropolitan-council lobby within the party lost decisively its battle for London against powerful regional and centralising influences and a new emphasis on efficiency and size.

These forces which shaped national Labour ideas also penetrated Labour's thinking at the local level and influenced the direction of the new authority. Implacably opposed to reorganisation, the new Councillors could not but see the increased powers of the new authorities, and the scope for new initiatives in public health, social services and housing. The stress on progress and technology from Labour nationally was caught and translated into a belief that the new-scale authorities could sweep away the problems of poverty and bad housing. There was continuing discomfort on the back benches, but the new and more powerful senior Councillors, surrounded by powerful officers, felt that with larger powers and greater resources something impressive could now be achieved.

2. The Effects of Reorganisation

Initially reorganisation led to a series of struggles between the Councillors of the three old authorities, over the name of the new Borough, the leadership of the new borough, and the chief officers. Manoeuvring was conducted on the basis of parochialism, rather than a Left–Right spectrum and, on that basis, Camberwell, with the highest number of Councillors, secured the positions of leader, deputy leader and chief whip, as well as the town clerk in the new authority.

In the years following reorganisation these divisions continued. Councillors and activists have continued to identify themselves with the old metropolitan areas, or by constituencies, rather than with the borough as a whole, and there has been little contact, or love lost, between the different groups, until the very recent past. Political divisions in the new authority were based on differences between the old ones. Bermondsey, with its record as a 'socialist' borough, was very suspicious of the new and more 'professional' methods that Camberwell brought with it. There was also resentment about what was seen as stinginess in the old borough of Southwark, where housing problems were very severe. As one

Bermondsey Councillor told me, 'We all said "God help us we have got to spend all our money on Southwark now" . . . we felt there was not enough for our own areas'.[33]

There were major confrontations over council rents. Camberwell's rents were considerably higher than Bermondsey or Southwark; partly because they had introduced means testing, partly because of their small non-residential rate base. Southwark's rents had been the lowest in London, and Bermondsey had seen low rents and no means test as an important political principle. The new Council proposed to level up all rents and introduce a rebate system. In Bermondsey, a mass meeting of Councillors, council tenants and trades-unionists was called to oppose rent increases and means tests; councillors stormed out of meetings; the Trades Council made representations; and, although the rent increases went ahead, councillor Alf Kemp was forced to resign as chairman of the Bermondsey party.

Service delivery throughout the new borough was reorganised into new, vast, departments, inevitably more remote and impersonal than before. This combined in many areas with an increasing professionalisation of the services. There were early new initiatives in health, maternity and child welfare, and social services, leading up to the reorganisation into a new Social Services Department in 1970. All were agreed, however, that the primary task for the new authority was housing. The new Minister of Housing and Local Government had announced targets of 500 000 new houses to be built per year, and Southwark were determined to be the front runners. Southwark set out to build 12 000 homes. This impressive figure was arrived at by the scientific process of adding together the building totals for all three boroughs before reorganisation, and doubling it!

> It was an enormously courageous dedicated attitude to housing – we are not going to be put off by financial constraints or anything – we are going to house the people of Southwark. There was a sort of religious fervour about it – I know it sounds funny – but if you'd lived as people in Southwark had lived . . . it arose out of peoples' experience of slums and slum landlords . . . no privacy . . . communal lavatories . . .[34]

> The only effective and coherent policy they had . . . was to knock down the whole of the borough and build a sparkling new borough.[35]

The borough began to assemble large land banks; officers and councillors plotted the existing slum clearance areas on a map, and

then drew wider and wider lines around them to define areas that
could logically be extended to provide clearance areas, until they
were large enough to produce the 1 200 homes a year that had
been asked for. There was no attempt at detailed surveying and,
on at least one occasion, the Borough Architect and chairs of
Housing and Finance drove round in a taxi to look at all the
proposed sites, before returning to approve clearance. Many of
the councillors had themselves been brought up in tenements and
slums, and had little sympathy with arguments of architectural
merit. At the same time, the architectural profession was firmly
committed to wholesale redevelopment and the creation of
classless communities in a modern environment.[36]

Densities were to remain high; the old crammed tenements were
within walking distance of the print works and the engineering
firms, and politicians and professionals agreed that local workers
could not be transferred out to the suburbs in any numbers. The
authority avoided building tower blocks, however, concentrating
on low-rise, high-density estates, on a vast scale. Several estates
were already in the pipeline on reorganisation; the Bonamy in
Bermondsey, the Acorn Estate in Peckham, and the Denmark Hill
Estate in Camberwell. Two huge new estates were programmed in
1966: the Aylesbury, a sixty-acre area in Walworth, to be built by
Laings using the Jehpson building system, and the North Peckham
Estate, almost equally large but using conventional building
methods and to be built entirely by the Borough's direct-labour
force. A third vast estate, the Heygate, was contracted to Laings in
1969.

The nature of these new developments had changed, as well as
the scale on which they were to be built. A planning spokesman
explained in June 1967:

> One of our main aims is to eradicate the old style terraced
> houses which live permanently in the shadow of a big factory.
> That sort of development is out.[37]

And another, discussing the Peckham slum-clearance programme,
confirmed that:

> The area used to be full of little terraced houses each with its
> own garden and front door. In some respects this sort of
> development was very desirable but today's pressure on space
> means that it has to be pulled down and replaced with
> something better.[38]

By mid-1968, the London Borough of Southwark had house-
building figures to be proud of. The Borough was building 1 750
homes a year, with more houses and flats under construction than
any other authority except Birmingham and the GLC. There were

problems looming on the horizon, however. The scale of the construction enterprise had led Southwark to create a massive direct labour organisation which became unmanageable, running into problems over staff shortages, delays, penalties and over-spending, with allegations of incompetence and fraud. The housing itself was beginning to cause problems. The introduction of cost yardsticks in 1967 had led to last-minute cuts in the design and specification of Southwark's mammoth estates, and problems of poor sound-proofing, rain penetration and poor building-finishes soon began to emerge. The new tenants began to complain about the 'barrack square' nature of the developments, the lack of playing facilities and social or communal facilities, and the growing repair problems. An article in the *South London Press* quoted a tenant's complaints about 'life in a concrete jungle' as early as October 1967: 'The animals in London Zoo at least have the advantage of exercise yards, we live in concrete cages with no provision for exercise or recreation.'[39]

The scale of the slum clearance programme also led to other problems. The creation of vast land banks meant that large areas of Peckham and Walworth were blighted, and vast numbers of houses were left empty for years. At the same time, in order to ensure the 'efficiency' of the decant programme, local people were offered precious little choice of where they wanted to live, and given little information about the plans for their area. The chair of Housing said to the *South London Press*:

> People must not be reluctant to move across the old borough boundaries – many properties for displaced people will be in the Bermondsey area and we don't want people to reject these places out of hand because they feel they are too far away from their old homes . . . we do not like to take a firm hand with people, but we shall have to with families who have chosen one particular spot and say they won't go anywhere else.[40]

The process of clearance, organised as it was on a vast scale, engendered a feeling of insecurity, alienation and uncertainty. There were few attempts to communicate directly with people in clearance areas, or to let them know what was going to happen to them and when. Seven years was a long time for the build-up of rumours and anxieties. There was little meaningful consultation. Public meetings tended to be centred around grandiose schemes for the future of the area, and to ignore or treat as illegitimate local people's concern about their own future. The Chief Valuer is quoted by Ungerson, in her study of Southwark in the 1960s, as saying:

I learned a lot from the Newington public meeting – mainly
that people are not interested in the Borough's problem. They
are only interested in their own problems and how the
redevelopment affects them in particular.[41]
Indeed, the Council itself seemed to feel that consultation was
counter-productive. As one housing manager said 'I don't know if
you've found this, but the great majority of folk are prepared just
to sit back and wait'.[42] Ungerson reports that Council officers were
unhappy about public meetings, seeing them as an 'excuse for
minority activists'.[43] She quotes an officer as saying 'we give as
much information as we can, but not too much to commit
ourselves or upset the residents'.[44]

As the scale of local authority housing activity increased, more
and more local people were drawn into the process. Housing
allocation was no longer the cosy and somewhat élitist process it
had been in the past. The increasing professionalism of the
planning and housing service led to the introduction of points
schemes, but waiting lists operated alongside, and secondary to,
the decanting of redevelopment areas. However, it did mean that
housing allocation could no longer be restricted to the better off
and respectable sections of the working class. In slum clearance,
the majority of residents had to be rehoused. Nevertheless, a
remarkably harsh set of rules was established to determine
eligibility for rehousing after clearance. The qualifying period for
rehousing was surprisingly long. To be rehoused, residents had to
have lived in a redevelopment area before the proposals were
made public, for one year if they were unfurnished tenants and for
three years if furnished. But because areas were declared at least
seven years before possible clearance, as part of the forward plan,
an unfurnished tenant might well have to have lived in their home
for a minimum of eight years, and a furnished tenant for eleven, to
qualify for rehousing. These strict rules were backed up by an
'information' campaign of dire warnings to dissuade anyone from
moving into the area once it had been declared. If new arrivals
remained until clearance they were reluctantly housed as homeless, in substandard accommodation.

These rules were racially discriminating in effect, since few
black families would meet such long residential qualifications. This
approach does seem, however, to have had the support of local
people, who expressed concern, according to Ungerson, about the
possibility of 'outsiders' getting new homes in preference to local
people. In the opinion of one Walworth resident:

I really think they do so many things that are wrong – bringing
in people from the outside – coloured people from Paddington
and other places. Well housing ought to be for us that's always

lived here. It's all wrong isn't it? I suppose they do their best – I don't like to criticise but really we should come first – we belong, don't we?[45]

In the years immediately after reorganisation, 1965–8, Southwark drew up plans for, and began work on, if it did not complete, the bulk of its massive clearance programme. In May 1968, the collapse of Ronan Point, and the ensuing scare over high-rise buildings, marked a shift in policy away from clearance – partly for financial reasons. The Labour government's White Paper 'Old Houses into New Homes'[46] proposed a shift away away from redevelopment and towards rehabilitation, and was implemented by the incoming Conservative government. Southwark remained determined, however, to fulfil its ten-year programme. Southwark's spending peaked in 1968 at £33 million, after a decision that, despite cut-backs, the housing programme would not suffer.[47] Cuts were made in plans for welfare spending on old people's homes and homes for the physically handicapped, but housing spending was financed by substantial rate increases in 1968 and 1969.

Reorganisation had more far-reaching effects than the shift in policy in the years 1964–8. The sheer size of the authority had important consequences. Camberwell had been large for a metropolitan borough, but for Southwark and Bermondsey the switch from a population of 83 000 and 56 000 respectively to 300 000 was dramatic. Councillors, officers and residents alike had to get used to a new boundary that was totally unfamiliar. Residents in Downtown, Rotherhithe had little in common with those in suburban Dulwich.

The new size and scale meant that the nature of local politics was permanently altered. The detailed, painstaking work of local councillors was to be replaced by policy decisions, planning and strategic considerations. The population, if they had ever identified with their local council, would find it difficult to do so now. As one councillor said, comparing the old metropolitan councils with the new, London borough:

> The size of the area relative to officers was one that allowed for more personal contact between officers at all levels and the local populace, they identified far more with the Town Hall . . . now it has just become an administrative centre.[48]

Or another, representing the south of the new borough,

> . . . being a smaller council you were nearer to the people, you knew the problems of your area. Since coming on the new Council, the problems of Docklands seem to be so far away, they do not seem relevant.[49]

This feeling of distance was compounded by the fragmentation of services, with different offices in different parts of the new borough. This led to a lengthening of lines of communication, and to delays.

This is not to argue that the old boroughs were more democratic or politically responsive than the new Borough. The old councils sometimes had powerful hierarchies and élites, and guarded their independence from the local party jealously, but there had been informal links which brought councillors and political activists in the party and the trades unions into constant contact. Nevertheless, it was often forcefully argued that, in relation to the old Southwark Borough, reorganisation had positive effects, ending the secretive style of the old metropolitan borough and opening up debate. The extent to which a handful of councillors could control the business of local parties diminished, although, during this period, the Labour parties showed no inclination towards independence.

The relationship between officers and councillors changed as a direct result of reorganisation. One of the effects was a considerable increase in management-level officers, since none of the existing officers from the metropolitan boroughs could be sacked or demoted. Wistrich points out in her study of Camden that, as a result of reorganisation, the growth of staff in Town Clerk's and other central departments was general.[50] The new departments were thus top heavy, with large numbers of officers concentrated at the centre, rather than at the level of direct provision of services. As one Councillor told me:

> You could not get rid of officers, you had supernumary officers on high salaries . . . when we were talking about it before reorganisation they said we would have new executive officers, but you got the same tired old officers you had before, with highly inflated salaries, calling themselves directors when before they had been merely officers.[51]

Officers, particularly at senior levels, became far more remote from their 'patch', and far less familiar with the area in which they worked. Councillors constantly talked about the diminishing standards of 'loyalty' and 'service'. In parallel, the relationship between Councillors and officers changed. Councillors were less familiar with the new council areas, they were dealing with a larger and more impersonal machine, and were further away from the arena of decision making.

Even the Senior Housing Officer, in a reply to a MHLG questionnaire on reorganisation mentioned the 'lessening of democratic control due to the increased number of electors per member and the larger administrative area, but this is more apparent in matters of detail than of policy'.[52] Councillors could no longer be involved in the detail of policy and day to day decisions, and no longer had a clear view of everything that went on within the council. The back bencher was particularly affected, as group decisions no longer dealt with matters of detail, and as committee chairs became more powerful and surrounded by senior officers, back-benchers felt more and more excluded. Representing a local ward became more fraught with difficulties, councillors no longer had the information, the contacts or the familiarity with the council's business to 'get things done'. One back bencher said bitterly:

> In the new borough officers became so difficult to get at, they were always busy off out . . . the new borough was much too large . . . it was set up to achieve easier communication and more efficient and economic services. The opposite happened.[56]

In addition, the relationship between officers and manual workers changed, and between councillors and work-force. In the old boroughs, particularly Bermondsey, where trades-union principles had been strong, relations had been good. Departments were small, and manual workers and senior officers knew each other. Links between the unions and the councillors were strong. After reorganisation, partly because of the influence of Camberwell, with its willingness to experiment in new methods, and far less of a trades-union tradition, the officers in new Southwark began to restructure staff relations.

As part of reorganisation, Southwark had committed itself to building up a large, direct-labour organisation. New managers were determined to use new methods; as the new manager of the building department put it, 'the village character must be wiped out, we are now a vital, dynamic and large community'.[54] Soon there were unofficial strikes throughout the work-force; bonus disputes, protests against the reorganisation of the direct labour organisation, and against the flying in of labour from Scotland and elsewhere. When an 'imported' workman from Hull reportedly replaced a local man, a strike of over 2 000 Southwark council workers was called; dustmen, drivers, cleaners, maintenance gangs, plumbers and town hall messengers joined in. A Southwark Trades Council member was quoted in the *South London Press* as saying:

> In old Bermondsey Council we had team spirit with cooperation and goodwill. Southwark has destroyed this goodwill, the principle of 100 per cent trade unionism has been wilfully violated.[55]

The nature of local representation changed dramatically, simply by nature of the changed ratio of councillors to constituents. Whereas, under the old authorities, 180 councillors and 30 Aldermen had represented the population, this was reduced to 60 councillors and 10 Aldermen. The ratio of councillors to constituents went down from 1 to 1 000 or 2 000 to 1 to 5 000. Councillors were spread more thinly and were worked far harder. The new tasks of the local authority and new committees meant that councillors were far less able to combine successfully the job of local representative with political decision-making. The whole range of informal contacts with the local community, through living and working locally and through day-to-day contact began to break down. Traditional links between councillors and their constituents and between council officers and residents were severely weakened, but no new mechanisms took their place.

However, these changes had few visible effects at first. In the early years of the new authority it seems that there was considerable support for the priorities of the local authority. This support was passive rather than active, but councillors were convinced that the new policies and the large-scale redevelopment plans had local support:

> At the time we were doing what everyone wanted, everyone was screaming for them.[56]

> We thought we were going to house everyone cheaply and quickly . . . there was not a word said against it.[57]

What is remarkable looking back at this period from the standpoint of the 1980s is the absence of community organisations or campaigning. The only exceptions were the tenants' associations organised by the Communist Party in the old tenement blocks. And, even here, the tenants' agitation was directed towards getting old tenements such as Queens Buildings included in the redevelopment programme. There was no politically organised challenge to the direction of Council policies, or to Council priorities.

It was not until the effects of these changes began to work their way through, and the problems described above began to emerge, that passive support turned to apathy and the consensus around the Council's policies began to weaken. Nevertheless the effects were felt in terms of growing dislocation and anxiety, rather than in terms of political organisation.

> People perceived the council as something very far removed – working on the ground one was sometimes quite staggered about how ignorant people were about the work of the council

. . . people felt powerless – sometimes they felt angry, but often felt powerless to do very much about it.[58] The relationship between the councillors and the Labour Party also changed. Councillors who had previously dominated party activities were now a minority, and found it impossible to combine council work with leading positions in the local party. As one councillor put it:

> The Metropolitan Borough's council meetings were on Mondays, Tuesdays and Wednesdays, leaving Thursdays and Fridays free for party meetings. In the new council there was so much work and so many committees and sub-committees that it took the whole week, and if you have got to be at a council meeting, you cannot be at a party meeting.[59]

The Labour parties, however, remained quiescent, in some wards almost moribund, during this period. Real membership figures for individual constituencies ceased to be recorded once they slumped below the 1 000 minimum for affiliation to the national Party; parties affiliated on a nominal 1 000 members regardless of the actual constituency membership. Nevertheless, it seems clear from interviews that the active membership plummeted. The row over the introduction of means-tested rents had repercussions within the Labour Party, but, in general, the parties continued to support the Council, while drifting further away from active politics and towards a role as a rusty and seldom activated election machine. The Labour Party was therefore unprepared for the scale of Labour's defeat in London in the local-government elections of 1968. Labour lost control of every local authority in south London except Southwark, Labour's bedrock, and in Southwark Labour was returned with a substantially reduced majority. Not a single Labour councillor was returned in Camberwell, which meant, amongst other things, that Bermondsey councillors were to take over the leadership. Worse was to come. After a landslide victory in the local-government elections, the Tories regained control at Westminster two years later. The reasons for Labour's drop in support were complex, and related more to the unpopularity of the Labour government than to local factors. Nevertheless, it was a warning sign, and demonstrated the beginnings of Labour's vulnerability in what had been previously assumed to be electoral strongholds.

3. Summary

There are two reasons why London government was reorganised in 1964. The first is the one made by Rhodes, who traces the complex history of the Commission, the White Paper and the Act, and puts it down in the last analysis to a few strong personalities; to the pressure of the LSE, the absence of other proposals and the partisanship of individual Tories.

It can perhaps be summed up by saying that in the Conservative Cabinet of 1961 there was no very great enthusiasm for London reform, only an inability in the face of Mr Brooke's enthusiasm, to think of an alternative other than simply preserving the existing system. Great decisions may often be taken for no better or worse reason.[60]

The second, if we are to look at underlying forces, is more complex. The Labour Party's conviction that reorganisation was a Tory plot to destroy the powerful Labour LCC is a good starting point. However, the forces at play were more than 'party political'. We must include a whole series of academic and official assumptions about the nature and needs of local government, which appear neutral, but which had a powerful effect on the relative balance of forces within London. As I shall argue, this was not limited to the breaking up of Labour authorities and the injection of Conservative suburbia into London, but had powerful effects on the relations of Labour authorities to their constituents.

I have argued that the reorganisation of London government cannot be explained merely in terms of party politics, because the support of the Labour government in 1964 for reorganisation played an important part in its final form. What took place was a shift in Labour's thinking at a national level, a belief that it was important to disentangle Labour from the parochial 'village' concerns of working-class communities and to appeal to a wider cross-section of the country on the basis of new efficient, scientific, government. I explore these ideas in greater depth in Chapter 6.

Reorganisation had important structural effects locally. Structures and traditions that had created a series of links within the old metropolitan boroughs between council, party and local people were dissolved and not replaced; partly because of the size and scale of the new authority, partly because of the stress on large new departments and the increasing professionalisation of service delivery. The massive redevelopment programme launched in the mid-1960s was a success in its own terms, and was not deflected by central-government cut-backs in the late 1960s and early 1970s. Over this period around 7 000 new homes were built and slums cleared. But I have suggested that major new problems began to emerge. Blight and uncertainty were created by the scale of the clearance programme, and the new homes turned out not only to have serious repair problems, but to create bleak environments for family living.

Finally, I suggest that 1968–9 was a turning point in terms of support for Labour locally, as well as nationally. Labour's new approach, presented in terms of technological solutions for social problems, led to disillusion locally. During this period, this was manifested through apathy, but in the next period major conflicts began to develop within the community.

NOTES AND REFERENCES

1. Robson, W.A., *The Government and Misgovernment of London.*
2. *The Royal Commission on Local Government in Greater London 1957–1960*, 43.
3. Ibid., 47.
4. Ibid., 62–3.
5. Robson, W.A., *Oral Evidence to the Royal Commission on Local Government in Greater London, Minutes of Evidence*, Thursday 5 November 1959, para. 13 018.
6. Ibid., para. 13 070.
7. op. cit., 12–16.
8. In *Greater London: The Politics of Metropolitan Reform*, 32.
9. Mr Fred Willey MP, House of Commons Debates, 11 December 1962, Hansard col. 230.
10. *South London Press*, 5 December 1961, 4.
11. For a detailed description see Smallwood, op. cit., 228–38.
12. Lord Morrison of Lambeth, House of Lords Debates, 23 April 1963, Hansard col. 1146.
13. In the introduction to Rhodes (ed.), *The New Government of London: The First Five Years*, x.
14. Mr Michael Stewart MP, House of Commons Debates, 10 December 1962, Hansard, cols. 72–3.
15. Mr Michael Stewart MP, House of Commons Debates, 2 April 1963, Hansard, col. 399.
16. Bob Mellish MP, addressing a meeting of London Labour groups at Caxton Hall, 2 November 1964 (from Minutes, in Papers of London Co-ordinating Committee, Labour Party Archives).
17. Crossman, R., *Diaries of a Cabinet Minister*, vol. 1, *Minister of Housing 1964–1966* (London, Hamilton and Cape 1975), 74.
18. Reply given by Richard Crossman to a question from Arthur Lewis MP, House of Commons Debates, 2 February 1965, Hansard, col. 891.
19. Bassett, K., Political Responses to the Restructuring of the Local State (SAUS Conference Paper, 1981), 48.
20. Wilson, H., 'The New Britain', *Selected Speeches*, 15.
21. Wilson, H., 'Housing and Planning' *Selected Speeches*, 68.
22. Dunleavy, P., *The Politics of Mass Housing in Britain 1945–75*, 100–1.
23. Wilson, quoted in Coates, D., *The Labour Party and the Struggle for Socialism*, 99.
24. *South London Press*, 1 December 1961, 1.

25. Reg Goodwin, quoted in *South London Press*, 23 February 1962, 1.
26. Sam Silkin, quoted in *South London Press*, 3 August 1962, 1.
27. Reg Goodwin, quoted in *South London Press*, 5 December 1962, 1.
28. Interview with Southwark Councillor.
29. Interview with Southwark Councillor.
30. Bermondsey Council Minutes, 26 September 1962.
31. Letter from Southwark Labour Group to NEC 31 August 1964, in Papers of Greater London Co-ordinating Committee (Labour Party Archives).
32. Southwark's response to Greater London Co-ordinating Committee's Questionnaire, 17 July 1964 (Labour Party Archives).
33. Interview with Southwark Councillor.
34. Interview with Southwark Councillor.
35. Interview with ex-Southwark Councillor.
36. See, for example, Burns, W., *New Towns for Old* (London, Leonard Hill, 1963).
37. Planning spokesman, quoted in *South London Press*, 30 June 1967, 13.
38. Timothy Tinker from Southwark's design team, quoted in *South London Press*, 20 May 1966, 15.
39. *South London Press*, 27 October 1967, 5.
40. Charlie Sawyer, chair of Housing, quoted in *South London Press*, 15 December 1967, 1.
41. Quoted in Ungerson, C., *Moving Home: A Study of the Redevelopment Process in Two London Boroughs* Occasional Papers in Social Administration no. 44. (London, Social Administration Research Trust, 1971), 55.
42. Ibid., 46.
43. Ibid., 55.
44. Ibid., 46.
45. Ibid., 42.
46. Ministry of Housing and Local Government, *Old Houses into New Homes*, Cmnd. 3602, 1968.
47. London Borough of Southwark, Minutes of the Council, 15 March 1969.
48. Interview with Southwark Councillor.
49. Interview with ex-Southwark Councillor.
50. Wistrich, E., *Local Government Reorganisation: The First Years of Camden* (London, London Borough of Camden, 1972), 243.
51. Interview with Southwark Councillor.
52. Interview with Southwark Councillor.
53. Interview with Southwark Councillor.
54. Quoted in *South London Press*, 2 April 1965, 17.
55. Bermondsey Trades Council member quoted in *South London Press*, 26 April 1966, 1.
56. Interview with Southwark Councillor.
57. Interview with Southwark Councillor.
58. Interview with Southwark Councillor.
59. Interview with ex-Southwark Councillor.
60. Rhodes, G., *The Government of London: The Struggle for Reform*, 241.

Four

1970–82: Collapse

DURING this period there were dramatic changes both in the local economy and in the politics of the area, which were to have important repercussions within both the Labour Party and the local authority. In section 1, therefore, I examine the changes in the local economy and the emergence of a series of community campaigns. In sections 2 and 3 I follow the results of these in the Labour Party and the local authority.

1. Local Economy and Local Community

Attention has been drawn in previous chapters to the gradual exodus of manufacturing industry during the post-war period. But during the 1960s and 1970s this accelerated to a rush. In 1966, Crosse and Blackwell, employing 1 200 people, had moved its plant to Scotland. Other firms, such as Beach and Sons the jam manufacturers, left in the same year. Dewrance, employing 400 people, moved to Skelmersdale in March 1968, and in August 1968 Sainsburys closed their food factory employing 1 700–2 000 workers. IPC closed their printing works in 1970, making 758 workers redundant. Shuttleworths closed the chocolate factory in Gallywall Road, making 1 100 workers, mainly women, redundant. Other factories began to leave, including Pearce Duff, Oxoid, Briant Colour, Burrup Matheson, Pye, Rocola, Brooke Bond, Oxo's Haywards factory and numerous small concerns, primarily from the area of north and mid-Southwark.[1] In 1978 there were only eight manufacturing firms which employed more than 500 people. By 1986 there was one: Peak Freans.[2]

Between 1966 and 1974 Southwark had the highest rate of industrial decline in inner London, at 38 per cent.[3] Between 1961 and 1971 55 000 jobs disappeared, 52 000 in manufacturing. The highest proportion of job losses was in printing (22 per cent), food and drink manufacture (37 per cent), metal engineering (25 per cent) and textiles and clothing (23 per cent).[4] By 1978 manufacturing and port-based jobs declined to only 29 996, a loss of 53 per cent.[5] The Surrey Commercial Docks were also declining. Ever since decasualisation in 1967, work had been steadily transferred down river to Tilbury. By September 1969, the Port of London Authority was discussing the real possibility of closure. During 1969 Hays Wharf closed their six wharves between Tower Bridge and London Bridge, arguing that the number of unofficial strikes had made them unviable. A massive campaign launched by the unions, Trades Council, councillors and MP failed to halt the closure of Surrey Docks, which took place in 1971.

There has been considerable controversy over the extent to which the exodus of industry from inner London was caused in part by the impact of government policy, designed to encourage industry to move out of London to the regions.[6] In the early 1960s many of the closures in Southwark were due to relocations to development areas or new towns, or because of zoning changes. But by the early 1970s the vast majority of closures were due to plant deaths. Griapos, in a study of south-east London from 1970–5, indicates that over 65 per cent of all closures were plant deaths, with deaths representing a higher proportion of closures in small firms.[7] It has been argued persuasively that the decline of industry in inner-city areas has been due to the long-term structural changes in the economy, and could not easily be created (or indeed, reversed) by a relatively ineffective government policy.[8]

Certainly, in Southwark, the issue of land and land values affected the riverside. Southwark was just across the river from the City of London, and thus 'a vital trigger mechanism – and the process that compressed the collapse of industry into such a short period – was the unprecedented boom in land values, starting in 1963 and reaching a peak in 1973.'[9] The process of office speculation was begun by the Hays Wharf company. As early as the 1950s, Hays Wharf, having acquired the freehold of their existing thirty acres of wharves and warehouses in Tooley Street in Bermondsey, proceeded to build a series of wharves and cold storage depots down river, thus 'freeing their entire Tooley Street operation for land speculation and eventual development.'[10] An ambitious prospectus was produced by the company, outlining the possibilities of office development, entitled 'City Within a City'.[11] While no offices were actually built here during this period, from then on commercial interests began to think of Southwark's riverfront as a 'golden mile'[12] of investment opportunities.

The local population continued to decline. By 1971, the population had fallen by 20 per cent compared to 1951; by 1981, it had fallen by another 16 per cent to 209 735.[13] A survey conducted in 1976 suggested that 'population loss is largely – though not entirely – a matter of migration.'[14] Families moved to outer London and the surrounding areas, primarily into owner-occupation and a better environment. The effect of migration was to alter the age structure and, to a lesser extent, the skill structure. The peak age for migration was 20–4, and few migrants were over thirty-four.[15]

Changes in the occupational structure of the local population reflected changes in the local economy: a decrease in the proportion of people in employment, an increase in the proportion of professional workers, and an additional fall in the proportion of skilled workers. The changes in occupational breakdown which had begun to emerge in 1961 continued apace. A comparison of figures for economically active males for the years 1951 to 1981 shows that by 1981 the proportion of employers, managers and professional workers had increased tenfold, of other non-manuals had doubled, of skilled workers had nearly halved, while unskilled manual workers had fallen from 25 per cent to 19 per cent. Aggregate figures of socio-economic class for women are only available for 1971–81, but, amongst women workers during that period, the proportion of employers, managers and professional workers increased from 3.6 per cent in 1971 to 6 per cent in 1981, of other non-manuals from 47 per cent to 53 per cent; that of skilled women workers fell from 7.6 per cent to 4.6 per cent, of service and semi-skilled workers fell from 22 per cent to 20.4 per cent, and of unskilled workers fell from 19.9 per cent in 1971 to 16.2 per cent in 1981.

Aggregate figures for men and women show that by 1981 nearly half of the population in work were in office or non-manual occupations, working in national or local government, personal, recreational and cultural services. Nevertheless, Southwark still had one of the highest proportions of manual workers in London, with 17.2 per cent of Southwark residents employed in manufacturing, 16.9 per cent in construction, 17 per cent in distribution, 10.9 per cent in transport. Unlike other areas of London, Southwark had an even balance of those in 'traditional' and 'new' employment. The 1981 census shows that Southwark had the second highest number of manual workers in London, next to Newham, and the highest number of unskilled manual workers.

In 1981, Southwark was still a relatively poor community. More than half the population had a gross income of under £100 per week, compared with a third nationally. Southwark had one of the highest proportions of households earning less than £3 000 p.a., and a high proportion (61 per cent) of households without a car.[16] The population has continued to age. By 1981, 15.7 per cent of the population were over 65. Since the turn of the century, the proportion of children aged 0–14 had halved, while the numbers of pensioners had more than trebled. The proportion of the population born in the New Commonwealth had increased to 16 per cent, although it is well established that the census considerably underestimates the proportion of black people in the community.[17] Unemployment was also rising during this period. By 1981 male unemployment had reached 16 per cent across the Borough, while recorded women's employment was 9 per cent. Importantly, however, these rates varied considerably in different parts of the Borough; unemployment was far higher in Peckham wards such as Barset (23.6 per cent) or Liddle (21.8 per cent) than in Bermondsey or Dulwich.[18]

Social changes have not taken place evenly throughout the Borough. The analysis of 1981 census data carried out by the Planning Department indicates a series of 'clusters' of population. The most widespread cluster, white, manual-working, mature families, was most common in the north of the borough (in Bermondsey), where there was also an overrepresentation of elderly people. In the middle of the Borough (in Peckham) were areas characterised by 'poor young families, often headed by a single parent, living in council accommodation'.[19] The centre of the borough also has the highest levels of unemployment, with the highest per square mile unemployment rate in the country recorded in Peckham. The area of Camberwell had become more affluent, with high proportions of white-collar single adults and mixed owner-occupation and private renting. Sections of Peckham, and East Dulwich further south, had a high proportion of black households, and were characterised by owner-occupation (especially black and Cypriot owner-occupation), less unemployment and more mature families than in the council estates of Peckham. Further south again, Dulwich Village remained a relatively undisturbed oasis of the affluent.

I have noted in earlier decades the absence of any political organisation or pressure outside the formal party political structures. During the 1970s, however, the calm surface of Southwark's political life was disrupted by a series of community-action campaigns, almost all directed at the local authority. Indeed, during this period, the political initiative moved away from the Labour Party. Indeed, the growth of 'community politics' had a considerable impact both on the local Labour party and on the local authority. New groups emerged from a variety of sources. Tenants' associations were established on many local estates, GLC estates were organised London-wide into a Federation of All

London Housing Associations. Southwark Trades Council, previously a fairly moribund body, began to represent a growing number of professional and white-collar workers, with a high proportion of delegates from local authority and civil-service unions. This new membership began to be far more active, commissioning reports on the local economy, setting up employment, planning and women's committees, and involving itself in campaigning activity and the growing community protest in the area.

A third development was the Community Development Project, located in Walworth. The CDP, one of the first community initiatives based in Southwark, in 1969 had constant battles for survival and little support from Council officers or members. Part of this stemmed from a confusion about the aim of CDPs. The project had been sold to the local authority by the Home Office as aimed at easing pressure on local-authority services through self-help and providing assistance to social services, whereas the project leaders soon discovered that the definitions of poverty and multiple deprivation with which they were supposed to be working were inappropriate, and began to reorganise on the basis of community action. The Southwark CDP soon wanted to get involved in the issues of redevelopment and planning, but met a brick wall. CDP workers were denied access to papers and given little or no help from any department outside Social Services. Councillors were especially hostile:

> Many local members saw CDP as a body that was trying to usurp their most basic function, that of being the representative of a particular neighbourhood.[20]

The project was reconstituted in 1973 after the resignation of the first project leaders in 1972, and again came into conflict with the Council. They eventually retreated into community services, education programmes for the elderly and housing casework. The final report of the CDP recommended that the Council introduce community development initiatives similar to those of neighbouring Lambeth, and suggested area management, neighbourhood resource centres, area committees and the dismantling of the departmental system.[21] The report was noted (having barely escaped rejection by the Council), and buried.

In addition to these more formal developments of new political structures, several single-issue campaigns, some of considerable strength and longevity, developed locally. The first related both to the Council's punitive treatment of the homeless and to the blight created in large areas of Peckham by the Council's policy of acquiring huge land banks ahead of its giant rolling housing programme. Thousands of homes were left empty and deteriorating. In September 1970, in a blaze of publicity, squatters led by Ron Bailey moved into three empty houses in Peckham. The group had successfully taken over properties in neighbouring Lewisham and Lambeth, and had set up a family squatting group in Lewisham, using properties on licence from the Council. In Southwark, however, the group was met with a hardline response, and a policy to evict 'queue-jumpers'. To deflect criticism, the Council housed some families they had already accepted as homeless in empty property, and set-up a 'newly-weds' scheme in which short-life housing was let to young people, with a compulsory savings element attached to the rent, so that they would be able to afford a Council mortgage when the properties were needed. Hence the Council attempted to demonstrate its willingness to help the 'respectable' population, while refusing to change its position on the homeless.

The squatting campaign was well organised. The squatters themselves were families who simply needed somewhere to live, but the campaign organised around them had a high profile and aimed at raising the issue of homelessness as a challenge to local authority priorities. They worked hard at sympathetic media coverage and answered councillors' arguments with detailed refutations. Court cases for eviction were delayed by countless quasi-legal defences which could be taken to appeal. When the Council remained unmoved, the squatters prepared for a siege. While continuing to protest their reluctance at being forced into such action, they organised marches and petitions. In April 1971 thirty members of the Southwark Family Squatters invaded the council chamber and hung banners outside saying 'Labour Southwark Fight the Homeless'.[22]

The campaign had two sets of objectives. The first was to pressure Southwark into making similar arrangements for licensed squatting as had been made in Lewisham and elsewhere. In this they succeeded. Several of the newer Dulwich councillors took up the issue of homelessness and, with the help of local clergymen and the local MP, a respectable 'front' was set up to create a formal self-help group with a proper management committee and a board of trustees to accept licensed short-life property from the Council. But there were also, on the part of the organisers, overt political objectives. They had hoped to 'spark off a squatting campaign on a mass scale and . . . start an all-out attack on the housing authorities with ordinary people taking action for themselves'.[23] They were committed to developing community campaigns,

'organisations and movements outside the normal political structure':[24]

> The people involved decided that they themselves were, for
> once, going to make the decisions affecting their lives. They
> didn't give a damn about the plans of those in power; they
> didn't give a damn when their pleas turned into bullying; they
> didn't give a damn about the discomfiture of politicians and
> their explanations that they wanted to help but couldn't or the
> political justification that they had to oppose the campaign in
> the general interest of the rest of the public. The hostel
> families and the squatters decided that they were going to
> decide what to do about hostel conditions and empty homes
> rather than councils.[25]

The squatters appealed to 'working people' and 'ordinary people'
to 'take control' of their own lives. But, as we shall see, it is not
clear that this represented 'a head-on conflict between the working
class and bureaucracy';[26] nor that their political analysis was
shared by many local residents. Several smaller scale campaigns
followed, waged, in particular, by local advice centres and
voluntary organisations, over the treatment of homeless families,
and the exclusion of single homeless people from the waiting list.

The Council, in response, attempted to mobilise public opinion
against 'queue jumpers' and 'problem families'. In suggesting that
homeless families were anti-social, they appealed directly to
assumptions shared in the wider community:

> We have a big problem in this borough with homeless
> families. You all know the type of people who become
> homeless . . . how many of you have seen a change in these
> people when they are put in decent homes? These people are
> anti-social and wherever they are put they are going to cause
> great frustration to any decent people.[27]

Observers within the Community Development Project noted
that, in taking this attitude, the Council

> seemed to have been reflecting the views of its electors. At a
> public meeting organised by a residents association that was
> addressed by representatives of the squatters there was very
> little support for the squatters.[28]

Indeed, there were sporadic counter-campaigns from local tenants.
The *South London Press* reports a campaign to 'save our streets
from squatters', and quotes a Mrs Taylor as saying 'it's not fair . . .
these people come into a nice neighbourhood and cause chaos'.[29]
Community action went both ways. One worker who had been
involved in the CDP records that:

We began to get squatters in the area and people would come
in and say there are squatters in no. 2 – and we'd say what do
you think we should do about it – and they'd say don't you
worry about it, we'll sort it – and a few hours later you'd hear
the fire engines.[30]

The punitive treatment of the homeless also met with approval
from some local people. When, under pressure, the Council
proposed to rehouse families from a poor-quality tenement block
for homeless families, tenants in Bradford House signed a petition
to keep them out; 'we don't want our estate turned into a half-way
house for the homeless or people with problems'.[31] Opposition to
homeless families mirrored attitudes to 'problem families', which
often meant single parents or black families.

Other campaigns developed into conflicts of interest. In Braganza
Street a successful campaign to prevent demolition was led by a
leading Conservative councillor who lived in the street, against
the wishes of neighbouring tenants. A similar split took place in
Moncrieff Street, where home owners campaigned to prevent their
houses being demolished to make way for a new Town Hall, while
private tenants backed the council's scheme, since it would mean
rehousing in council accommodation.

In north Southwark a very different campaign developed in the
early 1970s to try to prevent the redevelopment of the area for
offices. The pressure from the City had prompted the Council to
produce a draft strategy plan for the riverside which, while
ostensibly limiting office development in relation to the scale
envisaged by the 'City Within a City' report, accepted the logic of
re-zoning the area from industrial and housing to 'West End' uses.
The North Southwark Community Development Group, com-
posed of individuals and affiliated groups, was formed in the
Borough/Bankside area to examine the plan and make its contents
known to local people. A ten-point plan was drawn up, objecting
to the emphasis on 'luxury housing, large scale office building and
middle class amenities',[32] and arguing that the land in north
Southwark was needed for houses with gardens and for industrial
development. A second document put forward demands for
adequate consultation. They argued that the Council had failed to
publicise their consultation meetings adequately and that the
meetings themselves did not give local people a chance to express
their views:

> Confrontation arose because questions were not answered
> directly and because the meetings were not under the control
> of an independent chairman. The meetings had a 'public
> relations' flavour, rather than an attempt to involve people.

Sometimes criticism from the floor was apparently dismissed and this simply increased suspicion of a white wash.[33]

The NSCDG was based in a tradition of community action around the issues of participation and power, and the belief on the part of the professionals working for the project in the importance of involving local people in the planning process. The group was able to mobilise general popular support, with attendance of up to 200 at meetings and considerable local involvement, even if the day-to-day activities were left to a smaller number of activists. The campaign remained committed to going through established channels, and working with the tools of Skeffington, such as public inquiries, appeals and formal objections to planning permission. All these things professionalised the campaign. Some of its later publications have been politically sophisticated, arguing for greater use of the Community Land Act, land nationalisation and government involvement in local industry. The campaign was, however, able to link in to local traditions and myths – to the local concern to prevent change, to preserve jobs and homes, and to prevent the wholesale take over of their community by the City. The traditional imperative to 'look after one's own' and to 'keep out outsiders' extended to keeping out developers and office blocks.

Particular hostility was expressed by the Council towards the NSCDG. Their opposition was discounted as either ill-informed or as somehow promoted by government provocateurs:

I was convinced that a lot of the ferment in North Southwark was artificial and I still believe it was artificial.[34]

The NSCDG are so short sighted . . . you don't look ahead two years . . . you look ahead 10–20 years, everything is a risk that far into the future – but you can't look on such a short term perspective . . . if you're doing something for the next 50 years, can you base it on the existing population?[35]

Consultation was regarded as, at best, a pointless exercise. One ex-councillor told me that 'public consultation is not so important as long as you let people know what you're doing, and give them a chance to reply'.[36]

At worst, it was seen as giving unnecessary scope to those arguing against council policy. Any attempts to raise awkward questions or to protest about the forms of consultation often led to meetings being shut down.

People discovered a job in organising the people against [planning policy] – they might genuinely have held those opinions . . . but to try and organise people against the elected members wasn't very honest . . . if they weren't any good then there was an opportunity to pitch them out at the next election.[37]

Finally, in 1979, the Council withdrew their 25 per cent of the NSCDG's urban-aid grant, shutting off their funding. It was not until 1981 that the newly elected Labour GLC began to fund the centre again.

The community campaign, which perhaps put the final straw on the already bending back of the Labour group, was a campaign against the new Town Hall. Since reorganisation, the Council had proposed to build a new town-hall complex, bringing all the council's activities and offices under one roof. The site moved from the Elephant and Castle to Moncrieff Street and finally to Peckham High Street, but by 1979 the Council was ready to go ahead. The proposed scheme would have entailed major clearance in a popular residential and shopping area, and several years of blight before the scheme was completed. The proposed cost escalated alarmingly.

A campaign against the scheme was organised by the Peckham Action Group, comprising Peckham amenity groups and the local residents, shopkeepers and businessmen who stood to lose their homes and jobs. They organised petitions, marches and stunts, and were highly successful at getting media coverage. The Council responded for some time with the same hostility shown to other community groups. However, as I illustrate later in this chapter the escalating cost of the development began to cut across proposed cut-backs in council spending. Slowly the issue became more politically charged, and, while opposition parties began to make capital, the Labour party itself turned against the Council.

All this presents a much more complicated picture than the analysis Cockburn offers of community development and local authority responses in neighbouring Lambeth. Cockburn's argument is that the strategy pursued by councillors and officers in Lambeth during this period, of encouraging participation and setting up neighbourhood councils, was part of a comprehensive strategy by the local state to manage the local community and to diffuse dissent.[38] In Southwark during this period there was no attempt 'to manage the community', to listen or to try to absorb dissent through involving local people. Faced with a growing tide of community organisation, the Council stonewalled.

Hostility to some voluntary organisations was so great that any proposal put forward by them would almost certainly be rejected because it came from that group. Local advice centres found themselves ostracised. This opposition came not just from bureaucrats, but primarily from politicians. In some cases the response of council officers was far less hostile than that of councillors. They saw the need to adapt policies and were often more concerned about the fluency of administration than about who won the argument. Deals were made with middle-management officers, who would put forward community groups' proposals as their own, to ensure their acceptance.

Far from seeing their role as arbitrating between the competing demands of different groups, the Labour councillors had decided, in similar terms to those identified by Dearlove,[39] that attempts to influence council policy through community groups were illegitimate. Councillors argued that community groups were 'middle class' or represented 'outsiders':

> They used to say 'we represent the genuine working people of Southwark, and you don't'.[40]

> Representation was always a major issue – are you or aren't you . . . If you were in line with them you were representative and if you weren't you weren't. If you thought the same as them you were working class and if you didn't you were middle class.[41]

> The Council at that time actually believed that it knew best – and there was no room for involvement – certainly no organisations – and if there was outside involvement it certainly couldn't be outside the Labour Party.[42]

The councillors had forged their relationships with their constituents in the 1940s and 1950s when the Labour Party was the only real focus of social or political action. They saw their constituents as solid, decent, 'respectable' working-class folk, and saw any attempt to represent other groups – single people, single parents, black people, homeless families, etc, as illegitimate. At the same time, they developed a powerful suspicion of the new, young, middle-class professionals who put forward the interests of the underprivileged. Several councillors protested that what they did was 'community work', and resented bitterly the new professionals that came into the community to form links with local people and to speak on their behalf. They believed their traditional role as mediators between council and community was being usurped. The CDP reported that the majority of councillors had

> a general set of values embodying a high priority for policies favouring the main body of the Southwark population, a preference for the council providing services rather than

relying on 'outsiders' and a relative lack of sympathy for non-conforming minorities that might be thought to be in particular need. In these respects the councillors are probably in harmony with most of those who elect them.[43]

The burgeoning community groups, the new voluntary workers and professionals interpreted this as the Council refusing to listen to anyone but themselves. To them, the Labour councillors represented a virtually dynastic group, patronising and paternalistic in their insistence that they knew best and could be trusted to act on behalf of the people. But it is noticeable that the community campaigns gained most support when they were attacking office development or the waste of the new Town Hall, and least support when they defended the interests of the homeless or the single.

2. The Local Labour Party

In the late 1960s and early 1970s the Labour Party was virtually moribund in some areas of the borough, with membership of only a few hundred in the Peckham and Southwark constituencies. Bermondsey membership seems to have remained steady, but with little political activity. Dulwich remained the most sprightly party, badly shaken by the 1968 election result and working hard to recover lost ground. At about this time the parties lost their full-time agents, since the existing agents retired and the parties no longer had the membership or resources to continue as an election machine. All four parliamentary seats were held in 1970, but with a very narrow majority in Dulwich and a fall both in Labour's majorities and in the percentage poll. Compared with 1966, the poll fell from 55.8 per cent to 50.1 per cent in Peckham, from 73.87 per cent to 64.62 per cent in Dulwich, from 61.1 per cent to 53 per cent in Bermondsey and from 54.3 per cent to 48.4 per cent in Southwark.

A by-election held in Southwark in early 1972 was won by Harry Lamborn with an all-time low poll of 32.24 per cent. This was the last election for the Southwark constituency; later in the year, boundary changes, prompted by falling population, redistributed the constituency between neighbouring Bermondsey and Peckham. Similar patterns were demonstrated by the GLC and council elections: convincing wins by Labour, but with a falling poll. In 1974 polls rose in the February general election, only to fall back again in October to the same level as in 1970. By 1979 polls rose slightly, but Labour's share of the vote had again fallen. Majorities in Bermondsey and Dulwich were the lowest for several decades, falling to 8 509 in Bermondsey and 6 701 in Peckham, and to a knife-edge 122 in Dulwich, with sharp increases in the Conservative vote. In 1983 Labour lost both Bermondsey and Dulwich, and held on to Peckham with a sharply reduced majority.[44]

The only political issue to animate seriously the local parties in the early 1970s had been the Housing Finance Act. Slowly, however, the conflicts taking place within the wider community began to shift inside the Labour Party. New people began to join, many coming from tenants' associations or from community and voluntary groups. The Party membership began to reflect the changes that had taken place in the local population, but to over-represent young, community activists and public-sector profess-ionals. The 'new wave' was not entirely middle class, however. A considerable element of the new activists was made up of working-class radicals who had been alienated by the closed politics of the old Labour Party. Some socialist feminists and gay and black socialists began to edge gingerly into a party that seemed more open and less reactionary in its social attitudes. This influx was inevitably related to changes in national politics, and was also to an extent self-generating, as new members brought their commun-ity action experience, commitment to participation and an enthusiasm for membership drives.

There were conflicting views about the extent to which the movement inside the party was orchestrated. One local activist described the process in Bermondsey thus:

People in NSCDG decided that they ought to join the Labour Party – they were banging their heads against a brick wall and there was a door they could open and walk through.[45]

while George Nicholson, GLC Councillor from 1981, felt that it was less organised:

Frankly you could take over the party by accident and in a way that's what happened. It wasn't a hugely pre-mediated thing – just by half a dozen people joining the ward you changed the politics of the ward – you couldn't help it.[46]

Cathedral and Riverside wards in Bermondsey were 'taken over' by people from NSCDG and began to recruit new members rapidly. In 1978 the established Councillors in these two wards were replaced by several anti-office campaigners. New people joined the Peckham and Dulwich party during the years 1974 and 1978, and in the 1978 local-government elections several new councillors were elected. The new councillors began to take up the interests of homeless people, the black community, and squatters, and slowly these issues began to impinge on the General Management Committee meetings of the local constituencies. A row broke out in Bermondsey Labour Party when the Labour Club refused to admit a party member – allegedly because he was

black.[47] Bob Mellish provoked an outcry in the London Labour
Party by an anti-immigration speech in the House of Commons:

> People born and bred in our constituencies have been on the
> waiting list for as long as six years. But on the points system,
> one must give immigrants preference. How is the problem to
> be tackled unless we get the figures right? We must try to let
> the British people see that we are alerted to the problem –
> unless we do that our own people will take action which all of
> us regret.[48]

By now, however, he did not have his local party behind him.
Local parties had begun to question the actions of their representatives, in the Town Hall and in Westminster. Conflict arose
over the new Town Hall and, for the first time, the constituencies
passed resolutions firmly condemning Council actions. Indeed, the
new Town Hall debate marked a turning point in local party
politics, since, for the first time, the party itself began to join the
campaign against the Council. At first the political differences in
the local parties emerged over local issues; office development, the
sale of council houses, the sale of land, policies towards the homeless, harsh policies on rent arrears, and council policies that were
regarded as racist or sexist. Gradually, however, divisions over
council policies solidified into clearly distinguishable allegiances to
'Left' and 'Right'. These divisions emerged over the question of
responses to the cuts in local government spending which began in
1976, but most strongly over the question of responses to the
policies of the Conservative government elected in 1979. The
'Left' wanted to mount a political offensive against the Tories,
while the 'Right' were prepared to carry on as before. By 1980–1,
the local divisions had found parallels in the national divisions over
reselection and constitutional changes and in the struggle to
achieve a unilateral defence policy.

The old guard saw this process of change as one of infiltration,
of take-over by outsiders. Three long-standing councillors resigned
in disgust, and left to join the newly-born SDP. Councillor Kitty
Clun explained her reasons thus:

> In 1978 as in previous elections I had the honour of
> representing Newington as a moderate Labour councillor
> serving a moderate Labour Council. My political convictions
> have not changed – regrettably the Labour Party has. Over
> the years people have infiltrated the party, not may I add to
> benefit the electors but to push extreme left wing policies
> which I suggest are alien to the people of my borough.[49]

Other Labour councillors argued that the Labour Party was
moving away from local people:

I've got ward members who are totally confused . . . they
say what are you doing . . . you're doing nothing, you just
fight each other . . . they say why are you helping the homeless . . . why are you publishing things for gay liberation . . .
the ordinary people feel that the Labour Party has moved
away from them . . . they're no longer interested in their
problems.[50]

Amongst people whose commitment to the Labour Party is so
strong that one can weep, they've lost the confidence that it is
them that the Labour Party represents . . . that they are
talking about things they don't really understand while the
roof's leaking.[51]

The Left, on the other hand, saw the period 1980–2 as opening up
party membership, and turning a closed clique into an active campaigning party. Peter Tatchell, the new secretary of Bermondsey
Labour Party, referred back to the tradition of Alfred Salter:

Until recently, Bermondsey has been a dead and introverted
party drifting away from its radical traditions. . . . But in the
last two years we have tried to change all that . . . membership has doubled to over 800 . . . for the first time in years we
have organised petitions, demonstrations, newsletters, public
meetings and film shows to mobilise a vigorous local opposition to the Tories.[52]

The new Left was concerned to restate socialist principles and to
mount political campaigns over cuts in services, unemployment
and the attacks on local-government finance. The Left rejected
parliamentary politics, not because of anti-parliamentarianism
(although that was there too, sometimes) but because of a belief
that parliamentary politics could neither mobilise local people nor
build a socialist alternative. The Labour Party should take up:

struggles against the root causes rather than the superficial
manifestations of people's problems . . . encouraging them to
organise together to defend their interests and take a little
power for themselves rather than leaving everything to full-
time politicians.[53]

Many of the activities that held the party together in the 1950s and
1960s – casework and social activities, social support within the
community – were seen as 'non-political' and downgraded.
Meetings which had had a major social function were given a new,
more businesslike structure, so that important political issues
could be dealt with swiftly. Articulate professionals used to
dealing with matters of policy in the abstract were often impatient
with the day-to-day concerns of older members. A shift in

language, in structure, and in assumed knowledge may have
alienated local working people, as may the differences in lifestyles.
The Social Democratic Bulletin often accused the Left of
deliberately stringing meetings out into the night to sneak a
majority when the older members of the party went home
exhausted!

The conflict that was taking place was also about the role of local
government. The old guard saw themselves as administrators,
operating 'common-sense' policies in the interests of local people.
The Left saw local government as a way of creating alternative
democratic structures, to experiment with socialist possibilities.
The local parties gradually became committed to a new sort of
Labour council, based on participation from local groups, an
industrial policy based around trades unions and the Trades
Council, unemployed centres, and training initiatives; a planning
strategy based around community consultation and participation;
housing policies involving tenants' control; and the bringing into
political power of previously excluded groups, i.e. women and the
black community.

During 1980, there was a bitter struggle between the two factions
for control of the local Labour parties. In each constituency, every
position, every GMC delegate, and every resolution became the
subject of a power struggle between the two groups. Left and
Right accused each other of fixing elections, recruiting supporters
to pack meetings, and flouting Party rules. A rule book became an
essential part of political uniform. By 1981, all three constituency
parties had been 'won' by the Left. This was not, however, the end
of the affair. In 1981 and 1982 the battles began to hit the national
headlines. Late in 1980 the constituency parties met to consider
the 'long list' of candidates to be put forward for the 1982 council
election. As a result of the growing hostility to the Council's
policies from the local Labour parties, 31 of the leading councillors
were dropped from the list (out of a total of 64). The resulting row
hastened the defection to the SDP of eleven councillors who were
not reselected, bringing the total SDP group on the Council up to
14: in Southwark, as in Islington, the SDP was made up mainly of
defectors from the Right of the Labour Party. The rest stayed to
battle through a gruelling, although finally successful, series of
appeals.

At the same time Bob Mellish announced his intention to retire
at the next election, and in November 1981 Peter Tatchell was
selected as parliamentary candidate for Bermondsey. Ironically, in
the light of later events, he was not seen as the candidate of the
Left, but as a compromise, gaining considerable support from

older members of the constituency who preferred the popular constituency secretary, the 'local boy', to the 'outsiders' they met at the selection conference. He was, however, a candidate who polarised political opinion locally, and whom both Mellish and O'Grady saw as the incarnation of the take-over of their party by the Left.

I do not intend to rehearse the history of the Tatchell by-election fiasco here. 'The Battle For Bermondsey'[54] gives a fascinating blow by blow account. But the explanations for that defeat form part of the mythology of Left and Right. The Right saw Tatchell as representing everything that was going wrong with the Labour Party. He had been instrumental in overthrowing old customs and traditions and introducing a new sort of politics, the fact that he was gay put him at the far end of a spectrum of newcomers who were 'not like us', and his stress on extra-parliamentary politics seemed to the pragmatists of the old Bermondsey to be 'full-blooded Marxism'. In desperation, O'Grady, the previous council leader, stood as a 'real' Labour candidate with Mellish's support, convinced that Tatchell's politics and lifestyle would destroy Labour's vote, but that a traditional candidate would safeguard it.

The Left tended to see the struggle over the endorsement of Tatchell as yet another part of a struggle of Left versus Right and, at times, the National Executive Committee, in its role as mediator, was the target of the local party's anger. Tatchell to them was 'a good socialist', and they were confident that a working-class area like Bermondsey would inevitably support a shift to a politics that talked explicitly of socialism and democracy. In the event, both were proved wrong. Tatchell lost disastrously, and so did O'Grady, giving Simon Hughes a huge and unexpected success for the Liberals. But this was no by-election fluke. In the subsequent general election, John Tilly, a moderate, family man, failed to make any significant impact on the Liberal vote, and by-elections and council elections have subsequently consolidated the Liberal control of the area.   *L George Nicholson*

3. Labour in Local Government

The process of 'professionalisation' of the local authority described in the last chapter continued during this period. Southwark became one of the first boroughs to introduce new corporate structures. A 'community plan' was created to set out local authority policies and objectives, with study groups of members and officers to overview policy. A new post of Chief Executive was created, and the management structure reorganised, with a co-ordinating executive board. The new corporate structure was opposed by NALGO, and was greeted with unease by some back benchers.

> The back benchers felt lots of opposition, but they were flailing about, they had no idea how to deal with it, they just knew that things had changed . . . where they used to have a say they did not have a say any more.[55]

The new structures strengthened the power of the top-level officers and senior councillors, and a restructuring of Council committees considerably diminished the effectiveness of the Labour Group. The Policy Committee, which was a closed meeting consisting entirely of leading Labour Group Councillors and officers, made the major decisions. Once the Policy Committee had met, the agenda papers for the Council meetings were printed, before the Labour Group had formally met to decide policy. The success in creating a corporate structure within the Council was far more limited: the departments remained strong enough to undermine corporate initiatives when they chose. Indeed, Southwark's experience leads me to suspect that the effectiveness of corporate planning has been significantly overestimated both by its supporters and its opponents.[56]

The Council remained a relatively big spender: by 1981 the Council had the second highest average domestic rate in London (Lambeth's rates were the highest); had the third highest rate-fund contribution to the housing revenue account; was the highest spender on parks and open spaces, second highest on museums, refuse collection and town planning and fifth highest on personal social services.[57] Major housing clearance programmes continued until the late 1970s – well after the emphasis of government and many local authorities had switched to rehabilitation. By 1981 the Council was boasting of a housing surplus. The surplus was highly conditional, however, since it was based on a policy of excluding many of those who wanted council housing (through strict residence qualifications and waiting-list criteria) and discriminating against others in terms of the accommodation that was made available.

The Council, during this period, introduced a series of punitive policies, including the use of distraint in cases of rent arrears and the Criminal Law Act in cases of squatting, and proposed to introduce a number of 'sin bin' estates for problem families only. 'Problem families', in the eyes of many councillors and officers, were black families or single-parent families. Despite the Council's resistance to pressure to liberalise its housing policies, the Housing (Homeless Persons) Act in 1977 forced a limited redistribution of housing in favour of those who had previously been excluded; although homeless families, in which black households and single-parent households were disproportionately represented, were almost always offered the poorest accommodation.[58]

Soon, however, the supply of housing was shrinking. Capital programmes began to dry up after 1976, and the local authority had to abandon plans for new build and rehabilitation schemes. At the same time, it became apparent that the newest estates, the Aylesbury, the North Peckham Estate, and the Gloucester Grove Estate were hard to let, and even harder to live in. This was not only because of disrepair, but because of lack of security, vandalism, lack of play-space, shops or facilities. Growing numbers of tenants were dissatisfied, and competing for a small and shrinking numbers of houses with gardens and the more desirable estates. These changes led to increasing conflict over housing distribution, and over who had priority for the best council homes.

The Council was also forced to pay considerable attention to planning policy. The Hays Wharf scheme and the Council's response to it have been mentioned. Despite opposition from community groups, the Council decided to press on with its re-zoning proposals. They saw the development of offices on the riverside as a way of generating high-rate income that could be used to finance the housing programme. They argued that they did not, in any case, own the land, nor could they afford to purchase it, and they were therefore dependent on the private sector for development. The alternative would be years of blight and decay. Ironically, in view of the recent Docklands property bonanza, the riverside was seen as a poor site for housing, bleak and cold. Perhaps most important among councillors was a belief that the Borough's economy and employment could be regenerated by offices, and that this represented progress for their sons and daughters.

> We wanted to forecast what was going to happen and we forecast that improvement in technology and higher standards of education would mean that our youngsters wouldn't want the manual jobs there'd been before, they'd want something better . . . and rather than let them all go across the river, we thought we'd try to retain them here . . . instead of all the dirty mucky jobs there used to be, they'd be working in offices . . . [so] . . . we'd build offices.[59]

In 1977 the Council set up an Industry Fund to deal with the growing problem of unemployment in the area. The fund was to provide grants or loans to local firms and to launch an aggressive advertising campaign. The Council worked hard but unsuccessfully to encourage a huge, American-style Trade Mart to locate in Surrey Docks.

Throughout this time the local authority had steadfastly ignored community activists and pressure-group politics. Throughout the whole period of active campaigning by the NSCDG, not one major planning application was refused by Southwark. Minor concessions were made to the Family Squatting Group, by now 'respectable'; but local-authority policies towards the homeless remained punitive. Demands made by voluntary organisations for consultation with the Industry Fund, and by the Trades Council for representation on its board, were ignored for some time. That does not mean, however, that council policies were successful. As the Council decided to encourage office development, the bottom fell out of the property market, leaving companies with lucrative planning permission, but no offices were built. Trammel Crow, despite huge encouragement, pulled out of the Docklands Trade Mart venture. The Council's attempt to help local industry failed to prevent firms leaving the area or closing down, although many of them happily pocketed the Council's money.

By 1982 the passive support for the policies of the Council seemed to have ebbed away. The paternalistic pragmatism was seen as inadequate when service provision was deteriorating, and the secrecy of the Labour group was seen as inappropriate. A MORI poll commissioned by the local authority in 1980 to gauge local opinion about service provision revealed considerable disaffection. Interestingly, respondents in Peckham, the area of most recent redevelopment, and with the highest concentrations of black, unemployed and single-parent households, were considerably harsher in their judgements than the people of Bermondsey or Dulwich. Overall, 69 per cent agreed that 'the council wastes a lot of money', and 62 per cent disagreed with the statement 'the Council cares a lot about people like me'.[60]

4. Summary

In this chapter I have argued that the period 1969–82 was a period of fragmentation. The changes in the local population noted in earlier chapters continued, but the pace of industrial decline accelerated. The community had never been homogeneous but, during this period, differences became divisions. I have suggested that the growth of community action cannot be explained simply as a confrontation between 'the people' and 'the bureaucracy', or as 'the working class' versus the State. The community campaigns reflected a range of sectional interests, sometimes interlocking, sometimes conflicting. I have attempted to differentiate between the campaigns over homelessness and squatting, where the councillors often had sympathy from the 'respectable' sections of the working class, and campaigns over office development and the new Town Hall, where there was significant popular disapproval of Council policies. I have suggested that there developed, both through community action and within the Labour Party, a number of committed professional public and voluntary-sector workers, who saw their role both as representing those previously excluded from provision such as housing – black families, homeless families etc. – and as attempting to achieve access for themselves to council services and to the exercise of power.

During this period, automatic support for Labour was weakening. By the late 1970s, a major conflict emerged within the local Labour Party. I have described here the internal battles that took place; I will return in Chapter 6 to analyse the conflict of ideas that lay behind it. Each side blamed the other for the drop in Labour's support, without recognising the process of change that was taking place.

Finally, I have suggested that the role and perceptions of the local authority changed during this period. The Council became more professional, but there were clear limits to the effectiveness of administrative changes. Several issues in relation to the effectiveness of local-authority policy-making and influences on it have been raised. On the one hand, the local authority remained able for some time to ignore a series of active pressure groups. On the other hand, powerful influences, such as the City and central government, prevented the authority from meeting its policy objectives. On a cautionary note, however, it must be noted that these influences drew lines and forced limits, but they did not entirely restrict the authority's room to manoeuvre. Southwark's policies and their outcomes differed significantly from those in neighbouring Lambeth or Lewisham, for example.

The Council during this period, I suggest, lost much of its passive popular support. Most importantly, it could no longer be seen as acting straightforwardly to meet the needs of 'local working people'. It was far more clearly a site of struggle between competing forces, and the Council was seen as taking sides in the divisions fracturing the area: it was seen as *for* offices, *against* the homeless; *for* young married couples, *against* ethnic minorities; *for* the traditional community and *against* community groups.

NOTES AND REFERENCES

1. London Borough of Southwark, *Industrial Survey 1977*, 20.
2. LBS, *Making the Case for Southwark*, 2.
3. Dennis, R., 'The Decline of Manufacturing Employment in Greater London 1966–74' in A. Evans and E. Eversley (eds.), *The Inner City: Employment and Industry* (London, Heinemann Education, 1980) 45–65.
4. Southwark Trades Council, *Employment in Southwark: A Strategy for the Future* (London, Southwark Trades Council and Community Development Project, 1976).
5. LBS, *Making the Case for Southwark*, 2.
6. Cockrane, A., and Dicker, R., 'The Regeneration of British Industry: Jobs and the Inner City', *The State and the Local Economy* (Newcastle Upon Tyne, CDP/PEC, 1979), 5–11, 9.
7. Griapos, P.A., 'The Closure of Firms in the Inner City; the South East London Case 1970–75' in *Regional Studies*, ii. 1977 1–6.
8. See, for example, Friend, A., and Metcalf, M., *Slump City* (London, Pluto, 1981), 22; CDP Inter-Project Editorial Team, *The Costs of Industrial Change* (London, CDP, 1977), 68; Lawless, P., *Britain's Inner Cities: Problems and Policies* (London, Harper and Row, 1981), 27.
9. Ambrose, P., and Colenutt, B., *The Property Machine* (Harmondsworth, Penguin, 1975), 82.
10. Ibid.
11. Halford, W., and partners *City Within A City: The Redevelopment of Hays Wharf* (London, Halford and Partners, 1971).
12. *Commerce International*, March 1981.
13. See London Borough of Southwark Planning Division, *1981 Census Reference Report*, April 1983, 24. Unless otherwise stated, statistical information concerning population and occupation is drawn from the census figures for the period 1951–81.
14. Prescott-Clarke, P., and Hedges, B., *Living in Southwark* (London, Social and Community Planning Research, 1976), 7.
15. Ibid., 9.
16. London Borough of Southwark, *Making the Case for Southwark* 2–4.
17. London Borough of Southwark Planning Division, *1981 Census Reference Report*, 10.
18. Ibid., 22.
19. London Borough of Southwark Planning Division, *Towards a New Area Perspective: Social Area Analyses of the 1981 Census*, 14.
20. Interview with ex-Southwark Councillor.
21. Davies, A., McIntosh, N., and Williams, J., *Final Report of Southwark Community Development Project: The Management of Deprivation*.
22. Bailey, R., *The Squatters* (Harmondsworth, Penguin, 1975), 168.
23. Ibid. 34.
24. Bailey, R., 'Housing for People' in M. Loney and M. Allen (eds.), *The Crisis in the Inner City* (London, Macmillan, 1979), 108.
25. Ibid., 103.
26. Cockburn, C., *The Local State*, 75.

27. Charlie Sawyer, quoted in *South London Press*, 21 December 1971, 1.
28. Hatch, S., Fox, E., and Legg, C., *Research and Reform: Southwark CDP 1969–72*, 35.
29. *South London Press,* 18 May 1971, 3.
30. Interview with Southwark Councillor.
31. *South London Press*, 26 February 1971, 1.
32. *Architects' Journal*, 1 November 1973.
33. NSCDG, *Public Participation and Planning in Southwark*, 7.
34. Interview with ex-Southwark Councillor.
35. Interview with Southwark Councillor.
36. Interview with ex-Southwark Councillor.
37. Ibid.
38. Cockburn, op. cit., 98–103.
39. Dearlove, J., *The Politics of Policy in Local Government*, 155–74.
40. Interview with local community worker.
41. Interview with local community worker.
42. Interview with Southwark Councillor.
43. Hatch, Fox and Legg, *Southwark CDP 1969–72*, 35.
44. All election figures post-1964 obtained from London Borough of Southwark Electoral Registration Department.
45. Interview with local community worker.
46. Interview with ex-Southwark councillor.
47. Interviews with Anne Mathews and Alan Davies.
48. Mr Bob Mellish MP, House of Commons Debates, 24 May 1976, Hansard cols. 45–6.
49. Kitty Clun, quoted in *South London Press*, 17 July 1981, 9.
50. Interview with Southwark Councillor.
51. Interview with Southwark Councillor.
52. Tatchell, P., quoted in *South London Press*, 23 January 1982, 14.
53. Tatchell, P., *The Battle for Bermondsey*, 95.
54. Ibid.
55. Interview with Southwark Councillor.
56. In particular, the role Cockburn attributes to corporate planning in the restructuring of the local state is overstated. See *The Local State*, 31–40.
57. Chartered Institute of Public Finance and Accountancy, *Financial, General and Rating Statistics 1981/2*, asa3–A6.
58. See Goss, S., *Working the Act: The Homeless Persons Act in Practice*, SHAC Research Report 6.
59. Interview with ex-Southwark Councillor.
60. MORI, Research conducted for Southwark Council, *Public Opinion in Southwark: Views about the Council and its Activities* 31–49.

PART 2

Five

Class, Cleavage and Political Culture

1. The Construction of Class

I HAVE hitherto described the part of south-east London covered by my study as a working-class area. The term has been used in a common sense way, but, in the early years at least, there can be little quarrel with it. First of all, it describes the economic position of the vast majority of the work-force. If the occupational breakdown of the local population is examined, it is clear that, as late as 1951, over 90 per cent of employed men were manual workers.[1] Second, the term 'working class' also describes a social, political and cultural force. I have pointed to the restructuring of working-class institutions in the years following the First World War. This process followed the development of unskilled trades unionism, the industrial battles in the years from 1890 to 1914 and the radicalising effects of the war-time agitation. A new political culture was constructed based on a self-awareness and a pride in being working class. It was not until then that class became an important point of political identity and division, and acted as an 'organisational glue' which provided a coherence and a sense of solidarity in the local community. But, while the period between the wars can perhaps be described in these terms, it is clear that these two senses of class do not always hang so neatly together. We need to develop a more careful sense of what class means, not simply in classificational terms, but in relation to social and political formations.

Ostensibly, much of the debate about class has been about economic categories. The various sets of categories defined by different authors, however, lead to very different conclusions about who is or isn't working class – conclusions which bear little relation to the self-definitions established by working people. For example, within the terms set down by Poulantzas, Southwark's population in the 1980s is clearly no longer working class, because most of the community is no longer involved in manual work in the private manufacturing sector. The majority of the local population would therefore be categorised as part of an undifferentiated petty bourgeoisie.[2] For Carchedi, on the other hand, almost the entire community would be included as working class, as non-owners, non-exploiters and producers.[3] For Wright, a large proportion would be in contradictory class positions, but would primarily count as working class because of a lack of control of the work process,[4] Hunt,[5] would include a wider category of all waged labour, and would exclude virtually no one who is economically active. Authors defining class on the basis of occupational status would draw the line firmly down the middle of the community between the manual and non-manual workers, while the inclusion of characteristics such as tenure would, if anything, shift people into the working class. In passing, it is worth noting that none of this helps us to determine the class identity of those who are not economically active such as pensioners, single parents, or the unemployed.

Such an exercise is interesting in drawing attention to the wide range of definitions produced by different approaches to class categories. It exposes, for example, the problems involved in trying to reimpose a simple capital/labour dichotomy on increasingly complex social relations of production. Issues such as the growth of the public sector, the increasing number of professional and technical workers and the extension of the private service sector have all muddied the water. But, on further examination, it is clear that these are not intended as merely economic categories. They are meant to carry with them a luggage of class interests, political predelictions and possible alliances. As Laclau and Mouffe put it, the object of much of the Marxist debate about class is to 'determine that category of workers whose *economic* interests link them directly to a socialist perspective'.[6] Poulantzas states clearly that his objective is to answer the question 'what type of hegemony must the working class achieve in order to achieve the transition to socialism?'[7]

Poulantzas limits his conception of the working class to a very narrow group of 'productive workers' *because* his political analysis leads him to believe that a narrow definition of class will sharpen a political perception of the problems of alliances between workers with very different interests. As a consequence, however, he creates a tiny working class, which includes, as Wright points out in an excellent critique of Poulantzas, less than 20 per cent of the United States population,[8] while lumping together an extraordinary array of workers in a new 'petty bourgeoisie'.[9]

Wright, however, also assumes that by describing class position in relation to lack of control over capital or supervision within the work process, he has identified for those workers a 'real interest in socialism' around which mobilisation can take place.[10] Carchedi suggests that because divisions between productive and non-productive workers are over-determined by the domination of all production relations by capitalist relations, we can assume a congruence of interests between productive and non-productive workers.[11] In the same way, Hunt, because he wishes to argue that political mobilisation depends on the 'realisation of the hegemonic influence of the working class',[12] adopts an analysis of the working class as encompassing all waged labour *because* it is broad enough to support his analysis of the political formation.

It is the assumptions about political predispositions which lie behind the search for the 'true' working class that are illegitimate. Laclau and Mouffe have argued recently that the 'search for the "true" working class and its limits is a false problem . . . [because] fundamental interests in socialism cannot be *logically* deduced from determinate positions in the economic process'.[13] They suggest that such assumptions depend on the elision of two definitions of 'working class', one being the economic positions held, and the other the social agents that occupy them.

One response to this has been to separate the definitions of 'working class'; to revive the distinction, originally drawn by Marx, between 'class-in-itself' and 'class-for-itself', between class as an analytic category and class as a historical actor. Cohen, in his forceful restatement of orthodox Marxism, has insisted on a structural definition of class, but asserts that this does not entail an argument that production relations mechanically determine class consciousness.[14] However, as Jessop has pointed out, 'class determination (i.e. location in the relations of production) entails little about class position (i.e. stance adopted in class struggle)'.[15] If there is a class-in-itself and a class-for-itself, there is no necessary correspondence between the two. There are no straightforward connections, no inevitable processes whereby in studying class as an economic category we can draw conclusions about the behaviour of local people and the complex and messy circumstances in which they find themselves. Poulantzas, Wright and Carchedi may have spent many laborious and profitable hours defining who is or is not a member of the working class-in-itself, but there is no guarantee that when real people decide whether or not to join a struggle, they will, or can be made to, perceive themselves in those terms.

A mere separation of class into economic and political levels will not do. Orthodox Marxist approaches tend to reduce all other lines of cleavage to class, and to assume that class interests either exhaust the interests of the people concerned, or represent 'real' interests as opposed to the false interests otherwise identified. In recent years, however, the intellectual force of feminist work in particular has persuaded Marxists to recognise that some other social forces are irreducible to class. In *State, Power, Socialism*, Poulantzas says that 'we now know that class division is not the exclusive terrain of the constitution of power',[16] while Wright accepts that 'at least ethnic and sexual domination are not simply reflexes of class domination'.[17] Such concessions, however, weaken the argument both authors attempt to make for 'a general primacy of class'.[18] If there are forces outside, and irreducible to, class forces, then they can themselves affect other relations, including the economic base.

This does not just entail, therefore, the recognition of other social forces acting in the political arena. Hirst argues that, once one concedes the existence of political forces that cannot be reduced to class, there is a 'necessary non-correspondence'[19] of political forces and economic classes. One should therefore abandon attempts to find a correspondence between political superstructure and economic base, or to treat economic classes as having pre-existing interests in the political sphere. The constitution of political forces cannot be assumed to correspond to anterior class interests. They depend on actions and events within the political sphere.

The idea of *necessary* non-correspondence, however, assumes a complete separation of political and economic spheres which, as Laclau and Mouffe point out, may never fully take place. If there are no fixed or necessary connections, then there is no necessary non-correspondence. It is therefore possible, although by no means inevitable, that political configurations will coincide with economic positions at a particular historic moment in time.

Hindess moves on to suggest that classes cannot actually have interests. Classes, he argues, are conceptual categories, while interests can only be attributed to political actors, agents, institutions, or political parties.[20] But it is not enough to separate economic and political spheres and then treat agents and institutions within the political sphere as fixed, with interests attached to them. Laclau and Mouffe have sought to establish the indeterminacy of interests in relation to classes and the discursive nature of social formations. They suggest that fragmentation not only exists between diverse agents, but that it also exists within the social agents themselves. The difficulty of constructing interests consists precisely in the fact that an individual can be at one and the same time an office worker, a shop steward, a parent, a homeowner, and a Salvation Army trombonist.

Laclau and Mouffe argue that we must discard the 'idea of a perfectly unified and homogenous agent, such as the "working class" of classical discourse', and recognise that 'the working class was dominated by a plurality of weakly integrated and frequently contradictory subject positions'.[21] It is in this context that we must understand Jessop's contention that 'class struggle is first of all a struggle about the formation of class forces before it is a struggle between class forces'.[22]

None of this is to deny the central importance of the economy, and, indeed, it is its poverty in the face of economic changes that renders orthodox Marxist analysis so inadequate. It is precisely to the dramatic consequences of economic restructuring, as outlined in section 2 of this chapter, that I look for an understanding of events in Southwark. But these cannot satisfactorily be explained in terms of a true working class and its objective interests. The most important changes that have taken place relate back to the restructuring of the local and national economy and the effects on consumption patterns. But these neither exhaust the changes that have taken place, nor can they necessarily be translated back into an explanation based on individuals or parties as representatives of pre-existing class forces.

And yet class remains important, both because of the significance of economic location in structuring people's experience, and because class represents a 'contested point of intersection'[23] of institutions, practices, ideas and shared meanings, a 'language' through which people have defined themselves and their interests. Therefore, if the use of the term 'class' is to be helpful, the following conditions should be specified:

1. Classes cannot be seen to represent *real* or *objective* interests. Interests are defined and articulated in the course of argument or evaluation and their construction is problematic and open to dispute.

2. The construction of class at the political level is therefore also a discursive practice; class itself is structured through political organisations and institutions, and through cultural practices.

3. Other social divisions can neither be reduced to class, nor are class forces necessarily primary in any actual social conflict.

4. If class is treated discursively, we can see it as structured through a process of negotiation and accommodation with elements that are modified by, and modify, the notion of class itself. Hence class solidarities and divisions are formed by, and help to form, race, gender, and other social cleavages.

This does not mean that class interests cannot form the major determinant of struggles within a particular locality or a particular conjuncture. But it remains a contingent eventuality, not a necessary one. We can therefore understand the development of political institutions and of a political culture in terms of class, but not in terms of class as a pre-existing economic category, carrying with it an inevitable and necessary bundle of 'interests' and allegiances. The development of a self-confident working class took place on the basis of an overwhelmingly manual work-force, but through a process of negotiation and accommodation with other traditions and aspirations. Some of these came from a wider source than the local area: from absorbed ideas about British or English culture, from interpretations of the world learned from the media and from direct education and propaganda from schools, churches and institutions of the state. But these things are never simply transmitted downwards and 'received' by working people. Willis argues that working-class culture involves the

> active, collective use and exploration of received symbolic, ideological and cultural resources . . . to explore, make sense of and positively respond to 'inherited' structural and material conditions of existence.[24]

The traditions and institutions of local culture were also generated through the experiences, forms of organisation, shared meanings and institutions of local people. Thus the local working-class culture was neither entirely 'subordinate',[25] nor a revolutionary, organised, working-class movement. As Larrain states, it is possible for a working-class ideology to develop which is capable of organising oppositional ideas producing a 'common sense' or 'good sense',[26] which constitute

> forms of proletarian consciousness which are neither the clearest Marxist theoretical consciousness nor bourgeois ideology pure and simple.[27]

Byrne has called this 'radical reformism'.[28]

Such an ideology could thus constitute a major challenge to the status quo, while at the same time embodying many conservative values. As Forester has warned, we must be wary of a tendency to 'over-romanticise the "working class community"'.[29] While Forester seems to underestimate the strength of working-class politicisation and the role of the Labour Party, he does draw attention to what Seabrook describes as 'rigidly fixed patterns of behaviour and relationships',[30] and to the 'insularity, apathy, rivalry, superstition, deference, racialism'[31] and the victimisation of deviants among working-class communities. Evidence from Southwark and Bermondsey, for example, suggests that there was a fiercely self-protective community sticking together and looking for collective strategies to protect them from the outside world. The enemies were clearly identifiable: the landlords, the bosses, the rich, the government – all outsiders.

This interdependence, while strengthening solidarity, also bred a powerful traditionalism and insularity. Certainly, the special circumstances of the dock communities, where solidarity and discipline had to be carved out of a work environment of extreme deprivation, underemployment, insecurity and desperate competition for work, generated tightly-knit communities and powerful loyalties. Cohen has identified a similar quality in the East End communities he has studied. He suggests that the 'strengths of the East Ender could also be weaknesses' and points to 'an insularity, a narrow sectarian loyalty, which precluded any wider solidarity'.[32] These factors were less strong further south, in the newer communities of Peckham and Camberwell.

I stressed in Chapter 1 the extent to which the Church and a reverence for family values played a part in reinforcing traditionalism. Despite the fact that women were often an important part of the labour movement, providing much of the organisation, and an important part of the work-force, they were seen, and addressed, almost without exception as wives and mothers rather than as workers in their own right. At the same time in such an inward-looking community those from 'over the water' were virtual foreigners, and strangers came from no more than a few streets away. But to be an outsider was also to be outside the rules and cultural structures of society – to be a vagrant, a woman living outside traditional family structures, and later, to be black.

The image of the working class reflected that of the dominant section of the local community: white, male, unskilled and skilled workers. The dominance of that section of the local population, numerically, politically and culturally, meant that they were able to structure a local culture that appeared as consensual, as common sense. It was constructed through ideas of the family, and later of race and racism, which excluded some of the poorest sections of the community. The importance of class identity and shared meanings was precisely that they enabled sections of the population to be excluded without any consciousness of being divided against other sections of the working class. The belief that blacks should be kept out, or that women should stay at home and leave more jobs for the menfolk, or that vagrants should be kicked out of the borough, was held with no consciousness of contradiction, alongside beliefs in the need for local people to stick together, and for the community to look after its own.

2. Fragmentation and New Social Cleavages: Consumption Sector, Gender and Race

In Chapters 3 and 4 I noted a series of major and dislocating changes that took place locally. Of first importance must be the movement of manufacturing industry from this area of south-east London and the slow death of the docks. Economic changes significantly altered the occupational structure of the area between 1951 and 1982 and, as was spelled out in Chapter 4, this led to an increase in non-manual, professional and intermediate workers. However, in relation to other areas of London, Southwark still retains one of the highest proportions of manual workers. By 1981 there was an almost equal division of the work-force between manual and non-manual workers. In many ways, relative to other areas of London and the South-East, Southwark can be seen as a poor area, with a high proportion of manual workers.

Such a description, however, masks the changes that have taken place. Firstly, women's employment patterns have changed considerably. Secondly, the proportion of ethnic-minority households, while not large, has increased considerably. Thirdly, the population has been ageing, and there has been a disproportionate exodus of young, skilled workers. Finally, the unemployment rate has dramatically increased. The proportion of the total population that is unemployed or outside the working population affects the balance of the community. If the total population is examined, rather than just those who are economically active, and if one includes women, rather than examining only the employment of the male population, then in 1981 only 31 per cent of the total population were manual workers, 21 per cent were intermediate non-manual workers, 6 per cent were employers, managers or professionals, 12 per cent were unemployed, 18 per cent were economically inactive and 12 per cent were pensioners.[33]

Other changes have been made by the redevelopment of the borough in the 1960s and ever since. The effects of housing redevelopment have been discussed in Chapter 4. While, in the short term, living conditions for many people were improved, the process of upheaval, blight, reorganisation, the breakdown of communities and the wholesale transformation of local areas can be assumed to have had significant effects.

It has been the recognition of changes such as these which has led to a move away from a class-reductionist approach, and to the development of theories of interest formation based on other social cleavages, notably tenure, consumption groups, sectoral cleavages, race and gender. Much of this work, concerned with the 'plurality of social effects', is based on Weber's analysis of class as dependent not on production relations, but on market relations; on power, or potential power, in the market-place – through ownership or through the possession or lack of marketable skills.[34]

However, writers such as Saunders and Giddens have argued

that Weber's analysis is seriously flawed. One problem with a Weberian framework is its ideal-typical nature, and the tendency to produce taxonomic distinctions without there being any necessity to 'try them on' to real people or events to see if they fit. A second problem is a pluralistic approach which creates a multiplicity of parallel, but isolated categories based on ownership, access to skill and market position, or status, but without an internally logical way of dealing with situations in which people belong to one or more categories, or of attributing priority in a particular situation to one category rather than another. There is no way of dealing with the extent to which some divisions pre-date, create or distort other divisions. Indeed, it would be consistent within such a schema to treat each intersection of categories as a new category ad infinitum. As Saunders points out, such a schema

> leads logically to the conclusion that the number of classes is almost infinite, since there are as many differences in market situations as there are individuals in the population.[35]

The problem is perhaps most clear in the work of Dahrendorf, whose class system based on authority relations is essentially a classificatory or gradational one, in which there are no logical reasons to draw the line in one place rather than another.[36] As Giddens points out, it means that 'classes may exist in cricket clubs as much as in industrial enterprises'.[37]

The problem is particularly apparent in attempts to treat tenure as a source of division equivalent to economic class. Rex and Moore, for example, created first five and later six 'housing classes' using a Weberian schema: outright owner-occupiers, owners of mortgaged homes, council tenants, tenants of whole private houses, lodging-house proprietors, and tenants of lodging houses, and go on to analyse class struggle over housing and conflicts based on access to housing.[38] This analysis, as Saunders points out, falls into the trap identified earlier with Weberian class categories, since it is 'by no means clear how many classes should be distinguished',[39] and, indeed, these classes are by no means exhaustive. Haddon,[40] and Gans[41] have also criticised this position because it is based on present tenure and life chances, and not on potential or future life chances.

Tenure divisions cannot be seen in isolation from other points of division. While tenure distribution does not reduce to class location, it barely crosses class barriers. Almost the entire propertied, professional and managerial strata own their own homes, while the vast majority of council tenants are manual workers, unemployed or outside employment: owner-occupation has merely extended down into the working class. So we need to understand how access to tenure groups has been controlled, and by whom, and whether distribution between tenures depends on the market. If, for example, access to the most desirable tenures is restricted to certain sorts of people, either through the market or through an allocation system which privileges certain sections of the population, then tenure could be the result, rather than the cause, of social division.

In addition, struggles over housing have tended to be short-lived. Although often very effective for a period, they have seldom forged permanent solidarities. At the same time, the strength of tenure divisions may relate to other factors. For example, in inner-city areas with housing shortages and huge social contrasts, tenure divisions may be much stronger than in mining villages or rural areas. Correlation between tenure and other social divisions may be temporary, and depend to a certain extent on preferential subsidy systems that may not last indefinitely. In the nineteenth century, for example, the rich rented accommodation quite as often as the working class.

Saunders attempts, not very successfully, as he himself acknowledges, to reformulate a Weberian schema of tenure based on social classes rather than on ownership. However, while it is true that 'conflicts over housing, analysed objectively, cannot be reduced to the classic class categories of political economy',[42] it is not clear that this is best explained by assuming political divisions based on tenure, or attributing political interests to tenure.

A different approach is set out by Dunleavy, who argues that

a new line of cleavage has grown up which crosscuts occupational class divisions. This new cleavage is a sectoral one, with public/private-sector conflicts at its core.[43]

This public/private cleavage in the production sphere has a major impact on trades unionism, with the public sector having by far the highest unionisation rate in Britain for manual and non-manual workers. Public and private employees, he argues, are also likely to have different interests in a range of different issues, including 'attitudes to income policies and towards the extension or rolling back of state intervention'.[44] Dunleavy argues that sectoral divisions also emerge in relation to consumption processes which, he argues, are

social cleavages created by the existence of public and private (broadly speaking, collective and individualised, and often service and commodity) modes of consumption.[45]

However, for Dunleavy,

the relative importance of public (service) and private (commodity) forms of consumption seems to be the most important determinant of the salience of the social cleavage created by sectoral differentiation, and of the extent to which it comes to serve as a focus of ideological structuration and party political alignments.[46]

Thus sectoral cleavages will only achieve major political prominence 'when a substantial proportion of households lie on each side of the sectoral dividing line'.[47] He therefore suggests that major sectoral conflicts based on consumption can be expected in those areas, such as housing and transport, with a large, but still minority public sector. He asserts, but does not demonstrate, a connection between such cleavages and the production sectoral cleavages which spring up around public-sector employment and unionisation.[48] Finally, he points out that these sectoral cleavages do not cut across class evenly, since most of the owners of capital, the petty bourgeoisie and controllers of labour are located in the private sector. The working class, however, is fairly evenly divided on tenure, unionisation and car ownership. Therefore their effect is to fragment the working class as a political force.

This analysis has been very important in helping to understand attitudes to public services, and I return to Dunleavy's work in the discussion of local-government services in Chapter 7. Most importantly, he stresses social locations which cut across and cannot be reduced to social class, and in later work he brings into his analysis the question of interest perceptions and value formation, and of ideological and political structures. This dimension is given too little emphasis, however, and he tends to predict party allegiances and voting patterns based largely on social location. His analysis runs the risk of reducing social conflicts to social location. For example, while the tension between the interests of owner-occupiers and council tenants in recent years represents a clear public/private division with substantial numbers of people on either side of the dividing line, the same could be said for both private and council tenants in the 1950s when no such conflicts of interest were perceived.

Dunleavy also suggests that the effect of sectoral location is to create a politics of interest displacement, replacing fundamental long-term interests, i.e. class, with short-term ones. Such an assumption begs all the questions answered so unsatisfactorily by orthodox Marxists about the nature of objective or fundamental interests, and their correspondence with the interests which people themselves identify and live through.

Saunders and Cawson have attempted to use two different theoretical frameworks to deal with the two spheres of production and of consumption, a 'dual state' analysis. They argue that:

the state's productive activities are typically determined by means of corporate strategies involving representatives of the (class) interests of capital and labour, while consumption functions are more generally the product of competitive (non-class-based) political struggles.[49]

These two spheres correspond, ideal-typically, with a distinction between central and local government. In this way, central levels of government, concerned primarily with the production process, are analysed in terms of class conflict and a corporatist mode of decision making. Local levels of government, by contrast, are seen as dominated by issues relating to consumption, and are character-ised by pluralistic relations. They argue that there is:

> a good deal of scope at the local level for competitive politics, in which classes do not appear *as classes*, to influence important aspects of the provision of these services.[50]

This approach has been important in identifying a whole range of social locations other than class, in suggesting that consumption locations could be the basis of competition and of political organisation and in refusing a reductionism that would have seen these factors as mere aspects of working class 'interests' in the locality. However, the designation of separate spheres of class and non-class politics creates new problems. Firstly, because class relations are here assumed to be adequate to account for interests in the economic sphere, despite the wide range of differences in relation to control over the work process, public- or private-sector employment, or differences in skill. Class interests are assumed, which can be related to economic location on a functional basis, and 'represented' in a straightforward way. All struggles that relate to economic locations are therefore reduced to class. Attitudes on incomes policy, demarcation, trades-union reform and unemployment, are assumed to be represented by the corporate interests of labour and capital.

Second, within the sphere of non-class politics a range of other status groups are also assumed to have pre-existing interests 'as consumers of a particular commodity or service; as commuters, council tenants, parents, book borrowers and so on',[51] which are the subject of competitive struggle within a pluralism of interests. There is no consideration of the degree of overlap between these categories. All lines of structuration are treated as equivalent and separate, without any investigation of the intersection of lines of cleavage. Nor is there any consideration of those forces which make some consumption groups more powerful than others. But we know that, by and large, few social or consumption locations are transformed into axes of political struggle. It is therefore necessary, in each specific situation (rather than at an abstract or a priori level of analysis) to be able to say that some consumption groups are more important than others. Their importance will depend on their ability to transform themselves into arenas of political organisation. It is unlikely, for example, that the consumption group of 'book borrowers' will find enough in common, or a strong enough sense of opposition to other forces, to mobilise competitively. If a consumption group is to organise, there must be a sense of identity of interest with some, and of opposition of interest to others. It seems that it is those related either to tenure, or to public/private consumption divisions that have been most successful.

Thirdly, there is also a tendency to treat a state of affairs that has emerged only recently as a fundamental line of division. Dunleavy has criticised Cawson and Saunders for an ahistorical and ungeographical approach, as their dual-state thesis cannot be transplanted either to other countries, or to other periods of British history.[52]

The separation into a class and a non-class sphere inevitably suggests a complete separation between two different sorts of interests. But this separation occurs not only between groups of people, but *within* individuals, since every worker is also a consumer, and it is not clear how far people act as 'workers' in one sphere or as 'home owners' in another without the assumptions, ideas and traditions learned in one intruding into the other. Hence it remains a purely *formal* separation.

Alan Cawson's book 'Corporatism and Welfare' goes considerably further than the dual-state thesis. He restates the distinction between a competitive sphere characterised by pluralist politics, and a corporatist sphere characterised by class interests (a problematic distinction, as I have already suggested). But in other respects, Cawson's formulation involves some important indications of the way forward. Rather than seeing the two spheres as distinct, and therefore as amenable to separate forms of theoretical analysis, he stresses the need to study social policy in terms of the relationship between production and consumption. He suggests three categories of relations: associations of individuals, such as voluntary organisations or pressure groups; an 'objective' category of class relations; and, finally, functional relationships which are also objective, but which are given, not by class, but by vertical lines of social structuration, delineating sectoral location.

The problem with this formulation is that it combines very different sorts of categories and ascribes 'interests' to them all. His first category represents real groups of people organising in the real world, while his second two are conceptual categories. This creates an ambiguous definition of interests. On the one hand, Cawson argues that

> Both class and functional relationships are given by structure rather than by voluntary association; individuals in class and sectoral locations can in some sense be seen as deriving their interest from those locations.[53]

On the other hand he recognises that

> just as individuals *may* identify their political interests by reference to common class position, they *may* also do so by common functional location.[54] [My emphasis]

He goes on to say that

> clearly, not all interests which are important in the study of politics are so derived, and common location does not necessarily give rise to politically significant relationships.[55]

Hence, neither class nor sectoral location *necessarily* give rise to political organisation. In this way he argues that

> Political interests are articulated within a set of defined social relationships, and so political activity is manifested in groups comprising free associations of individuals at the same time that it is structured by a pattern of social cleavages.[56]

Interests can no longer be seen as attached to social location, but, rather, they are constructed through a process of mediation and negotiation between different structuring relations.

The other strands of criticism of a class-reductionist approach have come from the important and fast-developing work on race and gender. Not only has this work established the irreducibility of these points of division to class, but it has helped to develop an understanding of the interrelation of points of division, and the extent to which one form of cleavage can distort and remake another. I therefore intend to summarise in turn the debates about gender and class and about race and class.

Traditionally, even academics have tended to subsume issues of gender within other systems of stratification, and to ignore the specificity of women's position.[57] This has led to serious distortions of data, particularly in relation to occupational categories.[58] At the same time, Marxists attempted to deal with the 'Woman Question' using class analysis and value categories.[59] This approach led to an unquestioning acceptance of women as purely a 'reserve army of labour', and to the expenditure of considerable energy within the unresolved (and unresolvable) 'domestic labour debate'[60] as to whether domestic labour does or does not lower the price of labour power, and whether it does or does not constitute a separate mode of production. Moreover, none of the value-theory arguments explain why the family should be the preferable form in which labour power is reproduced. Nor do they explain why it should be maintained; in contrast for example with the process that Marx and Engels envisaged, by which all workers would be drawn into commodity production, and the necessities of life – cooked meals, clean clothes etc. – themselves become commodities bought and sold on the market.

At the same time, serious doubt has been cast on the 'reserve army of labour' approach which, at perhaps its most sophisticated, argues that married women are a 'preferred source' of the industrial reserve army because they can be paid at less than the value of their labour power, as part of the cost of their reproduction is met by the wages paid to their husbands.[61] However, this analysis cannot explain why it should be women who necessarily occupy these spaces, nor why married women should constitute a reserve army. Indeed, if they are cheaper than men for the reasons Beechey describes, they should be a preferable source of labour. In fact, recent studies have shown that it is difficult to substitute women for men whatever the fluctuations of the economy.[62] The assumption made at the beginning of the recent recession – that women would be the first to be forced out of work – has not been borne out.[63] Women have been segregated into very specific types of jobs, particularly those related to an extension of their role in the home.

Attempts to explain the role of women within society in terms relating solely to 'capital' and 'labour' have therefore proved unsatisfactory. At the same time, radical feminists have argued that gender represents the primary social division, and have sought to reduce other divisions to gender. At the most extreme, some feminists have sought to reduce questions of women's oppression to an essentialism based on biology, and 'to take procreation and its different consequences for men and women as the root cause'.[64] Such an approach runs the risks of reducing human society to purely biological characteristics, and neglects the powerful effects of culture, language and social institutions.

Both these sorts of reductionism have proved unfruitful in examining the complexity of women's social role. However, some Marxist feminists have attempted to describe a process of interrelation between two systems of dominance: capitalism and patriarchy. Patriarchy represents a system of dominance of men over women, built up over centuries through the organisation of production, the structure of the family, religious and social assumptions about the respective roles of men and women and the construction of masculinity and femininity. These relations are not separate from the relations of capital and labour, but operate on the same terrain. Hartman argues that capital creates 'empty places' in the production process that have to be fulfilled if accumulation is to take place but

There is no pre-determined way in which they should be filled and no *single* way that capitalist relations can develop. Capital has historically colonised existing social forms and worked through them, and, although these forms are then distorted, re-made and reproduced through the intervention of capital, this process is never one which operates entirely 'in the interests of' capital, nor one which capital entirely controls.[65]

More recently, feminists writing in the journal *m/f* have challenged the idea of a unitary patriarchy, and have set out to deconstruct a category of 'the feminine' produced through multiple cultural forms in relation to the law, the family, sexuality etc.[66] This approach has been subjected to a critique by Barratt,[67] and by Laclau and Mouffe[68]. The latter authors suggest that such an approach can identify a plurality of practices and meanings with no relation to each other. They suggest the need to understand an ensemble of social processes which reinforce each other in constructing the concrete forms of subordination, without seeing them as expressions of essential differences.

Nevertheless, much of the feminist analysis of recent years has been important in examining not only the sexual division of labour, but the way that this has been reinforced and recreated through the labour movement, and through cultural traditions and assumptions about the role of women and the family. Foreman argues that, historically, struggles over the division of labour and the nature of the family have been part of the struggles of working men against capital. Struggles to restrict women's labour were, at one and the same time, attempts to limit the gross exploitation of women workers and to safeguard the male working class from cheaper female labour used to undermine trades-union demands or as strike breakers. The strategy pursued by male workers was not to unionise women, but to exclude them. The trades-union movement organised to protect the family and, in so doing, to protect the privileged role of the male worker within the family. 'Gradually', says Foreman, 'the ability of the worker to keep his wife at home became a sign of working class strength, of prosperity, of better days to come.'[69]

Campbell and Charlton have argued that even more recently the trades-union movement has consistently argued for demands which benefit men over women. The demands for a 'family' wage are incompatible with a demand for equal pay for women.[70] If women are to be paid more, men will be paid, relatively, less.

They argue that trades-union demands for wage differentials, bonus schemes or overtime are consistently put forward in preference to demands for more flexible working hours, shorter hours, and child care; and increase, rather than reduce, inequality.

It is therefore not enough to see women's struggles as a subsection of class struggles. Women have not always perceived an automatic communality of interests with their male colleagues, and in some struggles there have been clear divisions between women and men workers. But, of most importance, gender divisions constitute part of the way that the labour movement was constructed, because, through the powerful assumptions about woman's role both in the family and in economic and political life, it was constructed primarily as a movement of men. The meanings attributed to 'working class-ness' in terms of the dignity of labour, of shared consciousness, of institutions and clubs, meeting places and feelings of identity, were constructed in ways that located women in a very definite and subordinate sphere in the home.

A similar analysis can be applied to questions of race and racism. Within traditional sociology and political science there has been a tendency to treat race in one of two ways. The first is to exclude the experience of black people entirely from any analysis of culture or politics in Britain. The second is to deal with race within an entirely separate literature concerning 'race relations', 'ethnicity', 'cultural assimilation' and, more recently, 'identity crises and culture conflicts'.[71] Within orthodox Marxist approaches there has been a tendency to treat black oppression as super-structural, and therefore as something that would be solved by a change of the economic base.

More recently, writers such as Stuart Hall have stressed the importance of setting racism within the context of Britain as an imperialist country. He argues that the colonial experience led both to the development of race as a cultural concept of differentiation based on the superiority of the white man and the civilising effect of empire, and to the protection and shielding of Britain and the British working class from the worst ravages of recession. The concrete experience of immigrant workers and the relationship between the economies from which they came and Britain as a colonial, imperial power, meant that they came to take up the worst jobs. Immigration was certainly induced through the labour shortages in Britain in the late 1940s and 1950s, but the manner in which immigrant workers joined the labour force was determined by relations of race as well as class. For Hall, therefore, race is important both in terms of the way that black workers have entered the labour force – creating a racial division of labour – and in terms of their role in political, cultural and ideological struggles. He goes on to argue that race is the crucial dimension through which 'working class-ness' is lived by black people:

> Race is thus, also, the modality in which class is 'lived', the medium through which class relations are experienced, the form in which it is appropriated and 'fought through'.[72]

However, there is a tendency in much of the work on race to place racism within the context of crisis as a divisive strategy, designed to secure the hegemony of the dominant group:

> Through racism it is able to defeat the attempts to construct alternative means of representation which could more adequately represent the class as a whole.[73]

It is, of course, important to analyse the institutionalised racism of the British State and the growing use of direct state intervention: immigration and nationality legislation, the criminalisation of black youth and saturation policing of inner-city areas.[74] But a formulation which equates racism with the intervention of the State in the interests of capital can also lead to a tendency to see the refusal of the black community to join alliances with their white, working-class comrades as a species of 'false consciousness'. Because black and white workers share the same relationship with capital, it is argued, it must be in their interests to work together. This approach understates both the extent to which the white working class has a stake in racially structured relations of production, and to which the construction of the labour movement has been through exclusive traditions and work practices. The white trades-union movement has a poor record of supporting black workers, and has often obstructed black workers in their struggles and colluded in discrimination. Sivanandan, and Miles and Phizacklea list a series of struggles in which white workers refused to support or opposed their black colleagues in industrial disputes.[75] Where overt discrimination does not occur, traditional trades-union practices of restricting entry to craft or skilled work can act to keep out black workers.

Nor can the effects of racism be analysed simply in terms of the work-place. I have explored in earlier chapters the extent of local discrimination against the West Indian arrivals in the 1950s and 1960s. Sivanandan mentions the extent to which tenants' and residents' associations organised to keep the blacks out of housing.[76] Rex has described the way that blacks were excluded from public-sector housing.[77] The colour bar existed not only in pubs and dance halls but in Labour Clubs and trades-union bars. The different experiences of black and white communities at home and work reinforced ideas of difference and alienation. Barker has explored the extent to which racism has been structured into our consciousness, not only at the level of prejudice, but in terms of assumptions about human nature, belonging and alien culture.[78] Hence, although black interests can be described in terms of tenure or class, and the vast majority of black Britons identify themselves as working class, it is important to analyse the extent to which white self-definitions have excluded blacks.

The white working class, just as much as the black working class, was created through race; through the exclusion of, and discrimination against, black people; through traditions of superiority, jingoism, and pride in the empire. This is not to deny that within sections of the labour movement there were elements working hard against imperialism, and a strong dimension of internationalism within the Labour and Communist parties. But local, working-class communities were, to an extent, constructed against outsiders; and this translated into hostility to immigrants. Joshi and Carter suggest that

> For the white working class in the inner-city areas, a black presence brought a sharp awareness that things had changed, awareness of the loss of community and their own sense of failure, of being left behind in the competitive struggle to live in the same streets as the people over whom 'they' had once ruled.[79]

That constant reinforcement of a sense of difference and of exclusion has, Sivanandan suggests, led black people to turn more to their own community for support when it was lacking from their comrades at work, and he stresses the growing identity of the black community, linking cultural, religious and social struggles against racism – 'Blacks by 1968 were beginning to fight as a class and as a people'.[80] However, Miles and Phizacklea deny any likelihood of 'black unity' because of the cultural, religious and political differences between various Asian groups and the segregation and even hostility between West Indians and Asians.[81]

At the political level, blacks are therefore subjected to diverse and conflicting forces, which construct points of identity and antagonism. These are not closed, however, but subject to constant negotiation, through real experiences and events. While an identity as black cannot be reduced to that of class, nor, a priori, can class or other interests be reduced to a unified struggle on grounds of race. There exists a parallel struggle for the formation of black identity, structured through other forces, a process of constituting new 'historical subjects', the outcome of which cannot be known in advance.

While I have made substantial criticisms of some of the formulations of new cleavages, they all point to a need to analyse other social groupings that cut across, and cannot be reduced to class. However, it is not enough to see these social locations in isolation, or to assume that social locations necessarily carry with them 'interests' or political affiliations. Recent theorisation of gender and of race has been positive because it has explored the interpenetration of different cleavages – of class and race, class and gender and, indeed, race and gender – and has examined the way in which some social groups are remade or structured by others.

I have suggested that the discovery of specific social locations is not enough to attribute political interests. Some of these locations have led to political struggles while some have not. Divisions, for example between those in public- and private-sector housing, are created at one point in time but not at another. If we are to distinguish social locations capable of political organisation, we need to understand more about the way in which a sense of shared identity is constructed. Social and economic locations generate conflicting sets of experiences and meanings, and interests are created through a process of accommodation and tension between these alternatives. Interests are specifically created through the identification of points, not merely of difference, but of antagonism. To have interests means therefore both to recognise the existence of lines of cleavage and consciously to identify actions or allegiances which place an individual on one side or the other. This makes the generation of interests in the sphere of politics both a conscious process and one that is constructed discursively, through disputed meanings and categories.

Summary

In the first four chapters I looked in detail at the socio-economic characteristics of the area under study, as well as at the politics of Labour and the policies of Labour local authorities. Studies of local politics or local government have, far too often, been carried out in isolation from changes in the economy and community. The fact that major structural changes have taken place creates an all-important context for the political changes which I intend to trace in the following chapters. However, it is wrong to assume, as many writers seem to, that political events at the local level can be explained merely by reference to the playing out of class interests. Socio-economic circumstances do not translate simply into interests which can be represented at the political level. An assumption that they have done so has led to confusion over the use of the term 'class', and to the conflation of an economic category with the cultural institutions, traditions and allegiances which inform political practices. I have pointed to the development of a strong political culture in the period from 1920 until 1950, based on an ethos of class solidarity which was also insular and narrow, and which excluded sections of the population which might be assumed to belong to an economically determined category of class.

Major economic and social changes have taken place which mean that, while the area remains poor, it is significantly different in composition from the old manual working community of the pre-war period. At the same time, while several writers have correctly pointed out the importance of other social locations, based, for example, on consumption patterns or tenure, they have also tended to treat these locations as automatically carrying interests and allegiances with them. I suggest that the formulation applied to class must also apply to other social locations and social groups that cut across class. It is not helpful, however, to turn to a pluralist analysis in which every social location is as important as every other, and which generates an infinity of different interest groups. While every social group and every social agent can be seen as a point of intersection of different material locations, some are more important than others.

While no single line of cleavage or potential cleavage can be assumed a priori to be dominant, it is possible at a particular historic moment that one may be so. Economic location can be assumed to have a far greater material effect on people's lives, and hence on organising ideas, than, for instance, book-borrowing. Thus the formulation of political interests and allegiances occurs around points of intersection of social and economic locations that generate conflicting sets of material and ideological effects. The emergence of lines of cleavage at the political level depends on the generation of lines of identity and antagonism, which must be a conscious process of interpretation, negotiation and accommodation. This is the sense in which, for Laclau and Mouffe, the struggle for hegemony is a discursive one.[82]

Part of the problem until now has been that both the class-based and the consumption/sectoral cleavage approaches lack a sense of historical change. Analyses which continue to explain events in traditional class terms have ignored the structural changes that have taken place in the last forty years. But one should also be cautious about treating new divisions, created around tenure or public/private sectors, as if they have always existed and can be assumed to be permanent. Many of them have only recently begun to have political effects, and I have noted the fairly recent emergence of black groups, women's groups, tenants' and squatters' groups, and the mobilisation around issues of social provision such as housing.

In Section 1 of this chapter, class was discussed in relation to the political culture constituted in the 1920s and 1950s, while in section 2, consumption and other forms of cleavage were discussed in relation to more recent changes. This is not to suggest, however, a simple historical progression. It cannot be argued that, while class was the main framework of interests and allegiances in the past, this has now given way to interests and allegiances based on new divisions such as race, gender and tenure. Similarly, as I demonstrate in examining the politics of Labour, it is not enough to see the torch of 'working-class interests', which was once carried by the traditional labour movement, as handed over smoothly to a new rainbow alliance of black women and unemployed groups. As I have argued, these points of division have not been absent in the past. Women's interests, for example, were not so much ignored as reinterpreted within the terms of an experience of working class-ness which they had little opportunity to form. The very strength of class as a point of identity meant that other forms of stratification were created first and foremost through a repertoire of class. Struggles could therefore be seen in terms of 'the working class' versus outsiders, or versus immigrants and vagrants.

At the same time, we cannot see class as having been superseded at the local level in recent years by pluralistic consumption divisions. It would be wrong to underestimate the importance of relations of production as a source of organised and interpreted experience and of political organisation, which are not left behind at the work-place, but which form political and cultural attitudes which are carried forward into other parts of life. But we must also recognise clear material differences, both between workers with different relations to the production process, and between those inside and outside the work nexus.

What has happened is that the increasing fragmentation of the local community has led to the breakdown of class as an organising idea and has created space for the opening up of other potential cleavages. But the traditional working class has not disappeared. Social changes have meant that manual workers are no longer dominant – numerically, culturally or politically – in the same way. However, the remaining, and still significant, section of manual workers (and pensioners who were once manual workers) provides a continuation of the political culture described earlier. There seems to be a time-lag between economic and social changes and the ideas which interpret them. Traditions and aspirations can survive long after the economic and social conditions in which they were created, and they continue to interpret the world in ways which have less and less relation to the changing realities. It is now, however, a disputed tradition, and exists in parallel with other cultural institutions and practices. When old communities disintegrate, the very traditions of solidarity and belonging which had united them are capable of becoming points of division within the new. Thus, as we shall see in later chapters, the idea of a political alliance between the 'working class' and the previously excluded groups, is neither simple nor straightforward. It would mean the redrawing of lines of identity and antagonism against the grain of long-established custom.

NOTES AND REFERENCES

1. Census of England and Wales, 1951, *County of London Report.*
2. Poulantzas, N., *Classes in Contemporary Capitalism* (London, New Left Books, 1975), 205–332.
3. Carchedi, G., *On the Economic Identification of Social Classes.*
4. Wright, E.O., *Class Structure and Income Determination*, 14–18, 23–32, 39–55.
5. Hunt, A., 'Theory and Politics in the Identification of the Working Class', in A. Hunt (ed.), *Class and Class Structure* (London, Lawrence and Wishart, 1978), 81–113.
6. Laclau, E., and Mouffe, C., *Hegemony and Socialist Strategy: Towards a Radical Democratic Politics*, 83.
7. Poulantzas, N., 'The New Petty Bourgeoisie' in A. Hunt (ed.), *Class and Class Structure*, 114.
8. Wright, E.O., 'Class Boundaries in Advanced Capitalist Societies' in *New Left Review*, 98 (July/August 1976), 3–43.
9. Poulantzas, *Classes in Contemporary Capitalism.*
10. Wright, E.O., *Class, Crisis and the State*, 108.
11. Carchedi, op. cit., 49.
12. Hunt, op. cit.
13. Laclau and Mouffe, op. cit., 84.
14. Cohen, G.A., *Karl Marx's Theory of History: A Defence* (Oxford, Oxford University Press, 1984), 75.
15. Jessop, B., 'The Political Indeterminacy of Democracy' in A. Hunt, (ed.), *Marxism and Democracy* (London, Lawrence and Wishart, 1980), 63.
16. Poulantzas, N., *State, Power, Socialism*, 43.
17. Wright, E.O., 'Giddens' Critique of Marxism' *New Left Review*, 138 (March/April 1983), 22.
18. Ibid., 23.
19. Hirst, P., 'Economic Classes and Politics' in A. Hunt (ed.), *Class and Class Structure*, 30.
20. Hindess, B., *Parliamentary Democracy and Socialist Politics* (London, Routledge and Kegan Paul, 1983), 73–5.

21. Laclau and Mouffe, op. cit., 84.

22. Jessop, op. cit., 63.

23. Stedman Jones, G., *Languages of Class: Studies in English Working Class History 1832–1982* (Cambridge, Cambridge University Press, 1983), 2.

24. Willis, P., 'Cultural Production and Theories of Reproduction', in L. Barton and S. Walker (eds.), *Race, Class and Education* (Beckenham, Croom Helm, 1983), 112.

25. Parkin, F., *Class Inequality and Political Order: Social Stratification in Capitalist and Communist Societies* (London, Granada, 1981), 88–96.

26. Gramsci, A., *Selections from Prison Notebooks* (London, Lawrence and Wishart, 1971), 328.

27. Larrain, J., *Marxism and Ideology* (London, Macmillan, 1983), 86.

28. Byrne, D., 'Class and the Local State' in *International Journal of Urban and Regional Research*, 6. 1 (March 1982), 83.

29. Forester, T., *The Labour Party and the Working Class* (London, Heinemann, 1976), 94.

30. Seabrook, J., *The Underpriviledged* (Harmondsworth, Penguin, 1973), 159.

31. Forester, op. cit., 94.

32. Cohen, P., 'Sub-cultural Conflict and Working Class Community' in *Working Papers in Cultural Studies*, 2 (Spring 1972), 38.

33. *Census of England and Wales, 1981.* Small Area Statistics 100% Southwark Inner London District.

34. Weber, M., *The Theory of Social and Economic Organisation* (ed.) Talcott Parsons (New York, The Free Press, 1964), 424.

35. Saunders, P., *Urban Politics* (Harmondsworth, Penguin, 1979), 68.

36. Dahrendorf, R., *Class and Class Conflict in Industrial Society* (London, Routledge and Kegan Paul, 1972), 165.

37. Giddens, A., *The Class Structure of the Advanced Societies* (London, Hutchinson, 1973), 73.

38. Rex, J., and Moore, R., *Race, Community and Conflict: A Study of Sparkbrook*.

39. Saunders, op. cit., 69.

40. Haddon, R., 'A Minority in a Welfare State Society' *New Atlantis*, vol. 2 (1970) 128.

41. Gans, H.J., 'Urbanism and Suburbanism as Ways of Life' in R. Pahl (ed.), *Readings in Urban Sociology* (Oxford and London, Pergamon Press, 1968) 95–119.

42. Saunders, op. cit., 68.

43. Dunleavy, P., 'Voting and the Electorate', in H. Drucker, P. Dunleavy, A. Gamble and G. Peele, (eds.), *Developments in British Politics* (London, Macmillan, 1983) 52.

44. Ibid., 52.

45. Dunleavy, P., *Urban Political Analysis* (London, Macmillan, 1980) 70–1.

46. Ibid., 71.

47. Dunleavy, P., 'Socialised Consumption and Economic Development', draft paper presented to Anglo-Danish seminar on

local-state research, University of Copenhagen, Denmark, September 1983, 33.
48. Ibid., 33.
49. Cawson, A., and Saunders, P., 'Corporatism, Competitive Politics and Class Struggle' paper for BSA/PSA conference on Capital, Ideology and Politics, Sheffield, (January 1981), 21.
50. Ibid., 15.
51. Ibid., 20.
52. Dunleavy, P., 'The Limits to Local Government' in M. Boddy and C. Fudge (eds.), *Local Socialism* (London, Macmillan, 1984), 76.
53. Cawson, A., *Corporatism and Welfare*, 62.
54. Ibid., 62.
55. Ibid., 62.
56. Ibid., 63.
57. See, for example, Wright, *Class Structure and Income Determination*, 209–18.
58. See Dunleavy, P., and Husbands, C., *British Democracy at the Crossroads* (London, Allen and Unwin, 1985), 124–9.
59. See Foreman, A., *Femininity and Alienation: Women and the Family in Marxism and Psychoanalysis* (London, Pluto, 1977), ch. 4.
60. For a review of the literature, see Gardiner, J., 'Women in the Labour Process and Class Structure' in A. Hunt (ed.), *Class and Class Structure*, 155–65; also: CSE Pamphlet no. 2, *On the Political Economy of Women* (London, CSE, 1976); Hanson, J., 'The Political Economy of Housework', *Bulletin of the Conference of Socialist Economists* (Winter 1973), 35–52; Molyneaux, M., 'Beyond the Domestic Labour Debate', *New Left Review*, 116 (1979), 3–29.
61. Beechey, V., 'Some Notes on Female Wage Labour' *Capital and Class*, 3 (Autumn 1977), 45–66.
62. See, for example, Walby, S., 'Women's Employment: Some Spatial Variations', paper presented to the Urban Change and Conflict Conference, Clacton, January 1983.
63. Segal, L., 'A Question of Choice' in *Marxism Today*, vol. 27.1. (January 1983), 21.
64. Barrett, M., *Women's Oppression Today: Problems in Marxist Feminist Analysis*, 85.
65. Hartman, H., 'The Unhappy Marriage of Marxism and Feminism: Towards a more Progressive Union', *Capital and Class*, 8 (Summer 1979), 8.
66. Editorial note, *m/f*, 1, 1978.
67. op. cit., 87–93.
68. op. cit., 117.
69. op. cit., 92.
70. Campbell, B., and Charlton, D., 'Work to Role' in *Red Rag*, 1979.
71. For a critique see Lawrence, E., 'Just Plain Common Sense: The "Roots" of Racism', in *The Empire Strikes Back: Race and Racism in '70s Britain*, CCCS, 95–142.
72. Hall, S., 'Race Articulation and Societies Structured in Dominance' in *Sociological Theories: Race and Colonialism* (Paris, UNESCO, 1980), 345.

73. Ibid.
74. Solomos, J., Findlay, B., Jones, S., and Gilroy, P., 'The Organic Crisis of British Capitalism and Race: The Experience of the Seventies', *The Empire Strikes Back*, CCCS, 9–46.
75. Sivanandan, A., 'From Resistance to Rebellion: Asian and Afro-Carribean Struggles in Britain' in *Race and Class*, vol. 23 (1981/2), 111–53; Miles, R., and Phizacklea, A., 'Class, Race, Ethnicity and Political Action' in *Political Studies* vol. 25.4 (December 1977) 491–507, 499.
76. op. cit., 120.
77. Rex, J., and Moore, R., *Race Community and Conflict*, 24, 26–7; and Rex, J., 'Race in the City', in *Five Years of Multi-Racial Britain* (London, Commission for Racial Equality, 1978), 12.
78. Barker, M., *The New Racism: Conservatives and the Ideology of the Tribe* (London, Junction Books, 1981).
79. Joshi, S., and Carter, B., 'The Role of Labour in a Racist Britain', in *Race and Class*, 15 (Winter 1984), 53–71.
80. op. cit., 128.
81. op. cit., 494.
82. op. cit., 176–93.

Six

The Rise and Fall of Local Labour

In the last chapter I looked at socio-economic changes and changing interests. In this chapter, I examine Labour's representation of those interests, and the impact on local political allegiance of socio-economic changes and of changing Labour Party organisation and ideas.

1. Labour Party Studies: Explanations for Decline

In Part 1 the changing support for Labour was traced through membership figures and polling data. Although membership figures can only be treated as approximate, a clear trend emerges. Labour's membership, Labour's votes and the percentage poll, all peaked around 1952, and declined thereafter. Individual membership figures in the early years cannot be relied on, since the Trades and Labour Councils were primarily federal structures, but in 1930 total individual membership for all nine constituencies reached an estimated 6 528, and by 1939 an estimated 11 588.[1] Recorded membership for all four of the reorganised constituencies in the post-war period reached 11 110 by 1950 and peaked in 1952 at 12 334.[2]

By 1961, this had begun to decline. Figures for 1960 are not available, but in 1961 Bermondsey recorded a membership of 3 200, Peckham 2 000, Dulwich 2 000 and Southwark 1 600 – totalling 8 800.[3] By now many parties were affiliating on standard minimum figures, rather than actual membership. By the late 1960s, it is unlikely that all four parties would have been able to muster 2 000 members between them. Indeed, it is likely that the rapid membership decline was the reason why the London region stopped publishing membership figures during this period. A slow increase in the late 1970s meant a membership in 1982 of approximately 2 500 across the three constituencies.[4] Thus, while the population had declined by a third, Labour Party membership had fallen to approximately a fifth of its 1952 level.

While there seem to be no other local studies with which to

compare these figures, they do broadly reflect the national trend. National figures must inevitably be taken as approximate, because until 1980 constituencies affiliated on standard rather than on actual membership figures.[5] Whitley estimates that individual membership, which grew to about one million in 1852, had fallen to about 250 000 by 1978.[6] Few authors have charted the growth of Labour support, preferring to concentrate on the dramatic figures of decline.

Studies concerned with the decline of Labour's support have paid more attention to voting figures than to membership figures. Labour's share of the vote, says Hindess, declined from 36.3 per cent in 1966 to 28 per cent in 1979.[7] Crewe says that 'at every election since 1951 with only one exception (1966) an additional slice of the population has stopped voting Labour; added together these slices amount to a loss of almost a third of Labour's support between 1951 and 1979'.[8]

Most attention has been paid to the defeats of 1979 and 1983. Crewe points out that in the 1979 election Labour lost through the 'desertion of its working class supporters'.[9] For the first time in 1979 the majority of manual workers didn't vote Labour. By 1983, Hobsbawm tells us, only 35 per cent of skilled workers, 39 per cent of trades unionists, and 17 per cent of first-time voters voted Labour. Hobsbawm argues that the remaining Labour vote consists largely of people living in

> Scotland and the North . . . or in decaying inner cities, of people employed in the traditional and rapidly declining industries of Britain's past and/or in the public sector, and is more apt than not to be elderly or black, and council tenants.[10]

However, it would be false to regard Labour's vote as receding to its traditional heartlands. Labour did particularly badly in some of its heartlands.

Locally, Labour's support grew almost continually until the 1950s. After 1934 all the local constituencies (with the occasional exception of Dulwich) returned Labour MPs, Labour LCC candidates and Labour councils. Labour's electoral success continued until 1979, when Dulwich was lost to the Conservatives, and 1982, with the defeat by the Liberals in the Bermondsey by-election. There were subsequent defeats in the 1983 election and in previously solid Labour wards in the local council elections. The change was not quite as dramatic as it may appear, however. Although Labour candidates continued to win elections, this was on the basis of falling percentage polls and falling majorities.[11]

This decline is obviously of crucial importance for a major

political party, and for the study of politics. How, then, has it been accounted for in studies of the Labour Party? There is no single body of theoretical work that we can turn to for a discussion of the Labour Party. There have been a number of studies of individual constituencies or Labour councils at particular times. While many of these have offered useful insights, they remain 'snapshots'. Indeed, in some cases, attempts have been made to generalise from single case studies in ways which take no account either of the differences in circumstances between areas, or of changes over time, and have therefore drawn the wrong conclusions. For example, Forester's evidence of inactivity in Brighton in the 1970s led him to disbelieve other studies which showed higher levels of activity several decades earlier.[12] Similarly, Hindess's account of Liverpool in the 1960s has been the subject of a critique from Liverpool historians.[13]

There are, by contrast, a number of excellent studies of Labour Party history which, although based on one area, trace the changing labour movement in relation to its social, economic and cultural surroundings, and which I have referred to in earlier chapters.[14] Sadly, most of these cover only the very early period of my study, and few cover the period after 1914. Work on the more recent fortunes of Labour seems to have been dominated by two powerful traditions. One is typified by Miliband's important book *Parliamentary Socialism*, and the other has been dominated by 'voting studies' literature. I want to examine these two traditions in turn, both because they have influenced thinking about the Labour Party, and because they have developed theories to explain Labour's decline.

Miliband's thesis is that the history of Labour is the history of an inevitable betrayal of a radical rank and file by a reactionary leadership. For Miliband, the Labour Party has 'not only been a parliamentary party; it has been a party deeply imbued by parliamentarism'. He asserts the 'similarity of the problems which have beset it throughout its history' and the 'permanence and similarity of crisis'.[15] These problems have stemmed, according to Miliband, from the constant attempts of the trades union and parliamentary leadership to seek accommodation with the capitalist parliamentary system, and thus inevitably to betray the interests of the rank and file. Thus in *Parliamentary Socialism*, Miliband argues that the party's leadership had an 'ideological and political commitment to the positions they hold, and which do not include the perspectives which animate their socialist followers'.[16] In *Capitalist Democracy in Britain* he again argues that

the pattern has been absolutely consistent: from the very

beginning of the Labour Party's history, its leaders have assumed the role of dedicated and indefatigable crusaders against what they judged to be ill-informed, stupid, electorally damaging, and in any case unattainable demands and policies, emanating from constituency parties.[17]

Coates draws similar conclusions. Hence he sees the dominant political perspective in the labour movement as 'labourist', by which he means an acceptance of the wage relationship in capitalism as unalterable, and a primary emphasis on parliamentary action. For Coates, Labour is not only 'not a revolutionary party but . . . it is not a successful reformist party either'.[18] Labour's reformism is always stymied by the conditions of crisis within which Labour is allowed to take power. He argues that:

> What makes Labour Governments so useful to the ruling groups in British capitalism now is precisely the way in which their roots in the labour movement give them a unique capacity to act as effective 'managers of discontent'.[19]

What these writers have in common, apart from their political perspective, is the generality of their arguments and the lack of real evidence. As Drucker points out, Miliband's thesis derives its force from the 'unargued and, so far as can be reasonably seen, untrue assertion that there was a revolutionary working-class consciousness to be betrayed'.[20] Indeed, although the radicalism of the rank and file is a constant reference point for Miliband and Coates, they make little attempt to study the rank and file at all. These studies concentrate entirely on the party leadership and assume the Labour Party equals the parliamentary party. There is no investigation of party activities at local level. The tension between rank and file and leadership is constructed by demonstrating the non-socialist nature of the leadership's policies, but there is no equivalent demonstration of the socialist commitment of the rank and file. Attempts by Miliband to show the labour movement as divided from very early days into a revolutionary wing, characterised by the SDF and a reformist wing, characterised by the Fabians, are misplaced.[21] Such distinctions are far from clear during the movement's formative years. I have illustrated in Chapters 1 and 2 the extent to which the local Labour party provided a federal structure for a wide range of attitudes, ideas and organisations. However, despite the extent to which socialist parties at times acted together, it was the Labour Party that won support, in preference to its more 'socialist' rivals.

Secondly, evidence from my study has made it clear that it is a simplification to refer to the Labour Party as suffering from an 'overriding commitment at all levels of the Party to Parliamentary politics',[22] or as constituting merely an 'electoral machine'.[23] As much effort and energy was committed to the attempt to win control of the municipalities, the Boards of Guardians and the LCC, as to that of gaining power in Parliament. They were seen, in the early years, as equally important routes to useful power. I have also established that, at times, local activity stretched far beyond merely working for elections and that the party was an important base for the extension of trades-union rights, and at times formed the base for local industrial struggles. Local parties, in the early years, engaged in considerable local political agitation: over housing, prices and poor relief, sometimes alongside other movements such as the NUWM, sometimes separately. Labour was also a centre for political education, lectures and classes, and for social activity.

Finally, evidence from several constituency parties over time does not support a universal picture of a radical rank and file opposed to the reformism of the leadership. Local parties, then as now, espoused a range of views, some to the Left of the national party, some to the Right, but predominantly concerned with issues with which they had direct experience. Socialism at a local level was not measured against a set of 'revolutionary' standards.

Miliband's final argument is that, to the extent to which one can identify 'an enduring conservatism in large sections of the working class',[24] blame for this, too, can be laid at the feet of the Labour Party, since the attack on socialist ideas by 'people speaking from within the institutions of the labour movement'[25] had an important impact on the political culture and in securing acquiescence. And yet, for Labour to have gained the influence that made this possible, it must first have won mass support in preference to other, more radical parties. Miliband's approach assumes a very simple transmission of ideology from the top down. As we have seen, the formation of ideas is neither a simple, nor a one-way, process.

While it may be true that the labour movement is firmly grounded in a gradualist and reformist tradition, its history is not that of a single uniform national trend, from which attitudes and political outcomes inevitably followed. Writers that have undertaken more detailed studies of Labour, especially in the localities, have found a picture that is infinitely more varied and rich.[26] Wright argues that:

> part of the neglect and misreading of British socialism derives from the easy attribution to it of such familiar labels as reformism, moralism, labourism, empiricism and collectivism. The point is not that such labels are inaccurate but that they

are inadequate. They do scant justice to the actual historical
contours of the tradition and reduce a diverse tradition to a
unitary one.[27]

A similar analysis to that put forward in academic circles by
Miliband and Coates has had a profound effect on political
activists. Most importantly, it has led to an explanation for
Labour's decline based on the theory of 'betrayal'. According to
this account, Labour's decline can be attributed to the progressive
abandonment of socialist ideals. Miliband argues that the record of
'failures, derelictions and betrayals' in the Wilson and Callaghan
years accounts for the 'progressive alienation of masses of
potential Labour voters from the Labour Party'.[28] Such arguments
have had powerful currency within the ranks of the Labour Party
in recent years. Tony Benn, for example, attributes Labour's
defeats in 1979 and 1983 to the fact that,

> Over the years the parliamentary leadership became separated
> from the party and . . . we have conceded basic arguments
> which no socialist party can afford to concede and still expect
> to win.[29]

Behind the betrayal thesis lies an assumption that the working
class possesses automatic and objective interests which predispose
them to socialism, an assumption which, as was argued in the
previous chapter, cannot be sustained. As Hindess argues:

> The argument requires that the interests of the working class
> be identifiable as existing independently of the practises of
> parties and other organisations in order that they can serve as
> the standard against which the practices of particular organis-
> ations (the Labour Party, trades unions, etc.) can be judged.[30]

The striking thing about these approaches is the failure to examine
processes of change. Those who see Labour's declining popularity
in terms of leadership failure, see it essentially as a short-term
problem, and argue that a return to socialist principles would win
back the 'traditional' Labour voters.

By contrast, writers who attribute Labour's decline to 'dealignment' conclude that it is inexorable. They do, however, examine
processes of social change. My criticism of much of this work is
that they examine precious little else. Butler and Stokes began a
tradition of looking at voting patterns in terms of class alignment.[31]
They argue that party support was predominantly derived from the
process of socialisation into which a prospective voter was born.
They predicted that, as voters socialised before the growth of the
Labour Party died out, support for Labour would increase. Butler
and Stokes's thesis has been (and it is rare in political science)
convincingly disproved by subsequent events. There has, however,

developed a strong literature of dealignment. These writers, despite their differences, all suggest that, while there *was* a working-class base to Labour's support, this has been eroded by social and economic changes, leading to a dealignment of class and party. They see the decline as inevitable. Abrams et al. suggested in 1960, for example, that Labour was bound to lose because 'Labour is thought of predominantly as a class party and the class which it represents is – objectively and subjectively – on the wane'.[32] Less crudely, Crosland argued that increasing affluence meant that working-class people had acquired 'a middle class income and patterns of consumption, and sometimes a middle class psychology'[33] which led them to vote less automatically for Labour, and to pay more attention to party image and performance. As Hindess points out, the arguments put forward by Crosland and by Abrams et al. entail the 'presumption of a straightforward association between class and voting behaviour'.[34]

More recently, a theory of 'class dealignment' has dominated voting studies. Crewe argues that the key to Labour's decline is the growing gap between working-class interests and the class-based Labour Party, as a result of changes in working-class life.[35] He suggests that Labour remains seen as the party of the trades unions and of the working class, but that class has less and less significance among manual workers. Crewe goes on to examine public-opinion polls in relation to a large number of policy issues and says that large sections of the population no longer support Labour's policies on nationalisation, the unions and public services. Indeed, Crewe implies that such policies may not have been popular in the past, but that class and partisan allegiance sustained a loyalty to Labour even when policy issues put it under strain. Crewe argues that the psychological and class ties have dissolved, and with them Labour's electoral insulation. Crewe fails, however, to account for the growth of support for Labour in the first place. If Labour's policies were unpopular, how did they ever win the loyalty he describes? Crewe also tends to assume that Labour is permanently locked into 'unpopular' policies when, in fact, there have been and can be major changes. One of Crewe's arguments, for example, concerns the unpopularity of Labour's position on council-house sales, and the impossibility of any policy change. But Labour reversed its opposition to council-house sales, with support from the party conference, in 1985. Crewe also falls into the trap of viewing the interests and views of the electorate as somehow formed independently from the world of politics.

However, two recent voting studies have paid more attention to the role of ideology and politics in *forming* the views of the electorate. It is this connection between patterns of social change, voting behaviour and political events that may begin to help us trace the changes in Labour's fortunes. Dunleavy and Husbands, for example, argue that attitudes cannot be separated from the events that give rise to them. They stress the importance both of ideology and the media. They argue that people's political alignments are formed both by their 'position in a complex structure of social inequalities and conflicts of interest', and by 'a set of dominant ideological messages formulated by institutions of central social significance. Chief among these are the mass media'.[36] They follow Parkin in suggesting that some social locations can insulate people from mass-media influence, in ways that other 'open' social locations do not.[37] Through the interaction of these two influences, people form collective perceptions of how the interests of their particular social location are integrated into the process of party competition. Dunleavy and Husbands argue that, within these perceptions, most people, most of the time, act instrumentally to further the interests of their social location. They draw attention to the 'growth of sectoral cleavages cross-cutting occupational class',[38] as an explanation for changes in voting patterns. These, they say, have created new fault-lines, around which people can define the interests of their social location. These include divisions between public- and private-sector workers, public and private consumers, and the increasing number of people dependent on state benefits. Dunleavy and Husbands, however, tend to give insufficient weight to the political and ideological processes of interest formation they have already identified, by treating voting patterns as predicted in a functional way by consumption and production locations.

Heath, Jowell and Curtice, in their influential book *How Britain Votes*, have also stressed the interaction between social locations (including a recast set of class categories) and ideological issues, such as party performance and perceptions of party stance. They suggest that arguments for class dealignment are overstated, claiming that

> the *absolute* level of class voting has declined as Labour has become less successful, but the *relative* level of class voting shows few signs of secular decline.[39]

They do, however, argue that the working class has contracted, reducing Labour's base, while the professional salariat, which provides fertile soil for the Alliance, has expanded. We must assume that since the 'Alliance' has fragmented, the same holds true for the new centre parties. In some interesting and original work they demonstrate that there is little evidence to support a consumer preference or 'instrumental' analysis of voting patterns. Party positions, they suggest, are not objective, to be measured against voter preferences. Perceptions of party position can change, and parties themselves can help to define or shape those perceptions and 'subjective awareness of class interests'.[40] They argue, therefore, that social location provides a voting 'potential' while ideology and party performance help to create a 'climate' within which voting intentions are evolved. Party loyalty is important because it provides brakes on electoral change, but it cannot necessarily stop it altogether. Parties can change perceptions of class and social location but 'cannot shape them just as they please'.[41] There are some weaknesses in this approach, including a tendency to draw an over-simple connection between class, voting and interests, and to use rather weak tests of voter perceptions. For example, attitudes to class awareness are explored in terms of answers to a question on nationalisation, while the relationship between tenure and voting patterns is considered in terms of an unsubstantiated assumption that the Conservatives represent an objective owner-occupier interest.[42] However, Heath, Jowell and Curtice's work is important in establishing the importance both of ideology and of political events in influencing voter perceptions and hence political allegiance, and in rescuing voting studies from a rarified atmosphere, removed from political reality, and returning it to the mainstream of political science.

Thus, while the earlier 'voting studies' theories were rather crude, later ones have been more sophisticated. It would be foolish to deny the importance of social locations such as economic class and tenure in affecting voting patterns. The correlations, particularly in relation to economic class, are powerful, and we would expect them to be. But we must be careful of moving from these to assuming that social location determines voting patterns, or that voting patterns in an area can necessarily be predicted from an analysis of occupational breakdown or tenure. Bermondsey is, perhaps, in this sense, a test case. Here is a case where all the indicators used by the dealignment theorists would lead to a prediction of a strong Labour vote. There are high proportions of council tenants, manual workers and the unemployed. And yet, since 1982, the Liberals have not only held the parliamentary seat, but have steadily gained ground on the local council. In contrast, in the more affluent white-collar areas of East Dulwich and Camberwell, Labour is gaining strength. This is not an instance in which an exception can prove the rule. If an exception of this starkness can be found, then social location alone cannot explain voting patterns – something that is also apparent when one considers that it took thirty years for Labour to win decisive control of the area earlier this century.

A sufficient explanation of changes in political allegiance would thus have to take account of a changing social and economic context, but would have to recognise that the context itself included, and could be altered by, political events, and the way people make sense of them. For example, as Heath, Jowell and Curtice say, 'parties' character and behaviour must be treated as sources of electoral change',[43] and there must be room for entirely contingent events, such as a strong political personality, or a mood created by war, to have effects. Political movements are capable of shifting the distribution of values and attitudes, of constructing new allegiances and lines of division and breaking down others. They do not do so, however, 'as they please', but in the context of powerful economic and social forces, past traditions, and unequal access to power and sources of communication.

2. The Conditions of Labour's Local Success and Decline

I have stressed the extent to which the young Labour Party was formed through, and helped to produce, the political culture described in the previous chapters. Thus, the Trades and Labour Councils and the ILP won support as part of the process of helping to organise the trades-union struggles and war-time agitation. The Labour Party helped to construct the cultural practices which structured the local community. The nature of that community, class-conscious, solidaristic, close-knit, was also both more closed to external influences and more open to penetration by ideas spread by word of mouth, by street-meetings and rallies and through the experience of collective struggles. Parkin has stressed the importance for the nurturing of 'alternative values' of close-knit communities which can reinforce internal values and resist pressure from the media and other forces.[44] At the same time, the local Labour parties built themselves into the local community through the strength of their organisational structures, through the surgeries, the street-stewards and magazines, and through social activities such as dances, lectures, swimming clubs and trips for the old folk.

Studies of Labour ideology have tended to concentrate exclusively on the writings of theoreticians and leaders.[45] But the message that reached local people did not come from books and theoretical arguments, but through leaflets, speeches at street-corners, rallies and local Labour papers. An examination of the *Walworth News* for example shows the recurrent themes of the 'welfare of the family and the security of the home',[46] 'making life brighter and more enjoyable than it is',[47] and a 'fair opportunity for every man, woman and child to live a healthy and happy life'.[48] While Labour lacked a coherent ideology, it was capable of giving voice to many of the values and ideas of the local community.

Labour reflected the concerns and worries of local people. It addressed trades unionists, and closely associated the Labour Party with ideas of 'fair' treatment for working people. But it also addressed working people at times of crisis: 'the harassed and careworn mother', 'the youth who starts on the threshold of life without a job', 'the veteran of industry whose only prospect is to spend his declining years as a "discard"',[49] and promised housing, health, education and full employment.

At the same time, Labour absorbed and retransmitted the inward-looking and insular nature of the local political culture. Thus the Labour Party was structured in terms of the experience and demands of male trades unionists, from which women were excluded. Women were addressed primarily as wives and mothers rather than as workers in their own right. Local Labour parties reflected the hostility to outsiders and the sense of 'looking after one's own' and, as I illustrated in Chapter 2, reflected the racism that developed within the local white community.

The concerns of Labour at local level had a strong local dimension, centred on problems of health, housing, and unemployment. I have pointed out that local elections and local government seem to have been as important a site of political struggle as national elections and national government. Labour-controlled local authorities were seen as important places in which to develop socialist policies. Authors such as Bassett and Gyford have pointed to the extent to which local government was placed at the centre of local strategies for reform.[50] This is not to argue that local elections could be seen as decided entirely on local rather than national issues. It is to suggest that the experience of collective provision in Labour areas, and strategies for local service provision in the period until 1939 played an important part in building support for Labour at local and national level.

It was clearly not enough for Labour to highlight the concerns of local people, it had to be seen to offer a solution to the problems it identified. And it was this which cemented Labour's appeal. The Labour Party was able to put forward not only a way of interpreting the realities of working people's lives, but an alternative, a vision of the future which, while couched in Utopian terms, had at its core a practical and limited programme. Again, an examination of local Labour publications shows Labour's appeal to be based, in the last analysis, on a simple proposition. The anarchy of the market and the search for private profit created misery and squalor. Private landlordism created slums, high rents and overcrowding. The private sector had neither the ability nor the will to meet the needs of local people for health services, for books, for recreation, for washing facilities, for good housing. But Labour in power, locally and nationally, could, through planned public provison, meet those needs collectively.

Drucker suggests that by the 1930s Labour had 'articulated a project which was gaining popularity amongst its potential voters'.[51] A 'project', for Drucker, has a special meaning. It is unlike a plan, or a programme, in that it is not structured by external experts, but, unlike a mere rebellion, a project does propose 'a resolution to a situation which was perceived as intolerable'. A project, suggests Drucker, is 'a will for the replacement of the present order of things, which embodies a conception of the new order'. Drucker sees the project as encapsulated in clause four of the Labour constitution, which he translates as nationalisation. But it was collective provision, not the form of ownership, nor the structure of the public organisation, that won support.

This project, then, made sense to local people, and gave shape and meaning to abstract ideas of socialism and democracy, while at the same time redefining them within the limits of the project. One aspect of the project which strengthened Labour's appeal and that of socialist ideas was the clear connection established between social provision and socialism, one which at times amounted to an elision of the two concepts. Two extracts from *Bermondsey Labour Magazine* illustrate this:

> Individually, we are helpless to protect our health, to secure our life, to dispose of our dust and house refuse, to get rid of our sewage to ensure a pure and abundant water supply or to obtain decent and proper housing. All together, acting as an organised community, utilising the resources of all for the benefit and service of each, we can provide all these things and we can make life fuller and richer and happier for everyone . . . every time you approve of these beneficient schemes you are approving of socialism. The socialists (with the Labour Party as their instrument) are simply out to extend and amplify these plans and to apply the principle that underlies them to all departments of our national and social life . . . you have all the time been a socialist without knowing it.[52]

To be social is to be chummy, to be pleasant, to be nice –
socialism therefore seeks to make life more sociable, to
promote the social idea. Instead of the idea of the individual
being the dominant factor in life, socialism seeks to make the
social factor the principal feature. Thus instead of competing
with one another for the good things in life, socialism asks
that we should cooperate with one another in order to
produce a good, full and free life for all.[53]

Labour's appeal was thus tied very closely to that of social
provision, and the effects of this are examined in the next chapter.
At the same time, it led to an uncritical acceptance of state
provision as at best benevolent and at worst neutral. Labour paid
little attention to the form of service provision or to the structures
created in the public sector. As we shall see, this elision has
hindered Labour Party analysis of shifts in support both for
Labour and local services. And it meant that, as people's
experience of socially provided services began to be negative, this
association, which had formerly strengthened Labour's appeal,
was to have a reverse effect.

It is in relation to all these factors, then, that one must look for
an explanation of the relative decline in support locally, and
perhaps also nationally. 1945 can perhaps be seen as the zenith of
Labour's achievements, the moment when Labour's project was
transferred to the national stage. The 1945 manifesto transferred
the language of collective provision for the common good into a
context of national interest and national reconstruction, a vision of
'the material resources organised for the service of the British
people'.[54] Labour's victory at national level has been represented
as a '"post-war settlement" between capital and labour',[55] an
'irreversible shift in the role of the state',[56] and as creating a
'qualitatively different social order'.[57] It institutionalised a new set
of social values, backed up by a level of support which meant that
future Conservative governments for three decades could not
entirely dismantle it. This period represented the peak of Labour's
hegemony.

But it was also, in some ways, a turning point. The local (and
local-government) dimension of Labour's concerns was replaced
by nationally structured economic and social strategies. As Keith-
Lucas and Richards point out, the 'labour movement was
interested in nationalisation rather than municipalisation'.[58] This
has been attributed at various times to the centralising tendencies
inherent in trades unions,[59] the increasing stress on macro-
economic planning,[60] and the assumed need for standardisation in

order to combat inequality.[61] Bassett refers to an 'uncritical but dominant Fabian view of the state [which] offered little resistance to a shift in emphasis towards the central state as the most effective agent of reform'.[62] Perhaps this shift should be seen as the result of a combination of all these, some resulting from the changed economic structure and changing role of government, some from a changing ideological framework, and new priorities within the Labour Party and labour movement. Inevitably the effects of the war in reordering British society should not be underestimated. Gyford, however, suggests that the shift began far earlier, and that, as the Labour Party emerged as a major parliamentary party in the 1920s, 'the focus began to shift away from the town halls to Westminster'.[63]

Locally, I have suggested that the reaction of the Labour Party to greater centralisation in 1945–7 was ambivalent. The local party welcomed the new services and their enforced provision in other less advanced parts of the country, but mourned their own loss of control. Later changes were to be met with greater opposition. However, the shift to greater centralisation seems to have had longer-term effects on political consciousness and the role of Labour locally. The role of local government changed slowly under Labour from that of a major provider of welfare services, to that of a secondary structure involved in the implementation of nationally determined programmes. Labour's task locally, therefore, was no longer to demonstrate 'municipal socialism' in action but to fulfill its share of national progress. The local Labour 'project' was diminished by its transfer to the national stage.

By the 1960s a number of organisational changes also affected Labour locally. Firstly, the dissolution of the Trades and Labour Councils had severed the links between local trades unionists and the Labour Party. Secondly, the reorganisation of London government in 1965, which, I have argued, broke links between the council, party and community and accelerated the process by which local services became professionalised and remote. Thirdly, the very fact of declining support and membership had an important effect, since it led to the abandonment of street-steward systems and local journals, and the loss of full-time agents. Social clubs and Labour Party dances, as well as political campaigning, fell into disuse. Labour's ability to influence the community drastically changed. When one in ten members of a community are Labour Party members, one can recognise the extent to which the party could act as an important cultural force. When, however, that figure is closer to one in a hundred, the link between people and party is considerably stretched.

The restructuring of the local economy and the fragmentation of the local political culture, described in the previous chapters, inevitably had major effects on political allegiance. But, as has been argued, the process of political change is far slower than has been assumed by those who see political allegiances as ready made, and as automatically attached to particular social or economic locations. While no immediate political changes were perceptible, socio-economic changes undermined the shared meanings and common sense that had developed, and weakened the extent to which Labour's project matched the aspirations of local people. In particular, changing lifestyles, consumption patterns and changing experience of public provision meant that the simple elision of social provision with socialism no longer made the sort of sense it had in the 1930s (see Chapter 8). Changing perceptions of public provision were to crucially affect Labour locally. The 'project' around which Labour's support had been built seemed incapable of developing or adapting in order to interpret changed realities. Attempts to restructure Labour's appeal in terms which related to the new economic plenty of the 1950s and 1960s failed to sustain any lasting allegiance.

Crosland and others attempted to replace 'the co-operative aspiration'[64] with an overriding concern for equality, social welfare and economic efficiency. But, as Warde points out, it was not 'social reformism', but what he refers to as 'technological collectivism',[65] which Wilson successfully took to the country in 1964. Technological collectivism was about modern technocratic solutions, and 'restating our Socialism in terms of the scientific revolution'.[66]

Devine suggests that for a while the attempt to regain national support worked: 'the 1966 result is the sole exception to the continuous decline in Labour's electoral support 1951–79'.[67] But by 1969 Labour had exhausted its renewed political credit. The failure of the Labour governments during this period is discussed elsewhere[68] and it is not possible in this study to enter into the debate about its implications. But this strategy, and its failure, also had its effects on Labour locally. An examination of Labour's attitude to local-government reorganisation has shown that the emphasis on large scale and the 'technological fix' meant that the 1964–9 Labour government had little sympathy for what were seen as amateurish and parochial local-authority concerns. Indeed, interviews with local people suggest that the new Labour style failed to penetrate effectively into local areas like Southwark. It sat uneasily with the traditions and institutions evolved at local level. The local party remained insular and traditional in its approach throughout the 1950s and 1960s. It maintained a powerful distrust of outsiders, which by the 1960s had developed into (sometimes overt) racism. I have indicated the existence of a time-lag, which meant that practices and traditions developed in one historic conjuncture survive well beyond the events that gave rise to their existence. The local consensus of support for Labour held, but by the 1960s, this support was passive rather than active, and by the end of the decade it had begun to waver. The rhetoric of Labour in the early 1960s failed to reanimate the local party or electorate, who continued to use the language of Labour's old 'project'. Its abandonment at central level thus weakened the connection between central and local party.

Indeed, Labour's technocratic vision was represented locally perhaps only by reorganisation and the vast scale of housing development in the late 1960s, both of which contributed to the fragmentation of the local community and to disillusion with social provision. Part of Labour's failure, then, must be seen as its inability to reanimate the project of collective provision to meet collective needs, in ways which adapted to social change.

During the early 1970s, Labour Party and public attention turned to national government and national issues, which are outside the scope of this study. The 1974 Labour government has been characterised as pursuing 'tripartite' or corporatist strategies; although arguments about a permanent corporatist trend in government have been severely weakened by the abandonment of tripartite structures during the Thatcher years.[69]

However, despite the lack of academic and political attention paid to local Labour parties during this period, we have noted that local parties were going through a transformation during this period. I have identified a new surge of activity in the local Labour party by the mid-1970s and the influx of new members, in part from the local community campaigns. Hain and Gyford have identified similar trends,[70] and Minkin and Seyd as well as Hindess have suggested an increasing party membership in other areas during this period.[71] Nevertheless, while this reanimated the debate within the Labour Party about socialist strategies, this cannot be seen as a period of regeneration of Labour's support, since electoral support continued to fall, nor as one in which the enthusiasm of new members for a renewed socialist vision was translated into broadly based support for a new 'project'. Indeed, both in Southwark and elsewhere the Labour Party during this period fought a series of serious internal battles.

Divisions in the local party in Southwark opened up primarily over local issues such as cuts in service levels, office development in the north of the borough and attitudes to homeless families, although these issues began to merge into the national disputes that split the Labour Party nationally, over opposition to the party leadership, cuts in public spending, reselection and unilateral disarmament.[72] These struggles, though widely interpreted as being between Left and Right can also be interpreted as taking place between very different sorts of people within the Labour Party, not only over the policies that the party should espouse, but over whom the party represented. Thus both sides not only came from different sections of the community, but they also had different conceptions of what representation entailed.[73]

The 'old Right', the majority of whom were older and had manual-working backgrounds, saw themselves as representing the traditional respectable manual-working families, who supported Labour 'on the basis of a rolled cigarette and a pint of beer'.[74] They saw themselves as representing their communities by a process of reflection; they were typical of them. They lived in their wards, they were council tenants, they did not stand out from their neighbours. They did not consult their constituents formally, because they saw it as their business to know what 'their people' thought. Indeed, since they were so similar to their constituents, it was argued, there was no need to consult anyone at all, since their views were the views of the community. If the community held common assumptions and traditions, then any member of the community could speak for it as well as anyone else.

This sort of idea of representation assumes a homogeneous community. It can only be possible to represent a community by being broadly typical of it, if the needs and wants of the whole community are similar. I have suggested that there were minorities unrepresented within the traditional labour movement of the inter-war and immediate post-war years. By the late 1960s, those groups that went unrepresented were no longer silent. Councillors, and many local party-activists and trades unionists, represented one section of the community, and could not or did not want to see that they didn't necessarily represent the interests of everyone. Indeed, because it was legitimate within the older traditional community to disenfranchise 'outsiders' or 'undeserving' groups, the new middle-class activists and the community-based groups were challenged as 'unrepresentative', as ineligible to be heard. It was this fixity that the new Left was challenging. Unable to be heard within the old rules, they decided the rules must be changed.

The new Left, it has been suggested, consisted primarily of white-collar professional and voluntary-sector workers, and put forward demands on behalf of the homeless, squatters, single people, women, blacks, gays and lesbians, which were often in opposition to the traditional 'working-class' community. An analysis of the community campaigns of the 1970s suggests the possibility that the concern of young professional activists to represent the excluded groups such as the homeless must be seen also in relation to attempts to wrest control away from a closed group of traditional Labour councillors in order to better represent themselves. It is important, however, not to over-simplify, since the new Left also included a second group, dominated by younger manual workers, mostly men, mostly in the public sector. These put forward demands on behalf of an idealised 'working class' for support for trades-union struggles and for confrontational positions based on socialist principles. This group held views on race, gender, squatting and homelessness which were indistinguishable from those of the 'old Right'. However, the differences between the two groups were submerged, at least initially, beneath a common opposition to the old Right.

The new Left espoused a very different concept of representation. They saw their representatives as delegates, acting on behalf of, or authorised to act by, the Labour Party. A councillor or MP was 'someone who is temporarily loaned the authority to speak and act on behalf of their party and constituents'.[75] Manifestos were to be binding, party representatives were to be mandated by, and accountable directly to, their party organisation. However, this approach can give rise, as Gyford has pointed out, to a form of preceptoral politics, in which party activists assume that they, and they alone, understand and can represent the real interests of local people:

> if the views of party activists are taken to be 'really' representative of the objective interests of the people, regardless of the actual views of the latter, then it is all too easy for them to begin that process which equates party and people, thereby reducing the very real problem of accountability to the people to the no less real, but very different, problem of accountability to the party.[76]

Neither of these two approaches actually involves turning outwards to discover what local people really think or want. Indeed, the working class seems to have been evoked by both sides of the conflicts that emerged in the 1970s merely as a totem, seldom identified, and never asked what it perceived its interests to be. Each side knew in advance what working-class interests were and had no reason to ask. The common use of a language which referred constantly to 'our people' and 'working people' did nothing to distinguish between the very different constituencies I have identified. Nor is there evidence of the formulation of any new project, capable of reinterpreting these changing realities.

Thus the Left and Right 'myths' that Hindess described in his study of Liverpool in the 1960s continued to have currency in the later changes taking place in Southwark.[77] And, indeed, while the profound Leftward shift in many local Labour parties might seem, at first glance, to confound the pessimism of *The Decline of Working Class Politics*, that is only because, as Hindess points out, the book is based on a reductionist concept of interests which assumes the working class is a political force 'whose essential character is determined outside of politics'.[78] It is by no means clear that a continuing rhetoric of concern for working-class interests necessarily has much to do with the local interests that have been self-consciously articulated.

Despite the increased levels of activity, the Labour Party was no longer involved with or related to large numbers of local people. Local people's aspirations and interpretations of the world were neither represented, nor necessarily understood, by the local party-activists. At the same time, neither side in the internal party struggles necessarily put forward a perspective that carried weight and resonance among the population around them. As Gyford has pointed out, it is not clear how far the conflicts within the Labour Party reach beyond a narrow group of political activists. He describes the extent to which the 'new urban Left' spends its time building bridges between different groups of activists, but 'what they do not do is bridge the gap between the various activists and the millions of people watching Dallas'.[79] Many of the views of the Labour Party during the late 1970s and early 1980s *from both sides* were seriously out of step with those developing within the local community, particularly in relation to public-service provision (see Chapter 7). However, the terms on which debate took place within the Labour Party during this period both obscured and studiously ignored these developments.

Both sides produced explanations of Labour's decline of the 'betrayal' variety. It is perhaps due to the strength of these divisions that the local Labour party has failed so seriously to analyse possible reasons for Labour's decline. Perhaps too much was at stake. If the real issue was the collapse of Labour's 'project', the inability of programmes from either the Left or the Right to represent the views and aspirations of local people, then some fundamental and uncomfortable rethinking will be required.

3. Summary

In Chapter 5 I examined the major socio-economic changes that have taken place in the area. These have had an important impact on support for Labour, but not in the simple way that has been suggested. It is apparent that Labour voting and support cannot be treated as a characteristic of classes or of consumption groups. These groups cannot be seen as possessing inherent 'interests' in socialist policies against which Labour's performance can be measured. Labour's decline cannot be accounted for by 'betrayal' or by 'dealignment'. Nor can it be seen as the shrinking of support back to Labour's heartlands, since the decline that I have traced in Southwark has been at least as dramatic as the national decline. I have noted that while Bermondsey, with the highest proportion of council tenants and the largest proportion of manual workers of the Southwark constituencies has become, at least for the time being, a Liberal stronghold, Labour voting in the south of the Borough, with a far higher proportion of home-owners and white-collar workers, has strengthened.

To account for decline, we also have to identify the special circumstances in which support for Labour was built up in the first half of this century. I have argued that political allegiance to Labour was won by the construction of a 'project' that found a resonance with working people, and created a common sense about the world, in a particular historic conjuncture. These circumstances no longer obtain. The decline in Labour's support must be related to the rapid social and economic changes and the fragmentation of the local political culture explored in the previous Chapter. But it is also important to examine changes in the Labour Party, changes in the project itself, and in the ability of Labour and Labour's message to relate to local working people.

This interrelation of factors helps to account for a considerable time-lag between social and economic changes and political changes. If we accept that political allegiances and traditions develop a momentum of their own, then we can understand that the loosening of political ties to Labour has been a long and almost imperceptible process, beginning in the 1950s, but with dramatic results in the 1980s. The process of fragmentation described in the last chapter means that there no longer exists a dominant cultural and political tradition, based on a white manual-working community, with shared interests and a shared lifestyle, that Labour can simply represent.

Labour is no longer able to hold together a local 'common sense' or 'project', which interprets events and shows a way forward. Labour policies and philosophy no longer provide the 'ideological glue' that can stick together the perceptions and allegiances of a fragmented community. And this must, to a considerable extent, be seen in terms of changing experiences and perceptions of collective provision (see Chapter 7). I have suggested that the shift towards central provision, increasing professionalisation of services, reorganisation and the change in Labour's ideology towards 'technological collectivism' have all affected the response of local people to a simple elision of socialism and social provision.

It is a mistake, however, to see these social changes as leading *inevitably* to a decline in Labour's support. Political allegiances are not determined solely by social position. We have suggested a complex interplay between intersecting social and economic locations and political ideologies, parties and events. The most likely response is increasing electoral volatility, and an increasing tendency for election results to be unpredictable, even in 'inner-city heartlands'.

Finally, I have suggested that the divisions within the community, far from being healed by Labour, are reproduced within the Labour Party at local level. Despite the fact that these are often played out as ritualistic conflicts between Right and Left they are more accurately seen in terms of a discourse of who constitutes the 'working class' and whose interests Labour represents – but this discourse has remained entirely internal, and fails to connect with the local people that both sides claim to represent.

NOTES AND REFERENCES

1. Figures taken from *London Labour News*, December 1930 no. 62, 5, and December 1939 no. 182, 3.
2. Executive Committee of London Labour Party, agenda 30 for 4/3/54, membership for 1952–3 and targets for 1954.
3. London Labour Party Annual Report, 1961.
4. Annual Reports of Bermondsey, Peckham, Dulwich CLPs, 1982.
5. Whitley, P., *The Labour Party in Crisis*, 53.
6. Ibid., 55; see also Hodgeson, G., *Labour at the Crossroads* (Oxford, Martin Robertson, 1981), 56.
7. Hindess, B., *Parliamentary Democracy and Socialist Politics*, 123.
8. Crewe, I., 'The Labour Party and the Electorate' in D. Kavanagh (ed.), *The Politics of the Labour Party*, 9–50, 12.
9. Ibid., 11.
10. Hobsbawm, E., 'Labour's Lost Millions', *Marxism Today* vol. 27.10 (October 1983), 7–13.
11. London Borough of Southwark, Department of Electoral Registration, Electoral Returns 1964–82.
12. Forester, T., *The Labour Party and the Working Class* (London, Heinemann, 1976), 107–17.
13. Hindess, op. cit.: see Baxter, R., 'The Working Class and Labour Politics' *Political Studies*, vol. 20.1 (1972), 97–107.
14. See, for example, Bush, J., *Behind the Lines: East London Labour*

1914–1919; Wyncoll, P., *The Nottingham Labour Movement 1880–1939*; Thompson, P., *Socialists, Liberals and Labour: The Struggle for London 1885–1914*.

15. Miliband, R., *Parliamentary Socialism, A Study in the Politics of Labour* (London, Merlin, 2nd edn. 1973), 13, 16.
16. Ibid., 273.
17. Miliband, R., *Capitalist Democracy in Britain*, 68.
18. Coates, D., *The Labour Party and the Struggle for Socialism*, 219.
19. Coates, D., *Labour in Power? A Study of the Labour Government 1974–79*, 260.
20. Drucker, H.M., *Doctrine and Ethos in the Labour Party*, 3.
21. Miliband, *Parliamentary Socialism*, 33.
22. Coates, *The Labour Party and the Struggle for Socalism*, 134.
23. Pimlott, B., *Labour and the Left in the 1930s*, 196.
24. Miliband, R., 'Socialist Advance in Britain' in R. Miliband and J. Saville (eds.), *Socialist Register 1983* (London, Merlin, 1983), 103–21, 106.
25. Miliband, *Capitalist Democracy in Britain*, 93.
26. See, for example, Byrne, D., 'Class and the Local State', *International Journal of Urban and Regional Studies*, vol. 6.1 (March 1983) 61–83; Dowse, R.E., *Left in the Centre: The Independent Labour Party 1893–1940*, Jupp, J., *The Radical Left in Britain 1931–41*; Thompson, *Socialists, Liberals and Labour*.
27. Wright, A., *A British Socialism: Socialist Thought from the 1880s to the 1960s* (London and New York, Longman, 1983), 5.
28. Miliband, 'Socialist Advance In Britain' 109–110.
29. Benn, T., 'From Defeat to Victory' in J. Curran (ed.), *The Future of the Left*, 148–158, 148.
30. Hindess, op. cit., 75.
31. Butler, D., and Stokes, D., *Political Change in Britain: The Evolution of Electoral Choice* (London, Macmillan, 2nd edn. 1974).
32. Abrams, M., Rose, R., and Hinden, R., *Must Labour Lose?*
33. Crosland, C.A.R., *Can Labour Win?* Fabian Tract 324, 1960, 12.
34. Hindess, op. cit., 131.
35. Crewe, 'The Labour Party and the Electorate'.
36. Dunleavy, P., and Husbands, C., *British Democracy at the Crossroads*, 18–19.
37. Parkin, F., *Class Inequality and Political Order: Social Stratification in Capitalist and Communist Societies* (London, Granada, 1981).
38. Dunleavy and Husbands, op. cit., 25.
39. Heath, A., Jowell, R., and Curtice, J., *How Britain Votes*, 87.
40. Ibid., 134.
41. Ibid.
42. Ibid., 38–9, 47.
43. Ibid., 172.
44. Parkin, F., 'Working Class Conservatives: A Theory of Political Deviance' *British Journal of Sociology* (1967) 278–90.
45. See, for example, Taylor, I., 'Ideology and Policy' in C. Cook and I. Taylor (eds.), *The Labour Party: An Introduction to its History, Structure and Politics*, 1–32; Foote, G., *The Labour Party's Political Thought: A History*.

46. *Walworth News*, February 1921, no. 1.
47. *Walworth News*, May 1925, 2.
48. *Walworth News*, January 1932, 1.
49. Ibid.
50. Bassett, K., 'Labour, Socialism and Local Democracy' in M. Boddy and C. Fudge (eds.), *Local Socialism* (London, Macmillan, 1984) 82–109, 84; Gyford, J., *The Politics of Local Socialism* (London, Allen and Unwin, 1985), 2.
51. Drucker, op. cit., 26.
52. Salter, in *Bermondsey Labour Magazine*, no. 9, January 1924.
53. Douglas, J.A.W., in *Bermondsey Labour Magazine*, no. 25, January 1926.
54. *Let Us Face The Future: A Declaration of Labour Policy for the Consideration of the Nation* (London, Labour Party, 1945), 6.
55. Bassett, op. cit., 90.
56. Gough, I., *The Political Economy of the Welfare State* (London, Macmillan, 1981), 70.
57. Warde, A., *Consensus and Beyond: The Development of Labour Party Strategy since the Second World War* (Manchester, Manchester University Press, 1982), 26.
58. Keith-Lucas, B., and Richards, P.G., *A History of Local Government in the Twentieth Century* 40.
59. Sharpe, L.J., 'Labour and the Geography of Inequality: A Puzzle' in Kavanagh (ed.), *The Politics of the Labour Party*, 135–70, 151–2.
60. Bassett, op. cit., 89.
61. Sharpe, op. cit., 154–5.
62. Bassett, op. cit., 89.
63. Gyford, op. cit., 3.
64. Crosland, C.A.R., *The Future of Socialism*, 69.
65. Warde, op. cit., 43–4, 106–10.
66. *Labour Party Annual Conference Report 1963*, 134–40.
67. Devine, P., 'The Labour Party: Why the Decline?' *Marxism Today*, vol. 24.1 (January 1980), 12–17, 13.
68. See, for example, Warde, op. cit., 106–18.
69. Warde, op. cit., 141–62; see also Winkler, J.T., 'Corporatism' in *Archives Européens de Sociologie*, 17 (1976), 100–36; Schmitter, P.C., 'Still the Century of Corporatism' in *Review of Politics*, 36 (1974), 85–131.
70. Hain, P., *The Democratic Alternative: A Socialist Response to Britain's Crisis* (Harmondsworth, Penguin, 1983), 144; Gyford, op. cit., 33–6, 44.
71. Minkin, L., and Seyd, P., 'The Labour Party and its Members' in *New Society*, 20 September 1979; Hindess, op. cit., 122.
72. For an entertaining, if slightly dated account, see Kogan, M., and Kogan, D., *The Battle for the Labour Party* (London, Fontana, 1982).
73. H.F. Pitkin has drawn attention to the range of meanings that 'representative' can have. See *The Concept of Representation* (Berkeley, University of California Press, 1967).
74. Interview with John O'Grady.
75. Tatchell, *The Battle for Bermondsey*, 46.

76. Gyford, op. cit., 90.
77. Hindess, B., *The Decline of Working Class Politics*.
78. Hindess, *Parliamentary Democracy and Socialist Politics*, 3.
79. Gyford, op. cit., 103.

Seven

The Politics of Local-Government Service Provision

IN the last chapter I suggested that support for public-service provision, especially locally based services, had played an important part in the construction of Labour's project. In this chapter I therefore examine the changes that have taken place both in the production and the consumption of local services; and the effect this has had on the experiences of different groups of consumers.

But, before doing so, I want to deal with those analyses of local government and service provision which would deny the importance of studying local-government politics, since they argue that local government is neither locally controlled by, nor of benefit to, local people. It is important to do this because I want to assert, firstly, that there is scope for political decision-making at local level and, secondly, that the question of who benefits from local services is less straightforward than has been suggested.

1. The Constraints on Local Government: Central Control, Economic Pressure and Social Consensus

In the 1960s Bulpitt suggested that 'we know very little about the activities of political parties in local government',[1] and, traditionally, studies of local government have 'lacked any political dimension'.[2] Despite a number of important studies which have highlighted the importance of local politics,[3] the nature of local political intervention and the role of Labour in local government have been inadequately studied, primarily because of the dominance of two sorts of literature, the traditional literature of local government studies and the Marxist literature on the local state, in both of which local politics are assumed to have no real effects.

The local-government literature has stressed the constraints exercised by central government. Thus, for a long time, within the local-studies literature the dominant assumption was that local government was concerned chiefly with administration and the 'devising of common sense solutions to concrete problems', and that 'much that local authorities do has no political content'.[4] A powerful lobby argued that local government had become simply the agent of central government.[5] This led to a fairly sterile central/local relations debate[6] within which it was argued convincingly that central control was neither as significant nor as effective as had previously been assumed.[7]

The efforts by central government since 1979 to impose new controls on local authorities have reanimated this debate, and reawakened concern that local government will become powerless.[8] However, the argument that formal or legal powers should not necessarily be assumed to be effective retains its force.[9] While in some areas the intentions of central government have been grimly carried out (for instance, the abolition of the GLC and Metropolitan Counties) in other areas they have been conspicuously less successful. The very quantity of recent controls is testimony to the ineffectiveness of earlier ones. Labour local authorities were able to maintain and increase spending in defiance of government controls for several years, through rate increases and, later, through creative accounting, although several high-spending councils, including Southwark, have eventually been forced to make real spending cuts. The fears that local autonomy will be stifled have been powerfully reawakened by the proposal to replace rates with the community charge and business rate. The new system proposes to end the redistributive nature of local public spending, in the hope of using pressure from those least able to afford the 'poll tax' to restrict service provision to a minimum. Many commentators argue that this will end all scope for local decision-making, and turn local government into the agents of central government. Nevertheless, while central government attempts to change the political direction of local government through administrative and financial controls, 'we must be cautious in assuming that these attempts will necessarily be successful'.[10] The lesson of history is not to write off local government too soon.

The Marxist approach, by contrast, has stressed not central control but structural constraints. Local councils have been portrayed by writers such as Cockburn as part of a national state in which 'all its parts work fundamentally as one', and its primary role is to 'reproduce the conditions within which capitalist accumulation can take place'.[11] This may seem, at first, a better starting point because, as Dearlove points out, it does 'situate local government and politics within the context of the encompassing political economy'.[12] However, on closer examination, it becomes clear that the structuralist framework renders any real examination of the scope for local political intervention impossible, since the initial theoretical assumptions are pitched at far too high a level of abstraction for a study of local politics to relate to them, and provide merely *post hoc* justifications demonstrating that any sequence of events served the interests of capital.

Cockburn's theoretical analysis has been the subject of a critique by Duncan and Goodwin,[13] and the structuralist tradition from which it is derived has also been the subject of a substantial critique by Cawson and Saunders, and by Jessop,[14] and I do not intend to reproduce those arguments here. While the importance of economic constraints has often been underestimated, they need to be considered, not in terms of the abstract need to maintain conditions favourable to capitalist accumulation, but through the concrete assessment of limits imposed by the local economy and the national economy. For example, employment and unemployment patterns, patterns of consumption and interest rates have a substantial impact on local-authority policy outcomes.

In addition to formal constraints and economic constraints there is also an important third set of constraints which has hitherto been neglected, and which relates to the social, cultural and political context within which the local authority operates. This can set assumptions about the proper role of local government, levels of service provision and, as we shall see, priorities for service allocation. This third level of constraint has, in part, been recognised by work which points to the increasing power of professionals to establish the pattern of service provision. Cawson has pointed to the power of professional bargaining groups, and stressed, in particular, the power of the social work profession and planners in determining policy.[15] Dunleavy has stressed the importance of the ideologies of professional communities as 'conduits of private sector influence on to state policy'.[16] The importance of professional ideologies needs to be carefully situated in time, however, since my study shows that in Southwark they held real sway only in the period after reorganisation, and it may well be that a reassertion of political direction in recent years means that such influence is now reducing.

It is important to recognise, however, that it is not only professional groups that can exert pressure and influence through the creation of an 'accepted wisdom' about the role of local government. Popular assumptions, traditions and expectations must also act as both minimum and maximum constraints. These assumptions and traditions, which go to make up a social consensus, are subject to change, not only in relation to the changing economic context, but in response to political intervention either at the formal or informal level. At the same time, changes in 'common sense' can alter the unwritten rules within which local government operates. It is thus important that an analysis of the framework of constraints is a dynamic one, centering on the processes of change, of redistribution of power, and on shifts in the extent to which formal politics influences, and is influenced by, economic, social and ideological constraints.[17] This necessitates an analysis over time to avoid falling into the trap of assuming that the constraints or balance of forces that exist at one historical moment can be generalised into a theory of 'central/local relations', the role of the State, or of service provision.

While there are several interrelating sets of constraints on local decision-making, the extent of these constraints changes over time, as does the relative importance of different limits. For example, in the 1920s there were major confrontations between local and central government at the formal level. I have suggested that the 1920s were a time of relative flux when, after the period of radicalisation in 1914–18, local councils felt able to challenge central government in situations where the outcome was uncertain. Similarly, during the 1980s, central-government control over local authorities has been far more powerful at the formal level than at any other period; and yet it is clear that many authorities have been able to avoid the policy changes required by central government. These can therefore be seen as periods when the formal constraints were most apparent, but were not necessarily completely effective.

By contrast, those periods were interspersed with other periods when a blanket-like social consensus around local-service provision muffled the conflict between central and local government and damped the concern of local government to test its powers. Disagreements between central and local government existed during the 1940s, 1950s and 1960s, but never erupted, because they existed during a period of expansion and of powerful social consensus. This consensus was built around a particular sort of service provision, and accepted both the shift of power to central government and the relatively pragmatic administration of local government. The power and freedom of local government may well have been greater on a day-to-day basis than was perceived. But so strong were the popular and professional assumptions about the role of local government that it never flexed its muscles. Hence, during this period, it could be argued that political constraints in the form of social assumptions and self-imposed political limits were stronger than formal constraints. There are times when the real battles take place at the level of formal constraints. But there are others when the real battles take place at the level of social attitudes or local economic forces.

Thus far I have attempted to establish that there are major constraints on political intervention from central government, from wider macro-economic forces and from a social consensus about the role of local government and its priorities. But these constraints are not fixed, they move over time, and they can shift as a result of intervention at a political level. It is that which ensures the scope not only for political direction of local government within the constraints that have been identified, but for action at the political level which can, at times, change or move the boundaries.

2. Local Service Provision: Who Benefits?

Having examined the scope for political intervention at local level, I want to examine how this scope has been used. This means looking at the nature of the services provided and at who benefits from them. Can Labour in local councils intervene successfully to represent the interests of local people?

On a simple level, there is clear evidence that Labour councils have pursued different policies, and spent more money, than Conservative-controlled ones. Jackman and Sellars find evidence that

> Politics has a statistically significant impact on expenditure; while Conservative councils tend to spend less, Labour ones tend to spend more over and above any difference in their spending needs.[18]

Sharpe and Newton confirm that, of the British output studies, 'there has been a clear majority of studies suggesting that party colour does have an effect'.[19] In the early part of this study, I established that for example in the early years Bermondsey spent considerably more than its Conservative-controlled neighbours, and developed housing, health and other programmes to a greater extent.

However, I have also established that not all Labour councils act in the same way, and that different local histories and circumstances have led to different policies being pursued in different Labour authorities. Thus I have drawn distinctions between the policies of Southwark and neighbouring Lambeth over responses to community involvement, and between the policies of the three metropolitan boroughs, of Camberwell, Southwark and Bermondsey. Caution must therefore be urged before it is assumed that all Labour councils can be seen, in any generalised or automatic way, to serve the interests of local people. Indeed, I pointed in Chapter 4 to the growth in Southwark of community campaigns, the growing unpopularity of many council policies, and the creation and emergence of new tensions over service delivery. How can we account for this?

Two sets of literature have pointed to the negative effects of local-council provision. The first can be characterised as a radical planning literature, dealing primarily with housing and planning policies, and the second as a Marxist literature on welfare provision. Kirk has argued that local government 'in general terms supports the interests of big business and landowners'.[20] The literature on planning and housing policy, in particular, has portrayed local-authority policies as uncaring and bureaucratic, and as tending to dehumanise local people, rendering them powerless to affect their surroundings. Davies, in *The Evangelistic Bureaucrat*, sets out to demonstrate the effect that local authority bureaucratic uncaring had on people's lives.[21] Ron Bailey, in *The Squatters*, lists numerous examples of local-authority heartless-ness, such as homeless people being housed in hostels unfit for human habitation, families split up and husbands forbidden to visit their wives and children.[22]

Many of these accounts have tended to blame 'the planners', either because they ignore the demands of local people, or because they are committed to professional ideologies which operate in their own interests.[23] Pahl attempted in the 1960s to fit this often untheorised hostility to 'bureaucrats' into a theory of urban inequality which attributed a key role to the 'values and ideologies of local technocrats' who acted as 'social gatekeepers who help to distribute and control urban resources'.[24] However, as Pahl later accepted, an emphasis on the values of individual councillors and officers ignores the wider economic constraints.[25] He also ignores the effect of the political process. Kirk argues that 'it is wrong to blame the planners for short-comings beyond their control'.[26] Students of local welfare provision have increasingly situated their observations within a Marxist framework. Harloe points to the importance of the work of Castells in resituating work on urban sociology, and it is important also to recognise the importance of O'Connor's work in redirecting thinking about service provision.[27] As I have argued earlier, work which has established the extent to which local service provision takes place within a capitalist economic and social framework has been an important antidote to studies which have seen local service provision as a merely tech-nical, administrative exercise. However, on closer examination, much of the Marxist analysis of welfare provision is problematic.

O'Connor sets out two basic functions that the state has to perform. The first, achieved by social capital expenditure, is to secure the conditions of successful accumulation through social investment, and the second, achieved by social expenses, is to 'fulfill the State's "legitimization" function' by meeting, through collective provision, those needs that could not be met within the profit nexus, and thus preventing unrest and securing acquiescence. The best example of this is the welfare system, which, says O'Connor, is 'designed chiefly to keep social peace among unemployed workers'.[28] However, the mechanisms by which the State achieves this are not made clear. And, because, on even a cursory examination of history, it looks suspiciously as if welfare policies have been 'established by the efforts of the organised labour movement',[29] Marxist theorists fall back on the notion of contradiction. Hence, it is argued that, while public provision was won through political struggle to advance the interests of working people, such provision nevertheless, and at the same time, was *in reality* operating in the interests of capital. But, as Pemberton points out, the argument against such an approach is that it tends

> to conflate the origins of institutional arrangements with their effects; that it ignores a vital distinction between intended and unintended consequences; and that anyway, even if policy makers wished to use welfare for the purposes of control they may not find it easy to achieve that end.[30]

It is not clear, if services are designed to prevent social unrest, why many of them are provided for those groups in society least able to mobilise politically, or to pose a threat, such as the disabled and the elderly. Nor does it explain why services which clearly go beyond any basic minimum, such as record libraries, squash courts, theatres or ecology parks, can be sustained. In addition, it is not at all clear that the provision of State services can be assumed to secure legitimacy and social acquiescence. Offe has described a growing 'crisis in crisis management',[31] in which, he suggests, capitalism is becoming increasingly dependent for its survival on State intervention which takes a non-commodity form. This, however, threatens to undermine both accumulation and legitimacy, because it leads to decommodification, and undermines the ideology created by the dominance of the commodity form. A similar point is made by Habermas when he argues that increasing State intervention draws the primary contradictions, previously experienced in the realm of the economic, into the realm of the political.[32]

If it is true that services are provided, even in part, in response to organised demands of consumers, to secure acquiescence, then any analysis must allow space for levels of services to be driven higher than might be healthy for accumulation, and force capital to adapt to new and, at least conjuncturally, irreversible levels of social consensus about minimum service levels. Public provision can also undermine the ideology of the market and the commodity form itself:

> Partial victories won in this way, if they improve living conditions, will not thereby re-inforce capitalism. On the contrary, the public expropriation of real estate, the socialisation of housing construction, free medicine, the nationalisation of the pharmaceutical industry, public cleansing and transportation services, an increase in collective facilities, regional development planning (elaborated and executed under the control of local assemblies and financed by local funds) and the social control of all these sectors which are necessarily outside the criteria of profit . . . these things weaken and counter-act the capitalist system from within.[33]

While it may be true that some welfare provision is necessary to secure legitimacy, the concept only has meaning in the context of real demands and struggles on the political terrain. Securing legitimacy is about meeting minimum levels of demand, and thus the formulation of those demands, and the level of political organisation, must have an effect on determining what that minimum level of service will be. This means that legitimacy cannot be seen as a constant function. The level of service, and the distribution of services, necessary to secure legitimacy at one time may be inadequate at another.

Some theorists have put forward the more sophisticated argument that, although it was established to provide decent health-care and housing etc., social provision is also regulatory, and has the effect of controlling and reshaping people's lives. Hence Gough argues that the Welfare State

> simultaneously embodies tendencies to enhance social welfare, . . . and tendencies to repress and control people, to adapt them to the requirements of the capitalist economy.[34]

Cockburn has developed this argument, and sees the State as concerned to reinforce a normative notion of the family, and to coerce women into certain roles. Hence welfare services have led to a more intrusive state supervision of the family in order to regulate working-class lives.[35] A similar point is made by Donzelot, and this has been subjected to a substantive critique by Barrett and Mackintosh, which I will not repeat here.[36] A slightly different point is made by Bennington, who points out that 'present methods of state provision can be argued to reduce recipients' sense of status and increase a sense of inferiority'.[37]

However, the Marxist approach to welfare is focused at such a very general level that unsubstantiated generalisations are easily made, and any inconsistency can be explained away by introducing the concept of contradiction. There are some interesting ideas in all this, but they need to be disentangled from a structuralist or functionalist framework in which an eagerness to 'solve', in Marxist conceptual terms, the conundrum of increasing welfare provision within a capitalist society, means that all fine lines and distinctions are erased. In the first place, these formulations assume that all services have the same effects. And yet, common sense tells us that, while it may be possible to establish that regulatory systems or dependency can be created by housing waiting-lists or social services, it is less possible to establish such effects in relation to parks, swimming baths, street-lighting or the Christmas panto. Even in relation to social services, for example, it is not clear that every experience of help is regulatory. Secondly, they fail to distinguish between different types of consumers. And yet, as has been established in Chapter 4, the experiences of the homeless families described by Bailey, or the squatters described by Cockburn, are not typical of the experiences of other sections of the local population. Thirdly, there is an automatic assumption that the repressive effects of the service provision they identify are 'in the interests of capital'. But they may not necessarily serve any functional interest. They may even reflect the aspirations and priorities of sections of the local community, or the political party in power. And some of the repressive effects of service distribution may not really serve anyone's interests, but be partly due to the process of allocation itself.

An examination of 'who gets what' in terms of service provision requires more careful distinctions. Several taxonomies of the activities of the State or local government have been developed, but even within these, the vast majority of local government services are placed in a single category of 'collective consumption'.[38] The inadequacies of this term have been explored elsewhere, by Lojkine and by Pickvance.[39] Dunleavy makes a useful distinction between allocational services, which improve facilities for the community generally, and redistributive services which are financed by one group to provide benefits for another, poorer group.[40] However, as I will illustrate, it is not necessarily the case that all redistribution operates in favour of the poorest sectors. If we are interested in the effects and benefits of service provision, it is important to establish a set of distinctions that will permit an examination of the consumption patterns of different services, and will make a distinction between those collectively provided services which are accessible to, or used by, everyone, and those for which a process of allocation, or rationing, takes place.

Thus I want to distinguish two basic categories: *universal* services, those which are universally available and provided on demand through the rates; and *rationed* services, scarce services which are allocated bureaucratically according to need. Because of the specific concerns of my study, I want to confine discussion of these two service types to the local level. Thus, here, universal services include refuse collection, public libraries, street lighting, buses, sports centres, parks, health care, public health and, although I will not be considering it here, education. Some, but not all universal services are infrastructural, such as sewerage, water, roads and lighting; but it is not possible to sustain an argument that universal services are those necessary to perform an accumulation function, because they include, amongst other things, parks, galleries, baths and fireworks.

The distribution of services into these categories is not fixed. Services that were once rationed can become universal and vice versa. Similarly, services that are universally available here, such as free health care, are rationed in much of the rest of the world. The extent to which services are rationed or universal can be seen in part as a result of conjunctural political interventions, government programmes, and organised demands for provision.

Inevitably in categorisations of this kind, one is forced to simplify the complex realities of state subsidies (e.g. for private health-care, housing and education) and the hidden barriers to access to supposedly universal services (e.g. to those with disabilities), or variations in take-up. Nevertheless, I want to suggest that these two broad distribution systems for local services create very different attitudes to service consumption. Universally provided services reinforce ideas of citizen rights, and undermine the 'naturalness' of market provision. While it may be true that the better off consume more of these services,[41] there are few regulatory characteristics, and no stigma attached to consuming these services.

It is with rationed services that many of the regulatory characteristics identified apply, quintessentially in relation to housing. In the first place, the process of allocation itself has considerable effects on the consumers of these services. They are, by definition, scarce relative to demand. Scarcity in the market context leads to high prices, and the poorest are priced out of the market. Scarcity in the allocative context leads to policing, the need to organise queues, to test merit, to prioritise need and check against fraud. That process of policing in its turn affects the nature of the services themselves, they become inevitably overregulatory and paternalistic. Hence the allocation process generates consequences for those dependent on service provision. This need only carry with it a sense of stigma, however, if the public sector is seen as a last resort, or if only the poorest families have to turn to the State for help. Strict tests of housekeeping standards in the 1930s, 1940s and 1950s reinforced the 'respectability' of those allocated council housing.

Secondly, allocation takes place on the basis of priorities that are not neutral, or technical, but open to political contestation. The concept of need itself is far from objective, and carries with it a number of 'common sense' assumptions. Thus, for example, the needs of local residents or families with children have been considered to require greater priority than the needs of single people or new arrivals, and the needs taken into account when allocating nursery places are often those of the children, rather than those of the parents. Housing and social service allocation has met some 'needs', while entirely overlooking others, and a whole series of minimum qualification periods and special categories have been introduced which, far from prioritising need, give expression to divisions between the 'deserving' and the 'undeserving'.[42] The question of whose needs are to be met can thus be seen as potentially always a subject of political conflict. The absence of conflict over priorities could be taken as evidence of a social consensus at a particular time, but not as evidence that these priorities are objective.

Rationed systems of allocation have primarily been used to squeeze out the poorest section of the community, and to privilege a 'better off' or 'respectable' stratum of working-class families. Evidence from a study of Southwark supports Harloe's contention that, for example, the supply of housing has been 'confined to a relatively restricted section of the working class', and

> served for many years to exclude large numbers of those at the very bottom of the housing market from access to social housing – people such as the elderly, the young, mobile and less skilled, blacks and other immigrants such as guest workers, or those with a history of unapproved social behaviour, such as single parent families or even large families.[43]

That privilege is of course only relative; it has meant 'respectable' sections of the local community have had greater access to scarce services than they might otherwise have had. Services remain scarce, however, and the most privileged sections of the community do not depend on them at all; money can always buy you out of this particular struggle.

Traditionally, the groups that have been most excluded from service provision have been those outside the traditions and structures of the local working-class community. These include homeless families, single parents, vagrants, the less 'respectable', and the immigrant community which began to arrive in the mid-1950s. Categories of need also tended to exclude young middle-class or professional people who, by the 1970s, had begun to compete in working-class areas for housing, nursery provision and other services. Women have not been excluded from service provision as such, but the low priority given to services which, for example, reduce the burden of care for dependents, has reinforced structures of discrimination. Dominant assumptions that caring is primarily the role of women within the family have resulted in social services that are provided only when family structures break down, rather than as support services to which everyone is entitled. These assumptions have been generated and reinforced within the labour movement, as well as within the wider social formation.[44] Political demands for childcare and caring services have never been sufficient to ensure more than strictly rationed provision.

It is rationed services that give the most scope for direct political influence on distribution. At the formal level, this influence is exercised through the political party in power, and I examined in Chapter 6 the nature of the local-government project established by Labour. At the same time, however, that project emerged from, and to gain local support had to reflect, the priorities and social assumptions of the local community. So we must also look at the nature of the demands put forward by local people. I have cited examples where, rather than voice a demand for the universal provision of a scarce service, such as public housing, the political demand formulated by sections of the community was for the exclusion of other sections, such as homeless families or immigrants. To the extent that local government is 'vulnerable to working class demands, pressures and even control'[45] the priorities and assumptions of the community, the labour movement and the Labour Party in an area like Southwark, have an impact on the distribution of services. Thus certain groups have been excluded with the tacit agreement of the rest of the community. I suggest that these tacit rules determining access to certain services have been disturbed by the major changes that have taken place within both consumption patterns of services, and the experience of those services.

3. Changes in the Production and Consumption of Local Services

In Part 1 I argued that the services provided by local Labour councils were a source of popular pride and enjoyed considerable local support in the period between the 1920s and 1960s. Not everyone could gain access to council provision, but the majority of local people aspired to it. Public services met needs that could not be met in other ways. But it was not merely that there was no alternative. The health care that could be obtained in Bermondsey was in advance of much that could be obtained in the private sector. Council housing included electric lights before many homes in the private sector. Council homes had baths, electric fires, cupboards, sculleries and separate bedrooms, at a time when few private houses could boast such luxuries. I have suggested that, while some of these services were available for all, others, particularly council housing, were allocated to the better off, 'respectable' working class. However, since the 1960s, there has been growing criticism of public provision. I have suggested that some of this has arisen from the identification of processes of exclusion outlined in the previous section. But that is not a sufficient explanation, I outlined in Part 1 the enormous changes in the production, consumption and distribution of public services. I want here to recapitulate these changes and to point to their effects.

Firstly, there have been considerable changes in the production and the nature of services. In Chapter 3 I stressed the importance of the effects of reorganisation, of the centralisation of service provision, and the consequential breaking down of links between community and council. The creation of a single borough with none of the old networks and links with the community coincided with new initiatives in service provision, and the introduction of huge new departments. Service delivery was increasingly dominated by professionals, who, as Dunleavy has argued, developed professional ideologies which overtook the day-to-day political direction of even the most insignificant details that had existed in the old councils.[46] Councillors found they no longer had much control over decision making. While this, in some ways, loosened some of the more paternalistic policies that had previously been operated, it did so at the cost of shifting policy out of the local political arena and into one dominated far more by national concerns and professional ideologies. In Chapters 3 and 4, I traced the effects of the major redevelopment programme pursued in the

1960s, in terms of planning blight, uncertainty and dislocation, and the rapid emergence of problems in the new estates. Thus an expansion of service provision and of council spending during this period may in fact have resulted in the perception by consumers of a declining quality of service.

Secondly, given the distinction that I have made between the possible effects of universal and rationed services, it is important to note the extent to which the balance between these two types of services has changed. While it is difficult to make more than a rough assessment of the distribution of each council's spending in the early years, it is clear that universal services made up the bulk of net revenue spending. In 1939, for example, the majority of council spending in Bermondsey, Southwark and Camberwell went on lighting, refuse, roads, public baths and public health – all universal services. Rationed services, housing, maternity and child welfare and sick benefits, accounted for just over 7 per cent of net revenue expenditure in Camberwell and Southwark, and for nearly 10 per cent in Bermondsey.[47] By 1951/2, housing had grown as a proportion of spending but was no more than 12 per cent even in Bermondsey, while most of the other rationed services had been transferred to central government and the NHS. Local social-service spending was still embryonic during this period.[48] An examination of net revenue spending in 1980/81 reveals, of course, that total spending has increased in real and money terms but, more importantly, that the balance of universal and rationed services has changed dramatically. Highways and general services accounted for 15 per cent and public health for 1.2 per cent, while housing accounted for 32.5 per cent and social services for 28 per cent. Thus, by the 1980s, rationed services made up 60 per cent of net revenue spending.[49]

Thirdly, as has been demonstrated by Dunleavy and Saunders there has been a shift from public to private consumption, particularly in relation to housing and transport.[50] Advances in productivity in the private sector, the cheapening of capital, mass-production techniques and the search for new markets have led the private sector to begin to compete with State provision, primarily through the commodification of housing and transport, and the introduction of new, mass, consumer goods, such as televisions, washing-machines etc. Hobsbawm draws attention to this process, and to the spread of the 'mass-produced economy of mass consumption',[51] and its effects in fragmenting the 'common style of proletarian life'.[52] A perception of these trends formed the background against which Goldthorpe et al. conducted their studies into working-class embourgeoisement, although, by assuming an automatic relationship between changed social location and changed interests, they failed to take account of the time-lag in sustaining assumptions and traditions from the past.[53]

However, the shift from public to private consumption does not take place evenly throughout the population. Dunleavy has argued that it is begun by the better-off sections of the population, although this may, in its turn, lead to 'coerced exchanges' further down the income scale.[54] Because some, more wealthy people, make the transition, it eventually coerces others into making the exchange in order to avoid the steady welfare-loss inherent in staying within public consumption. Lowe points out that this only occurs if both systems are assumed to produce basically the same benefits. However, it may be the case that 'exiting' from one sector to another 'confers qualitative advantages and not merely sustaining standards'.[55] Certainly the process of exiting must reflect a changing view of the relative quality of the services concerned. Private consumption is now seen as offering prestige, greater choice and flexibility, and, in the case of housing, capital gain. Thus those who are able to exercise choice are less likely to choose to stay in the public sector. Those who are unable to exercise choices, the poorest section of the community, remain dependent on the public sector. This has led to a process of residualisation, particularly in relation to public housing. Gray, for example, notes that the 'commonly held views of council tenants as relatively well-off households requires substantial modifications',[56] while Forest argues that there are developing

> increasingly dependent relationships between state welfare benefits and those who occupy council housing, sub-groups within the working class which are being progressively marginalised from the labour movement.[57]

From an examination of Southwark, it seems likely that what is slowly taking place is a change from one set of allocation priorities which privileged the better off and respectable working people, to another set which caters primarily for the poorest, residual section. At the same time as better-off working people have moved into private-sector consumption, local authorities have, in the last few years, through a combination of governmental, professional and local political pressure, liberalised allocation policy and begun to make provision for single people, for the homeless, the black community, extended families and gay men and lesbians. Some of this has been justified at the professional/ technical level as refining definitions of need. In other respects service allocation and priorities have been the subject of political struggles to include certain previously excluded groups. I suggested in Part 1 that some of the political struggles fought around the local authority and local Labour Party can be explained in this way.

Finally, we must recognise the importance of cuts in central government funding to local authorities. The extraordinary range of new government controls on local spending introduced since 1979 have been explored in detail by Boddy; Jones, Stewart and Travers; Schott; Midwinter; and Gyford and James;[58] I do not intend to reproduce these analyses here, but rather to look at the effects these have had on perceptions of local service provision, since these have been neither simple nor uniform. It was pointed out in the first section of this chapter that central government is not able to control local authorities in quite the straightforward way that is often assumed. Thus, while there has been a sustained attempt by central government to control local spending, the extent to which individual councils have cut services has been mediated by a number of factors: the political will of the local authority, the success of direct political campaigning and of less direct lobbying, the financial room to manœuvre within each authority, the scope for increasing rents, rates and charges, the level of balances, and the relative ingenuity of creative-accounting measures.

Some government controls, such as housing-capital allocation, have been unavoidable, and have had powerful effects in increasing shortages of rented housing and in depressing the relative desirability of public housing in all areas. But cuts in revenue support to local authorities have met with varying responses in different local authorities. Where cuts have been made, and have resulted in a fall in the quality of the service, this is likely to intensify the coerced exchange effect, since people able to substitute private consumption for public consumption will do so. It may also increase conflict between groups of potential consumers for scarce provision.

In boroughs such as Southwark, however, the cuts in revenue subsidy have been offset to a considerable extent by rate increases. Thus, while the supply of services in poor inner-city areas is dramatically outweighed by demand, spending levels have actually increased. Here the effect of cuts has been to shift the burden of financing local services from central government to the local ratepayer. Issues such as 'value for money' and 'waste' have hence become far more politically significant, and struggles have intensified over the distribution of resources. For a while, substantial rate increases funded constant or increasing spending levels, and created a potential division between those who are most dependent on rationed services, but who pay at most rebated rates, and those who pay full rates, but use fewer services. As Dunleavy has pointed out, there is a tendency for the continuation of local services to depend on the willingness of those sections of the population who don't benefit from them to finance those who do.[59] It is worth noting in passing that the effects of rate-capping, and the consequent shifts in many authorities to creative accounting to sustain expansion, have helped to ease this conflict.

The widely declared purpose of central government and sections of the Right to reduce the scope of public provision and dismantle the 'choice-denying universality of the Welfare State'[60] has encountered considerable obstacles. Public support has hardened behind certain services, such as the National Health Service, and behind the need for a minimum level of public provision.[61] Nevertheless, the changes that have taken place and the poor experience of public-sector provision[62] have contributed to a growing ambivalence about state provision, even amongst its consumers. Mishra argues that the 'broad consensus concerning the mixed economy and the welfare state . . . has weakened a good deal in recent years'.[63] Taylor-Gooby has argued that this stems in part from 'the perceptions of welfare benefits as serving the illegitimate interests of undeserving groups'.[64] Recent surveys have revealed growing ambivalence about the privatisation of services.[65]

Judge, Smith and Taylor-Gooby argue that support for public services coexists with a commitment to parallel private-sector provision: 'permissive views about the privatisation of welfare can co-exist with support for public spending on the welfare state'.[66] While many people see public-sector provision as an important safety net, they aspire to private-sector provision. This means that it is too simplistic merely to represent cuts in local services as 'an attack on working class living standards, real wages and quality of life',[67] or to expect a coherent working-class response. Far from evoking a unified response, the withdrawal of government subsidy is more likely to widen the gap between different consumer experiences, and to exacerbate the potential divisions that are emerging.

The changes in consumption patterns outlined above have been analysed elsewhere in terms of conflicts based on sectoral cleavages and social location. Dunleavy has stressed the emergence of what can be seen primarily as a public/private division.[68] However, I have suggested that the identification of interests and of political allegiance cannot be assumed to stem simply from social location. We must also take account of the way a sense of shared identity and division is created, and of the importance of institutions and traditions, and the time-lag effect I have identified earlier.

The new forces at work cannot therefore be limited to simple cleavages between those consuming in the public, and those consuming in the private sector. The following observations illustrate this point. Firstly, as we have seen, changes in the nature of public and private services have changed aspirations; and hence differences may evolve, not around present consumption patterns, but around the possibilities and aspirations for future consumption. For example, until the 1950s, while the majority of local people were private tenants, they aspired to council housing, and therefore there was a consensus across the tenures about the need for council housing. Now, although the majority of the local population are council tenants, we cannot assume that they will support the development and expansion of council housing if they aspire to home ownership. Secondly, Southwark has seen considerable development of political organisation around consumption, and yet it is not an area where the vast majority of the population has switched to private consumption. Indeed, it has one of the highest proportions of council tenants in the country, and high levels of public-transport users, social-services clients, etc. But the increasing pressures I have identified have intensified divisions *within* the public sector.

I have argued that, while certain groups used to have privileged access to some services, patterns of allocation and consumption have shifted. In Southwark – and in other similar areas – there is now a population not only far more heterogeneous, but with widely varying experiences of service provision. The consensus around service delivery, a consensus which structured local support both for local services and for Labour policies, seems to have broken down. We can no longer identify an overwhelmingly manual-working class, held together by strong social and political bonds, the majority of whom consume, or aspire to consume, public housing and services. This leads me to suggest the potential formation of new divisions, formed not on the basis of simple consumption locations, but on an interplay of production and consumption locations, of past tradition, of aspirations and of access to political power.

Firstly, there is the better-off section of the traditional working class, those in full-time skilled or semi-skilled work in the traditional industries such as the print, the riverside industries, and in public-sector manual work, and new, service industries. This is the group which had, until recently, most access to the political structures within the labour movement, and which still dominates the tenants' movement and the local trades unions. They are most likely to own their own home or to have bought their council house, and to own a car. Despite a trades-union and labour-movement background, they are very much part of the move towards what Raymond Williams called 'mobile privatisation',[69] centred on the home, DIY, the family and leisure. They are also, especially the younger families, the group which has predominantly moved out of the borough to other London suburbs such as Bromley, Bexley and Croydon.

Secondly, there are those in the less well-off sections of the traditional working class. Many of them are elderly, in low-income households, who, in their earlier years, did best out of exclusionary allocation procedures restricted to white 'respectable' working people. This group also includes poorer white households who have no option other than public-sector provision, but resent its growing stigmatisation. It is from this group that we should expect the most powerful consciousness of things having 'changed for the worst'. This is not only because of the changes in the quality of services identified earlier. Shifts in allocation towards previously excluded groups have led to a relative shift in the position of this group, and a removal of previous privileges over other people. Those in this group often seriously resent the intrusion of new groups whose needs coincide with their own.

The third group consists of those who have traditionally been excluded from service provision; homeless families, single parents, the homeless and rootless, non-conventional households including gays and lesbians and, most importantly, the black community. While the 'poor whites' *perceive* a shift of relative privilege towards those groups, black people and single parents still experience considerable discrimination in relation to access to local-authority services. They tend to be residualised within the public sector, offered the worst accommodation, given access to the most stigmatised services. It is this group who are most dependent on State services, and who might be expected to be most consistently supportive of the public sector, but this is complicated both by experiences of discrimination by the regulatory nature of rationed services, and by their underrepresentation in structures of political representation at local level. The demand by this group for greater political representation has implications which will be briefly explored in the concluding chapter.

Finally, there are the growing numbers of professional and managerial workers concentrated in the public and voluntary sectors. Young, active middle-class people, politically active and articulate, I have suggested that they have disproportionate access to structures of interest representation. While they attempt to 'represent' the underclass, they do so in the context of improving their own access to services and to employment.

Conclusion

In this chapter I have argued that there is scope for local-government decision making, despite the fact that there are constraints; from central government, from macro-economic forces, and from limits set by levels of consensus and social attitudes. In the first part of my study, I described the extent to which local Labour councils have, at times, achieved significant policy changes, and have moved the boundaries of local service provision.

However, local-service provision cannot be seen in a simple sense as 'in the interests of the working class'. A radical literature on planning, and a Marxist literature, have pointed to the regulatory effects of service provision. However, there has been a tendency in this literature to assume that all services have the same effects, that all consumers are affected in the same way, and that the repressive effects of service provision can be read as 'in the interests of capital'. I have questioned all these suppositions. In contrast, I have developed a distinction between universal and rationed services, and argued that, while universal services can be seen to promote ideas of citizenship rights, rationed services create dependency by their very structure, and have traditionally been used to squeeze out the poorest sections of the community and to privilege more 'respectable' working-class families.

I have traced the changes that have taken place in service provision: changes from predominantly universal to predominantly rationed services, changes in the organisation of service production through reorganisation and centralisation, and major changes in consumption patterns, reflecting the changes described in Chapter 5. I have suggested also that cuts in service provision, or a shift of the burden of services towards local taxation, exacerbate the effects of these changes; that different groups of the population now have very different perceptions of, and experiences of, service provision.

I have identified four interests based on differences in consumption and production location, traditions, expectations and political power. This is not to suggest that these categories represent coherent social or political groups with a self-consciousness of interests. They represent 'potential' groupings, and whether or not they congeal into political forces would depend on their ability to develop a sense of shared identity, common meanings and coherent traditions. However, evidence from my study shows that these sorts of divisions have been transformed into short-term conflicts, for instance over access to housing, or rate levels. In the light of these trends I perceive a growing dilemma for Labour in local government, and this is the subject of the concluding chapter.

NOTES AND REFERENCES

1. Bulpitt, J.G., 'Party Systems in Local Government' in *Political Studies*, 11 (1963), 11–35, 11.
2. Gyford, J., *Local Politics in Britain*, 9.
3. See, for example, Green, D.G., *Power and Party in an English City* (London, Allen and Unwin, 1981); Gyford; Hampton, W., *Democracy And Community*; Newton, K., *Second City Politics*; Dearlove, J., *The Politics of Policy in Local Government: The Making and Maintenance of Public Policy in the Royal Borough of Kensington and Chelsea*.
4. Jessup, F.W., *Problems of Local Government in England and Wales* (Cambridge, Cambridge University Press, 1949), 193.
5. See, for example, Robson, W.A., *Local Government in Crisis*; Green, L.P., *Provincial Metropolis* (London, Allen and Unwin, 1959); Jackson, R.M., *The Machinery of Local Government* (london, Macmillan, 1965); Jones, A., *Local Governors at Work* (London, Conservative Political Centre, 1968).
6. For a review of this debate see Rhodes, R.A.W., *Control and Power in Central–Local Relations*; and '"Power Dependence" Theories of Central–Local Government Relations: A Critical Assessment' in M. Goldsmith (ed.), *New Research in Central–Local Relations*; Cawson, A., *Corporatism and Welfare: Social Policy and State Intervention in Britain*, 88–9.
7. See Griffith, J.A.G., *Central Departments and Local Authorities*; Boaden, N., *Urban Policy Making: Influences on County Boroughs in England and Wales* (Cambridge, Cambridge University Press, 1971), 15; Sharpe, L.J., and Newton, K., *Does Politics Matter*, 38, 135–170.
8. The effects of these new controls, see Boddy, M., 'Financial Control and the Politics of Central–Local Government Relations in the 1980s' paper presented to the Urban Change And Conflict Conference, Clacton, January 1983; Jones, J., Stewart, J., and Travers, T., *Rate Control: The Threat to Local Government* (London, Local Government Chronicle, 1983); Midwinter, A., *The Politics of Local Spending*; Gyford, S., and James, M., *National Parties and Local Politics*, ch. 9.
9. Cohen, G.A., *Karl Marx's Theory of History: A Defence* (Oxford, Clarenden Press, 1984), 238.
10. Cawson, op. cit., 90.
11. Cockburn, C., *The Local State*, 47, 51.
12. Dearlove, T., *The Reorganisation of British Local Government: Old Orthodoxies and a Political Perspective*, 217.

13. Duncan, S., and Goodwin, M., 'The Local State and Restructuring Social Relations – Theory and Practice', *Urban and Regional Studies Working Paper* (Sussex 1980).
14. Cawson, A., and Saunders, P., 'Corporatism, Competitive Politics and Class Struggle' paper prepared for BSA/PSA Conference on Capital Ideology and Politics, Sheffield (January 1981); Jessop, B., *The Capitalist State*, (Oxford, Martin Robertson, 1982).
15. Cawson, A., *Corporatism and Welfare*, 44, 90–104.
16. Dunleavy, P., 'The Limits to Local Government' in M. Boddy and C. Fudge (eds.), *Local Socialism* (London, Macmillan, 1984), 49–81, 79.
17. Offe has made a similar point. See 'Some Contradictions of the Modern Welfare State' in *Critical Social Policy*, vol. 2 (Autumn 1982), 7–16.
18. Jackman, R.J., and Sellars, M., 'Local Expenditure and Local Discretion' in *CES Review* (May 1978), 63–73, 20.
19. Sharpe and Newton, op. cit. 10.
20. Kirk, G., *Urban Planning in a Capitalist Society* (London, Croom Helm, 1980), 181.
21. Davies, J.G., *The Evangelistic Bureaucrat*.
22. Bailey, R., *The Squatters* (Harmondsworth, Penguin 1973), 7–20.
23. See, for example, Dennis, N., *Public Participation and Planning Blight* (London, Faber and Faber, 1972); Gladstone, F., *The Politics of Planning* (London, Maurice Temple, 1976).
24. Pahl, R.E., Whose City? and other Essays on Sociology and Planning (London, Longman, 1970), 215–18.
25. See, Pahl, R., 'Managers, Technical Experts and the State' in M. Harloe (ed.), *Captive Cities* (London, J. Wiley and Sons, 1977), 49–61, 57.
26. Kirk, op. cit., 182.
27. See Harloe, M. (ed.), *New Perspectives in Urban Change and Conflict*, 4; Castells, M., *The Urban Question* (London, Edward Arnold, 1977); O'Connor, J., *The Fiscal Crisis of the State* (New York, St Martin's Press, 1973).
28. Op. cit., 7.
29. Pemberton, A., 'Marxism and Social Policy: A Critique of the "Contradictions of Welfare"'. *Journal of Social Policy* vol. 12. (July 1983) 289–308, 298.
30. Ibid., 300.
31. Offe, K., 'Crisis of Crisis Management: Elements of a Political Crisis Theory' *International Journal of Politics* vol. 6. 930 (1976), 29–67.
32. Habermas, J., *Legitimation Crisis* (London, Heinemann, 1976), 50–52, 68–75, 93.
33. Gortz, A., *A Strategy for Labour: A Radical Proposal*. (Boston, Beacon Press, 1967), 97.
34. Gough, I. *The Political Economy of the Welfare State* (London, Macmillan 1981), 12.
35. Cockburn, op. cit., 58–62.
36. See Donzelot, J., *The Policing of Families; Welfare versus the State*

(London, Hutchinson, 1979); Barrett, M., and McIntosh, M., *The Anti-Social Family* (London, Verso, 1982), 95–105.

37. Bennington, J., *Local Government becomes Big Business* (London, CDP Information and Intelligence Unit, 1976), 17.

38. See O'Connor, op. cit.; Cawson and Saunders, op. cit.; Dunleavy, P., 'Socialised Consumption and Economic Development', draft paper to Anglo-Danish Seminar on Local State Research, University of Copenhagen 1983.

39. Lojkine, J., 'Contribution to a Marxist Theory of Capitalist Urbanisation' in C.G. Pickvance (ed.), *Urban Sociology* (London, Tavistock, 1976), 119–47; Pickvance, C.G., 'Historical Materialist Approaches in Urban Sociology' in C.G. Pickvance (ed.), *Urban Sociology*, 1–33.

40. Dunleavy, P., 'The Limits to Local Government' in M. Boddy and C. Fudge (eds.), *Local Socialism*, 49–52, 61.

41. Le Grand, J., *The Strategy of Equality* (London, Allen and Unwin, 1982), 46.

42. See Damer, S., 'A Note on Housing Allocation' in M. Edwards, F. Gray, S. Merrett and J. Swan (eds.), *Housing and Class in Britain* (London, Political Economy of Housing Workshop, 1976), 72–4; Gray, F., 'Consumption in Council House Management' in S. Merrett (ed.), *State Housing in Britain*, 196–232, 207–225; see also Means, R., *Social Work and the Undeserving Poor* (Birmingham, CURS, 1977).

43. Harloe, M., 'The Recommodification of Housing' in M. Harloe and E. Lebas (eds.), *City, Class, Capital*, 17–51, 40–1.

44. See Goss, S., 'Womens' Initiatives in Local Government' in Boddy and Fudge (eds.), *Local Socialism*, 109–33.

45. Dearlove, *The Reorganisation of British Local Government*, 245.

46. Dunleavy, 'The Limits to Local Government', 79.

47. Councils of the metropolitan boroughs of Bermondsey, Southwark and Camberwell, accounts estimates March 1938 for the year ending 31 March 1939.

48. Councils of the metropolitan boroughs of Bermondsey, Southwark and Camberwell, accounts estimates March 1951 for the year ending 31 March 1952.

49. London Borough of Southwark, Annual Report and Accounts 1980–1.

50. Dunleavy, P., 'The Urban Basis of Political Alignment: Social Class, Domestic Property Ownership and State Intervention in Consumption Processes', *British Journal of Political Science*, vol. 9 (1979), 409–43; Saunders, 'Rethinking Local Politics' in Boddy and Fudge (eds.), *Local Socialism* 22–49, 41–2.

51. Hobsbawm, E., *Industry and Empire* (Harmondsworth, Penguin, 1969), 281.

52. Hobsbawm, E., *The Forward March of Labour Halted* (London, Verso, 1981), 7.

53. Goldthorpe, J.H., Lockwood, D., Bechhofer, F., and Platt, J., *The Affluent Worker: Industrial Attitudes and Behavior* (Cambridge,

Cambridge University Press, 1968); *The Affluent Worker: Political Attitudes and Behavior* (Cambridge, Cambridge University Press, 1968); *The Affluent Worker in the Class Structure* (Cambridge, Cambridge University Press, 1969).

54. Dunleavy, P., *Socialised Consumption and Economic Development*, 25.

55. Lowe, S., *Urban Social Movements: The City after Castells* (London, Macmillan, 1986), 71.

56. Gray, 'Consumption in Council House Management', 201.

57. Forest, R., 'Residualisation and Council Housing: Aspects of the Changing Social Relations of Housing Tenure', *Journal of Social Policy* vol. 12.4, 453–68, 462; see also Murie, A., 'Council House Sales mean Poor Law Housing', *Roof*, vol. 2.2 (1977), 46–9, 48.

58. Boddy, 'Financial Control and the Politics of Central–Local Government Relations' 24; Jones, Stewart and Travers, *Rate Control: The Threat to Local Government*; Schott, K., *The Economic and Political Determinants of Aggregate Local Authority Expenditure and Revenues 1948–1980*, paper presented to Socialist Economic Review Conference, London 1982; Midwinter, *The Politics of Local Spending*; Gyford, and James, *National Parties and Local Politics*.

59. Dunleavy, 'The Urban Basis of Political Alignment'.

60. Harris, R., and Seldon, A., *Over-Ruled on Welfare: The Increasing Desire for Choice in Education and Medicine and its Frustration by 'Representative' Government* (London, IEA, 1979), 203.

61. See Bosanquet, N., 'Social Policy and the Welfare State' in R. Jowell and C. Avery (eds.), *British Social Attitudes 1984: Social and County Planning Research* Farnborough, Gower, 1984) 75–97, 84; see also MORI, *Breadline Greenwich,* research conducted for Greenwich Council (London, MORI, 1983).

62. Hall, S., 'The Culture Gap' in *Marxism Today*, vol. 28.1 (January 1984), 18–24, 19.

63. Mishra, R., *The Welfare State in Crisis*, 25.

64. Taylor-Gooby, P., 'The New Right and Social Policy' in *Critical Social Policy*, vol. 1.1 (Summer 1981), 18–31, 26.

65. Bosanquet, 'Social Policy and the Welfare State', 76.

66. Judge, K., Smith, J., and Taylor-Gooby, P., 'Public Opinion and the Privatisation of Welfare: Some Theoretical Implications' in *Journal of Social Policy*, vol. 12.4 (1983), 469–90, 475.

67. Boddy, 'Financial Control and the Politics of Central–Local Government Relations', 24.

68. Dunleavy, *The Urban Basis of Political Alignment*.

69. Williams, R., 'Problems of the Coming Period' *New Left Review*, 140 (May 1983), 7–19, 16.

Eight

Conclusion

WITH only a few exceptions, the study of Labour in local government is a comparatively recent phenomenon. New research has been stimulated by the recent controversies over initiatives by Left Labour councils, and over struggles between Labour councils and the Conservative government. In this study, I have looked at Labour in local government in Southwark over a sixty-year period. In a sense, then, this has been an exercise in clearing the ground, in examining the explanatory power of different approaches and theories. It seemed to me that before we could fruitfully analyse the political problems that now face Labour, particularly in local government, it was important to examine carefully the pressures and changes that condition present developments.

Much of the study of local government, and of the debate surrounding the recent struggles between central and local government, has been ahistorical, and has been weak because of that. I have therefore looked backwards in time, in order to examine, not only changes in local government and in the local Labour Party, but in the social and economic context within which those changes took place. I have argued that without an understanding of the socio-economic trends which shape a local area, we cannot analyse the formation or fracturing of political interests and political support.

A careful examination of Southwark has shown that what has often been treated as a static formation – an inner-city working class community with a solid Labour base, where Labour has controlled the authority for fifty years – has in fact been the site of parallel processes of transformation. These have involved a build-up of collapse in the local economy, in the local political culture, in the establishment of Labour as the expression of that culture, and in the consensus surrounding Labour's policies in local government.

Secondly, I have stressed the interrelation of interest formation, interest representation and local government. I have argued that the formation of interests and the determination of policy outcomes do not take place in separate boxes from which the effects of political cultures, consciousness, allegiances, traditions, organisations, parties and demands are excluded.

Thirdly, I have argued that political conflicts in a particular conjuncture are the result not only of discontinuities, but also of continuities from the past. The processes at work are not simply those of fragmentation but involve a complex process of layering in which new structures and practices are built on the old, and neither replace, nor entirely dissolve the explanatory power of what went before. Therefore, I have not merely examined a process of change, I have also indicated the underlying continuities, and it is this combination which creates conditions for emerging conflicts.

Finally, I have argued a need for more local studies. Studies of the Labour Party, and of local government which have only examined the national dimension have missed a rich seam of evidence which casts doubts on some theories and adds depth to others. The evolution of Labour at a local level has been a very different process from that suggested by simply studying the national party. And local government practices and policies differ too widely to be understood by an examination of changing local government legislation. There is a need for other local studies over time with which to compare my findings about Southwark.

It will be useful to summarise these findings, before going on to consider their implications for any wider analysis of the problems facing the Labour Party, and of the issues concerning local government. Here, therefore, I want to relate the evidence from Part 1 of the book to the theoretical analysis in Part 2, and to stress the interdependence of the three areas of study set out in the introduction: social and economic changes affecting the local community; the evolution of the local Labour Party; changes in local government.

1. Social and Economic Change in the Local Community

In Part 1 I examined the significance of economic, and resulting social, changes in the area. Southwark in 1919 was a poor, industrial area; it still is, but this surface continuity hides the extent to which the community has changed. I have shown the emergence in the years until the 1950s of a local political culture, structured through the institutions and practices of working people, with an emphasis on the trades unions and Labour movement. This culture was based on powerful ideas of class solidarity, 'looking after one's own', and hostility to outsiders. The

1950s represented the zenith of this self-confident community. In Chapters 2, 3 and 4, I traced the collapse of the local economy. This led to changes, a reduction in the proportion of manual workers, an increase in the proportion of white-collar and professional workers, and increasing proportions of black people, elderly people, the unemployed and single parents. In Chapter 4, I pointed to the effects of these changes in the fracturing of the local political culture, and traced the emergence of political conflicts within the local population.

In Chapter 5 I explored this process of build up and fragmentation with regard to the formation of political interests and the development of class and other social cleavages. In the early years, working-classness could be seen to describe not only the economic location of the majority of local people, but also a self-conscious identity constructed through local political practices and institutions. Class was constructed as a dominant point of identity, but it was constructed *through* other divisions.

Thus the local self-awareness of working-classness was constructed through male traditions which excluded women's experience. In addition, white self-definitions excluded blacks. It was consistent within the language of class for sections of working people to be excluded from the self-defined working class. I have stressed the importance of economic restructuring, but the effects of this on the formation of political interests are far from simple. Social changes have broken open a previously closed community; those groups excluded from the previously dominant political culture have grown, and the presence of young professionals has added a new dimension. However, the process of fragmentation must be seen as incomplete since old assumptions and traditions survive long after the economic and social conditions in which they were created. New structures and cultural practices are superimposed on the old. While the old traditions of class-belonging are no longer capable of constructing social cohesion, they are able to act as points of division. This is especially so in Southwark, where the population is now evenly divided between a traditional manual-working class, and the rest.

An explanation of the trends I have identified depended on an analysis of class cleavages and interests. But in exploring this, I found that much of the existing literature was inadequate. In particular, while recognising the importance of class within the organisation of interests, I have rejected the work of those who attribute pre-existing political interests to Marxist class categories, and assume, a priori, that class is the primary determinant of interests. I have drawn attention to a more recent literature on social cleavages such as consumption groups and tenure, which raises important questions, but which is problematic for three reasons. Firstly, this literature also tends to assume that social and economic locations carry pre-existing political interests. Secondly, studies within a Weberian context create a multiplicity of parallel but isolated categories. It is therefore impossible to examine overlaps between categories or to attribute priority. Thirdly, dual state formulations which attempt to overcome this problem do so by proposing a purely formal separation of interests into two spheres, and thus one which can not inform political practice.

In reality, while material interests must be a crucial starting point for any examination of social change, they do not determine the political process, and they may conflict within social groups, or even within individuals. The points of intersection of social and economic locations generate contradictory social and ideological effects. I have therefore found that the most useful work has identified interests as being constructed at points of intersection between social locations. Work on race and gender which has explored the intersection between these points of division and class has been particularly useful. The construction of political interests and allegiances must be seen as an open and dynamic process, taking place in the context of existing traditions and assumptions as well as changing realities, and through cultural, ideological and political practices.

2. Labour

The second and perhaps most central theme of this book, has been the development of the Labour Party at local level. The social and economic changes and continuities discussed above form an important context for any analysis of the local Labour Party, since they structured both the political practices of local Labour and the ideas for which they sought support. At the same time, the emerging Labour Party helped to structure the political culture in its formative years.

In Part 1, I traced the changes in Labour's fortunes locally. I pointed out that Labour could not claim an automatic local working-class base. Support was won slowly, based on trades-union connections, social links with the community, and effective communication networks within a fairly closed society. Most crucially, however, it depended upon Labour's ability to reflect local concerns and the traditions and assumptions which made up the dominant political culture. Nevertheless, Labour did not merely reflect these ideas, it also built support around a project that interpreted the experience of local people, offering the practical alternative of social provision for social need. Support for this project peaked in the 1950s, and since then a slow decline of membership, party activity and electoral support has occurred. I have drawn attention to an influx of new members in the 1970s, and to a regeneration of political campaigning. But this did little to repair the fraying links between Labour and the fragmented local community, since conflicts which had affected the local community now began to emerge within the Labour Party. A great deal of the new energy was consumed in a series of struggles within the Labour Party, and between the party and the Labour council. Most important of all, this revival of activity failed to stem a draining of political support from Labour.

In Chapter 6, I interpreted these changes through an inter-relation of factors. A crucial starting point must be the economic and social changes outlined above, since changing occupation and consumption patterns have weakened Labour's ability to construct a common sense that interprets increasingly disparate experiences. Changing lifestyles and the experience of public-service consumption have weakened the persuasiveness of Labour's project, and in particular of the elision of social provision and socialism. I have described attempts to redraw the lines of Labour's appeal, but argued that these failed to sustain any lasting allegiance. Labour's project has failed to adapt to changed realities or to provide a new 'ideological glue'. This has been compounded by a shift away from local concerns, towards more centralist strategies and by organisational changes in the Labour Party, which weakened links between it and the local community. I have identified a downward spiral, since, as membership shrinks, and links are severed, Labour is increasingly less able to intervene in the structuring of political ideas and practices within the community. This combination of factors has not led to local electoral defeat, but instead to electoral volatility, even in – perhaps especially in – an inner-London area such as Southwark. While the divisions within the local party are usually simplified, as splits between 'Left' and 'Right', they are more usefully analysed as in Chapter 6, in relation to a discourse about who Labour represents and how it can be seen to do so. In part these disputes can be seen as the result of superimposing the new on the old. Those ideas which structure the experience of local Labour parties and local communities change slowly, and they carry with them a weight of social traditions and loyalties. There is a time-lag between changing economic and social structures and changing ideas.

An explanation of the rise and fall of Labour's local support involved an examination of the existing literature on the Labour

Party, and this material is dominated by two traditions, each with its own explanation for decline. I have rejected the literature which presents 'Labourism' as a problem, since it gives an over-simplified interpretation of the nature of Labour's politics, and neglects the Labour party at a local level. While I have less argument with some of the observations of the second tradition – that of 'dealignment' – I take issue with the crude underlying assumption that interests are formed outside the political process. Discussions about Labour's decline are inseparable from those about the nature and formation of interests discussed above. Both these traditions assume that political allegiance is derived from interests which are attached to particular social locations, or to economic class, in ways which I have argued are inadequate. Of more use, I have suggested are the more recent voting studies which examine political allegiance in relation to the effects of cross-cutting social locations and to the importance of ideas and party performance. While political parties can be seen to influence the context within which allegiances are developed by changing the values people hold, or the perceptions they have of the realities around them, they cannot do so simply 'as they please' without any analysis of the realities of people's changing life experiences.

3. Council

The third area covered by my study is local government. An examination of the politics of the Labour Party in Southwark is inevitably bound up with a study of local government. Labour controlled local government in Bermondsey for sixty out of the sixty-three years covered by my study, and in Southwark and Camberwell for fifty-one. I have stressed the extent to which the political practices and ideas of Labour have affected the policies and priorities of local councils and the nature of service provision. At the same time, issues of service provision are central to Labour's project, and the experience of and demand for that provision has affected the context of Labour's political allegiance.

In Part 1, I traced the changing nature of local government. In the early years, local authorities received less subsidy and possessed less power, but that created scope for a more overt political direction of policy, despite conflicts with national government. Within powerful constraints, local authorities were able to provide badly needed services for their communities, and did so within a strong local consensus over priorities.

Nevertheless, certain groups were excluded from provision. I have described a shift towards control from the centre after the war, and a changed consensus as to the role of local government. Reorganisation (triggered by Conservative attempts to shift power and an academic consensus about dismantling parochial communities), strengthened these trends. The creation of new impersonal departments and the effects of wholesale redevelopment in the area severed the remaining links between the local community and the council. By the 1970s, local-community campaigns developed, and I have traced a series of clashes between these campaigns and an inflexible council.

In Chapter 7, I set out a framework for analysing these events. Changes in local-government service provision can be seen as dominated by economic transformation, but as mediated by political intervention at local and national level. It is therefore important to recognise changes in consumption patterns and changes in the production of services, through centralisation and the shift to large scale, professional departments. In addition, I have identified a shift from a time when services were predominantly provided universally, to one in which the majority of them were allocated bureaucratically, or rationed. This, I have suggested, widens the gap between different experiences of local, service provision. The effect of any cut in services is therefore to intensify divisions and amplify ambivalence, rather than to create a unified response. These differences in experience do not simply occur between public and private consumption, but, importantly, also occur within the public sector. Consumption experiences differ between those able to buy private goods and services, and those who remain dependent on the public sector; but also between those accustomed to relative privilege within the public sector and those previously excluded; and between both of these groups and young 'middle-class' arrivals, temporarily dependent on the public sector. These divisions do not necessarily create conscious interests or cohesive points of identity; they are open rather than closed, and they interpenetrate other cleavages such as class, race, gender and sexuality. But some recent conflicts have reflected these divisions.

Responses to change are also structured by continuities from the past, since these divisions are based not only on social location, but on the accretion of past practices and assumptions. Assumptions about need, categories of deserving and undeserving, and exclusion and privilege, structure responses to even minimal redistribution of service provision. Political perceptions of public-service provision and its importance are often judged through assumptions built in the past.

These changes cannot be understood within analyses of local

government which deny any scope for political intervention at local level, or which argue that all public provision in reality serves the needs of bureaucrats or of capital. The first part of Chapter 7 was in part a critique of these approaches. I stressed the importance not only of economic and central controls on local government, but also of constraints established by political practices and the development of social consensus about levels of service provision. I drew attention to the fact that constraints were not fixed – they changed (and could be changed by political intervention) over time. •I then examined more thoroughly the argument that service provision had the effect of regulating the lives of consumers. While this raises interesting questions, I argued that it is important to distinguish more carefully between different sorts of services and different sorts of consumers. While recent work has started to do this, I have taken it further by distinguishing between universal services and rationed services. It is rationed services that give the most scope for political priorities to develop, and these priorities derive from lines of identity and division within the community, and are open to political and ideological contestation: Social fragmentation can undermine a political consensus about 'who should get what' and create the possibility of emerging divisions between different sections of the community based on access to or dependence on service provision.

There are two reasons why an analysis of the present problems facing Labour and Labour in local government requires a keen sense of the past. In the first place, an analysis of changes over time provides a necessary antidote to general models or explanatory theories drawn from studies of a single frozen point in time. In the second place, it stops us from assuming that events taking place now are inevitably permanent and irreversible. It helps us to treat with caution predictions that a loss of electoral support now means that the Labour party is a spent force, or that a struggle between central and local government being carried out now will inevitably end in the destruction of local democracy.

This study has looked at a small area in south-east London, but it has not been entirely local in its implications or conclusions. While I am conscious of the special circumstances in Southwark, the evidence would suggest similar trends and developments in areas with similar histories. And an examination of an area which has been one of Labour's heartlands, makes it possible to point to problems and possibilities for the Labour Party, and the Labour Party in local government elsewhere. Unless it can solve the problems it faces in Southwark it is unlikely to solve the problems elsewhere. I want now, therefore, to turn to some of the implications of my study for an understanding of the political dilemmas that face Labour, particularly Labour in local government.

4. Problems and Possibilities for Labour

Labour's third election defeat in 1987 confirms much of the analysis of the last two. The slight recovery since the disaster of 1983 did not alter the fact that this was the second worst result since 1918. Labour made gains in the north, strikingly so in Scotland, but hardly dented the south, and the Midlands. In London, the picture that begins to emerge is one of increasing electoral volatility, which simply cannot be measured by class composition or tenure or any of the other indicators that have been created. Results varied widely, including the loss of traditionally safe Labour seats such as Battersea. Evidence from Southwark and other traditionally Labour areas indicate that Labour's core support is melting – and while seats can be won, this is no longer certain.

The scale of Labour's disappointment has prompted a major rethink among politicians and academics. But this debate has not addressed the need, identified by a study of the political changes in Southwark, to win back support in Labour's old heartlands.

Sections of both the Left and the Right have called for a return to class politics; and for Labour to identify itself more clearly with the needs and concerns of 'working-class' people. The militant Left maintain that a return to a full-blooded socialist programme, involving, for example major nationalisation, and the defence of trades-union struggles, would increase Labour's support among working-class people. As the voting studies we have examined show, there is no evidence to support this. Indeed, I have attempted to explore the altogether more complex roots of Labour's support within a 'working-class' community.

From the Right, many traditional trades-unionists, and older members of the party who remember the years of power in the 1960s and 1970s with nostalgia, have argued that elections are being lost because local Labour parties have strayed away from traditional working-class concerns, such as health, housing and employment, into the lunatic fringe issues of lesbian and gay rights, women's committees and anti-racism. As Joe Haines put it 'we are losing touch with the people whose cause we were born to represent.'[1] The problem, as has been demonstrated by an examination of Southwark, is that the shrinking, male, manual-working class to which many traditional Labour activists and trades-unionists address themselves is no longer strong enough to drive through social transformation. In a poor inner-city area like

Southwark, which had, in 1981, the highest number of unskilled manual workers in all of the London boroughs, manual workers still only made up 31 per cent of the total population. The rest were white-collar workers, professionals, unemployed, economically inactive or pensioners. Even the remaining manual-working inhabitants no longer form such a coherent social or political community, and are themselves fragmented, holding a range of different and often conflicting beliefs and values.

Secondly, there has been a view from sections of the 'soft' Left, as well as from many of those, across the spectrum of the Left, involved in the 'municipal socialism' experiments of the 1980s that for Labour to win back support it has to address a rainbow coalition of interests. The argument goes that while the traditional working class is no longer a force for change, Labour can construct a majority by combining a number of oppressed groups – tradesunionists, the homeless, gypsies, the black community, the disabled, women, and lesbians and gay men. This approach recognises the limits of a purely class-based approach to social change, and to social experience, but most of the formulations are as reductionist and as keen to allocate people into categories with interests already attached, as the first group. As several writers have pointed out, the very structure of the Labour Party itself has been inhospitable to these groups – and often they are 'represented' through the self-importance of a tiny group of white, affluent activists. At the other extreme, many of those calling for Labour seriously to represent the women, the black community, lesbians and gay men, simply do not engage with the often powerful antagonisms of sections of the traditional manual-working-class community. Nor do they take account of the often clear political divisions between many of the minority groups they are attempting to unite, and the broad gaps between their experiences. The looseness of the language of class and of 'our people' and the assumption of common objective interests obscures these divisions.

Thirdly, there are a number of politicians and academics who are attempting to understand the realities from which 'Thatcherism' has gained its strength, and believe that Labour can win back support by adapting its policies to take account of the popularity of council-house sales, wider share-ownership and a wider role for the market. They have tended, however, to concentrate on the need to build support among the affluent suburbs and villages of the south; and have not yet come to terms with the diversity of experiences, needs and attitudes in the inner cities.

If it is to succeed in rebuilding political support, Labour has to face up to the problem of social fragmentation. Political unity involves more than a conceptual process of sticking together widely disparate groups with a glue called 'working-class interests'. At the same time, it will not be sufficient to canvass the opinions of a huge number of 'target voter-groups' and concoct a lucky dip of policies and ideas in which there is something for everyone.

Political interests are created at the level of conscious political practices and not through the attribution of social agents to conceptual categories. The divisions I have identified cannot be seen as either fixed or closed, they are inevitably partial and discursive in character. The fragmentation of community does not inevitably involve the fragmentation of political allegiance. Political interests can be constructed, in part through the activities of political parties. But if Labour is to reconstruct a mass base of support, rather than a short-lived electoral victory, it will have to develop a new political project, one which reorganises the political meanings of disparate experiences, demonstrates new connections, redraws lines of identity, and creates what Laclau and Mouffe refer to as a 'logic of equivalence' – a sense, across a majority of the population, of having equivalent but different interests in a transformative strategy.

It was that process which Labour underwent to establish the consensus of the post-war years. It is a similar process that the Thatcher government has conducted to reorder a sense of what is possible and desirable, and to win support among those for whom it is difficult to see a Conservative victory as representing material benefits – the unemployed, the young homeless and the old. Such a process has not, of course, been conducted purely at the level of formal politics. Through a network of self-reinforcing messages, policies have been redefined, and values reinterpreted. Choice has been redefined as choice based on ability to pay; vulnerability has been reinterpreted as independence; ruthlessness has been called strength. The Right has been seen as successful on law and order, while crime rates soar; on housing, while presiding over the biggest ever net shortage of homes since the First World War. A number of very powerful messages of race hatred, intolerance towards lesbians and gay men, and a willingness to crush civil liberties can now be given openly, when once they would have offended public decency.

These changes in the terrain of debate are, however, only partial. They overlay, and are constantly interrupted by conflicting interpretations. Ideas built up in the past retain a powerful hold, and are also continually reinforced. In some places traditions of solidarity, mutuality, 'looking after one's own' remain strong –

although I have pointed to the exclusiveness of such traditions. Elsewhere, values of equality, mutual support, social responsibility, the common sense of needing to build education and training, to care collectively for the old, the sick, the very young – cultural assumptions about democracy, fairness and a suspicion of profiteering and faceless bureaucrats emerge, for example, in a popular unease about the health service. And perhaps we can also point to unsatisfied aspirations for greater self-determination, greater control over opportunities and choices, greater sense of individuality in terms of work, consumption, leisure – which has been fanned but not satisfied by the Thatcher years.

These ideas do not stand in opposition to material interests. But they *organise* material interests, they make sense of them, fuse them into packages – projects – that function at the political level. And as perceptions of interests such as availability of child-care or housing, are not necessarily aligned with perceptions of interests in wage rates or dividends, the construction of such a project is a precondition for social transformation.

One thing is quite clear, the old project, bound up with a 'particular concept of socialism through state management'[2] has run aground on the experience of ordinary people. It would be political suicide to interpret Labour's successful project in 1945 as justifying the representation of it to the British people in the 1990s. The price of popular support is not a set of popular and harmless policies, nor an uneasy compromise between old-fashioned socialism and electoral realities; but a new project for social transformation which can make sense to, and link the experiences of, a majority of the population; and which is grounded in the social and economic realities of the 1990s.

Any such project will have to confront the stark changes that have taken place, even in an inner-city area like Southwark – changes of both experience and of perception. Central, must be re-examination of collective provision, recognising the failures of the past. Several Left theorists and practitioners are beginning to argue that State ownership and State provision are not necessarily appropriate to the modern age; and are turning to the market as an alternative. Others have argued that collective provision was introduced precisely because of the failures and shortcomings of the market. They have argued that ideas of socialist transformation have been bound up with and depend on, a central concept of society as based on collectives and not on individuals, and on collective rather than private provision of at least some key goods and services. It will be important for socialists to determine how far this is true, and whether there is another possible route to social change which does not involve State services of the sort that we have been used to. One thing is clear, if collective provision is to form an important part of any transformative project, then it must be changed and adapted to meet new aspirations. It will be important to challenge the paternalistic assumptions, bureaucratic procedures and the political privileging of some consumers over others that have all formed part of assessments 'based on need'. More seriously, the changing consumption patterns between public and private provision demand a radical response. If collective provision is to be limited only to the very poor, it will fail to build mass support, or to operate as a model for alternative forms of production and consumption.

There may be ways of exploring consumer-based and choice-based public services – which are not distributed according to ability to pay, but which nevertheless give consumers the ability to choose from a range of services those which best suit their needs and lifestyle. There are now areas of provision, such as child-care, training, leisure – where the private sector has failed to respond to demand, and where collective provision may well be more successful. And it may be possible for public provision to compete successfully in areas where the private sector has previously dominated, or to meet new and previously unvoiced demands. But it will require a change to consumer, rather than producer-based power; and a recognition of the diversity of different demands. The Labour Party has made tentative moves in this direction; campaigning around the idea of the 'enabling state', where collective provision is seen as liberating individuals, and extending opportunities that are not available in the private sector. But it needs to be more than a slogan. The whole structure of state provision needs to be re-examined. We need to look both at how services are provided and at 'who gets what' – at the authoritarian assumptions built into the policing of 'need' in relation to rationed services, and at the ideas which structure the provision of universal services.

The second set of issues to which such a project must respond relate to democracy, and, in particular, to local democracy. I have shown that local councils have been able, at certain times, to translate the ideas of a local community into action; and to make significant interventions into local lives. Over the next few years, Labour authorities will face two different sorts of attack. One will be an attempt to return local authorities to a purely minimal, administrative role – an attack on local democracy itself. The second will be an attempt to dismantle public provision. It will be important to distinguish the two different terrains of political debate; since there has been a tendency to elide questions of local government which relate to 'government', political power, and local decision-making – with questions of collective provision. They should be distinguished in part because despite the ambivalence with which many people regard collective services, there is a deep seam of popular support for the ideas of local decision-making, and a commitment to the role of local communities in determining local priorities – one that has been strengthened by the traditions of community politics, participation in planning, voluntary organisations and pressure groups that grew up in the 1970s. There is a commonsense distrust of centralising governments, and the transfer of power to Whitehall bureaucrats, or to the hidden mechanisms of profit, supply and demand. But to harness this, Labour would have to commit itself to a stronger and more radical concept of local democracy than it has been willing to do hitherto. A radical commitment to devolving local power would involve the abandonment of the tradition of 'representation' embodied in the paternalism of the old Right – in which councillors and MPs assumed that since they came from a community they could speak on its behalf and had no need of formal consultation. But it would also involve challenging a view of representative democracy put forward by the 'new Left' – which while it has involved some local people directly in decision making, still relies on a structure of mandates and lines of accountability which substitute the local party for the local people. Any transformative strategy requires a more participatory democracy than that; empowering people not only to take control of the services they consume, but to play a part in decision making across the spectrum of government and local-government policies.

Local government remains important for Labour, despite the difficulties it will face, since it remains an alternative site of power. Although local government can accentuate existing political divisions, it has the potential to be a direct channel of communication of alternative political values to those of Thatcherism between Labour authorities and local people; and to provide models and examples of what Labour might achieve in power. That is why, in part, the attack on local government from the Thatcher government has been so heavy, and why it has been directed not only at spending overall, but has attempted to restrain the local exercise of political power, and has concentrated on a handful of high profile and energetic Labour authorities. The struggle between central and local government over the past five years echoes the earlier struggles in the period between 1919 and 1927. It is possible to point to a similar testing of strength, a constant changing of the ground, and a similar clash between opposing concepts of local government's role. The quiescence of the intervening fifty years is due to the powerful consensus about local government as a centre for service administration rather than as a site of political intervention. The last five years have seen a dissolution of that consensus, and an extraordinary outburst of political activity, and a rennaisance of innovation and energy in local government. Despite forty-six Acts of Parliament and twelve changes in local-government finance, central government has been struggling to regain control, and local authorities have been able to find creative ways round both financial constraints and legislative controls. The Conservative Government has been attempting to return local government to a purely administrative role; first by restricting spending, then by capping rates, then by controlling propaganda and publicity; and finally by attempting to dismantle the redistributive nature of local-government spending. The experiments in municipal socialism have been an attempt to assert the centrally political nature of local-government decision-making, and the possibility of alternative choices.

Conflict between Labour councils and the Conservative Government must be left to another book. But if we examine them in the light of the changes identified in this study, the experiments in municipal socialism have been both fascinating and tragic. Fascinating, because Labour councils in London and other inner cities have begun to address themselves to the issue of fragmentation, and to try and respond to the needs of previously excluded groups, such as women, lesbians and gays and the black community. The result has been the dramatic emergence of new tensions and conflicts. Perceived conflicts of interest have emerged between trades unionists and consumers, between different groups of consumers such as council tenants and squatters, between the black community and a traditional white community and between all those groups and lesbians and gay men. Labour councils and Labour groups have been caught between competing claims, and conflicts over those claims have been reflected back as rifts within Labour groups and Labour parties. Indeed it is precisely in those authorities most aware of the problems and most willing to take radical initiatives that these conflicts have been most apparent. It is important to understand the reasons for this, since the value of these new local-authority initiatives in the context of exploring alternative forms of service provision should not be discounted by their failure to achieve the tasks they set themselves. Within the context of limited resources and rationed services, any attempt to reorder priorities to meet the needs of previously excluded groups is seen as an attack on the relative privileges of the traditional consumers. At the same time the expectations of women, the black community and of young, single people have been awakened but not satisfied. Hence we can identify the dual process of back-lash, when the traditional manual-working community perceives that services are being redistributed, and 'frontlash' from previously excluded groups when redistribution turns out to be minimal.

The tragedy is that this period of energy and innovation should have been so limited by Labour's old project in its conception of local government's role, and so distracted by strategies of confrontation from the formulation of radical alternatives. Labour councils have defended 'jobs and services' without an analysis of what sorts of services could meet the needs of local people in the 1980s. They have failed to analyse the changing demographic and consumption patterns in their communities, or to recognise the changing perceptions of the relation of public and private provision. They have seemed to promise 'more of the same' in a world in which traditional State services are increasingly being treated as residual. There have been exciting exceptions – Labour authorities which have developed and won support for new policies of employment generation, training, decentralisation to neighbourhood offices, the transfer of decision making to tenants and consumers, greater democratic participation and practical policies to extend services to women and minority groups. It is these initiatives that must form the beginning of any radical new approach.

It is to these issues that the debate must now turn. It is with these questions that local Labour councillors and politicians will have to grapple if they are to win back popular support for socialist strategies in the 1990s. Future studies of Labour in local govern-ment, and future strategies considered by political practitioners, should perhaps see these recent initiatives not as the end-product of a process of re-examining local government, but as the tentative beginnings of a more far-reaching reassessment of public services and their role.

Perhaps most importantly, this book has been an attempt to encourage other social scientists and political practitioners to examine current dilemmas in the context of social, economic and political changes over time. An understanding not only of the interrelating processes of change, but also of the continuities from the past is the key to understanding the present.

NOTES AND REFERENCES

1. Haines, J., 'Our Votes in Their Pocket' *New Socialist* no. 6, July/August 1982, 40.
2. Hall, S., 'The State-Socialism's Old Caretaker' in *Marxism Today*, November 1984, vol. 28, no. 11, 24–31, 24.

Bibliography of Primary Sources

NOTE. The research reported in this book relied on a number of different primary sources. I carried out a series of interviews over a three-year period with councillors, local Labour-Party members and community activists. In addition I studied a wide range of local material, including local authority minutes and documents, local Labour party and Trades Council minutes, Annual Reports and journals, private collections of papers and press cuttings and an assortment of books and pamphlets. In some cases they were read selectively (e.g. minutes of council committees) in others, only minutes or documents from certain periods were obtainable. War damage, neglect and the passage of time had led to the loss of many valuable papers.

Statistical and factual background came from a selective reading of government and national Labour-party publications relating to the area. This consisted of a survey of the County of London Census Reports relating to the Metropolitan Boroughs of Southwark, Camberwell and Bermondsey, and later the census reports relating to the London Borough of Southwark. Secondly, a selective reading of parliamentary debates in which MPs from the local area made contributions, and an additional study of debates relating to the reorganisation. Thirdly, a survey of resolutions to Labour Party Annual Conference and of Conference Reports in which resolutions from the local Labour parties featured. Finally, a survey of CIPFA statistics relating to expenditure patterns in the relevant local authorities, and London County Council comparative statistics.

In addition, a comprehensive reading of the *South London Press* throughout the period 1919–1982 provided valuable background and chronological detail, as did a survey of Labour journals during this period.

MANUSCRIPT AND ARCHIVAL SOURCES

The Labour Party

Manifestos.
Resolutions to Annual Conference.
Reports of Annual Conference.

Local Labour Parties

Minutes of Bermondsey Labour Group 1956–1964.
Minutes of Bermondsey Labour Party 1970–1982.
Annual Reports of Bermondsey Labour Party.

Minutes of Dulwich Labour Party 1956–1982.
Annual Reports of Dulwich Labour Party.
Minutes of Peckham Labour Party 1966–1982.
Annual Reports of Peckham Labour Party.
Records of the Southwark South East Labour Party 1919–1958.

The London Labour Party
Minutes of the Executive Committee.
Annual Reports of the Executive Committee.
Minutes of the Greater London Co-ordinating Committee 1964 (in General Secretary's papers 1945–1964, Labour Party Archives).

Trades Councils
6 Years of Labour Rule 1922–1928 (London, Bermondsey Trades and Labour Council, 1928).
12 Years of Labour Rule 1922–1934: Labour's Magnificent Record (London, Bermondsey Trades and Labour Council, 1934).
Papers relating to the Southwark and Camberwell Trades Council 1904–1953 (Dave Russell Collection, Southwark Local Studies Library).
Records of the Southwark and Camberwell Trades Council 1953–1977 (private collection in the possession of Rod Robertson).

Papers in the private possession of Fred Francis.
Papers in the private possession of John O'Grady.
Papers in the private possession of Ron Bailey.
Wal Hannington Collection (Marx Memorial Library).

BOOKS AND DOCUMENTS ABOUT SOUTHWARK AND THE LOCAL AREA
Avery, M.D., 'Industry in South East London (Bermondsey and Southwark)' MA Thesis, 1963.
Davies, A., McIntosh, N., and Williams, J., *Final Report of Southwark Community Development Project – The Management of Deprivation* (London, Polytechnic of the South Bank, 1977).
Halford, W., and partners *City within a City: The Development of Hays Wharf* (London, Halford and Partners, 1971).
Hatch, S., Fox, E., and Legg, C., *Research and Reform: Southwark Community Development Project 1969–1972* (London, Hatch, Fox and Legg, 1977).
Joint Docklands Action Group, *The Engineering Industry in Docklands* (London, JDAG, April 1978).
MORI Research Study conducted for Southwark Council, *Public Opinion in Southwark: Views about the Council and its Activities* (London, MORI, 1980).
MORI Breadline Greenwich, research conducted for Greenwich Council (London, MORI, 1984).
North Southwark Community Development Group, *Public Participation in Planning in Southwark* (London, NSCDG, 1973).
North Southwark Community Development Group, *The Property Market and the Redevelopment of North Southwark* (London, NSCDG, 1973).

Offord, J.G. (ed.), *The Book of Walworth* (London, Browning Hall, 1925).

Prescott-Clark, P., and Hedges, B., *Living in Southwark* (London, Social and Community Planning Research, 1976).

Russell, D., *Southwark Trades Council 1903–1978: A Short History* (London, Southwark Trades Council, 1978).

Russell, D., *The General Strike in Southwark* (London, Union Place Resource Centre, May 1976).

Stewart, J., Bermondsey in War 1939–45 (unpublished).

Ungerson, C., *Moving Home: A Study of the Redevelopment Process in Two London Boroughs*, Occasional Papers in Social Administration no. 44 (London, Social Administration Research Trust, 1971).

OFFICIAL SOURCES: LOCAL AND CENTRAL GOVERNMENT

Parliamentary Debates (Hansard) Fifth Series, House of Commons and House of Lords Official Reports (London, HMSO).

Census of England and Wales 1921, County of London Report (London, HMSO, 1921).

Census of England and Wales 1931, County of London Report (London, HMSO, 1932).

Census of England and Wales County Report: London 1951 (London, HMSO, 1953).

Census of England and Wales 1951 Occupational Tables (London, HMSO, 1956).

Census of England and Wales County Report: London 1961 (London, HMSO, 1963).

Census of England and Wales 1961 Occupation, Industry, Socio-Economic Groups (London, HMSO, 1963).

Census of England and Wales 1971 County Report: Greater London (London, HMSO, 1973).

Census of England and Wales 1981 County Report: Greater London (London, HMSO, 1983).

Royal Commission on Local Government in Greater London 1957–1960 Cmnd. 1164 (London, HMSO, 1960).

Oral Evidence to the Royal Commission on Local Government in Greater London (London, HMSO, 1960).

Ministry of Housing and Local Government *Old Houses into New Homes*, Cmnd. 3602 (London, HMSO, 1968).

Chartered Institute of Public Finance and Accounting *Finance, General and Rating Statistics 1981/2* (London, CIPFA, May 1981).

Metropolitan Borough of Bermondsey

Annual Reports of the Medical Officer of Health
Minutes of the Proceedings of the Council
Minutes of the Finance Committee
Minutes of the Housing Committee

Metropolitan Borough of Camberwell

Annual Reports of the Medical Officer of Health
Minutes of the Proceedings of the Council

Abstract of Accounts
Minutes of the Housing Committee

Metropolitan Borough of Southwark

Annual Reports of the Medical Officer of Health
Minutes of the Proceedings of the Council
Minutes of the Finance Committee
Minutes of the Housing Committee

London Borough of Southwark

Minutes of the Council.
Minutes of the Finance Committee.
Department of Electoral Registration, Election Returns, 1964–82.
Draft Strategy Plan for the London Bridge Area and Thameside (LBS, April 1971).
A Strategy Plan for Southwark's Thameside (LBS , March 1973).
Industrial Survey 1977 (LBS, September 1977).
Office Employment Survey 1979 (LBS September, 1979).
Community Plan: Employment Topic Paper (LBS Development Department, 1980).
Annual Report and Accounts 1980–81.
Community Plan (LBS, 1982).
1981 Census: Reference Report 1983/4, Policy and Research Report (LBS Planning Division, April 1983).
Towards A New Area Perspective: Social Area Analyses of the 1981 Census, Policy and Research Report 1984/1 (LBS Planning Division, January 1984).
Making the Case for Southwark: Making the Case for Programme Area Status Under the Department of the Environment's Urban Programme 1985 (LBS, 1985).

London County Council

Statistical Abstract for London 1919–1929 (LCC, 1930), vol. 23.
Statistical Abstract for London 1922–1932 (LCC, 1930), vol. 25.
Statistical Abstract for London 1927–1937 (LCC, 1938), vol. 29.

NEWSPAPERS AND PERIODICALS

South London Press 1919–82.
Southwark and Bermondsey Record and South London Gazette 1919– .
Daily Herald (1919 only).
London Labour News 1924–42.
Central Southwark Citizen 1935–7.
Walworth Clarionette (1933 only).
Walworth News 1925–39.
Bermondsey Labour Magazine 1920–53.
Rotherhithe Labour Magazine 1934–40.
North Camberwell Citizen
Miscellaneous Labour periodicals 1911–77 deposited in Southwark Local Studies Library.

Select bibliography

CLASS AND COMMUNITY

Barret, M., *Women's Oppression Today: Problems in Marxist Feminist Analysis* (London, Verso, 1980).

Barrett, M. and McIntosh, M., *The Anti-Social Family* (London, Verso, 1982).

Brook, E., and Finn, D., 'Working Class Images of Society and Community Studies', CCCS (ed.), *On Ideology* (London, Hutchinson, 1978), 125–43.

Carchedi, G., *On the Economic Identification of Social Classes* (London, Routledge and Kegan Paul, 1977).

Cohen, P., 'Sub-Cultural Conflict and Working Class Community' *Working Papers in Cultural Studies* 2 (Spring 1972), 38.

Hall, S., Critchner, C., Jefferson, T., Clarke, C., and Roberts, B., *Policing the Crisis: Mugging, the State and Law and Order* (London, Macmillan, 1981).

Hall, S., 'The State – Socialism's Old Caretaker' *Marxism Today*, vol. 28.11 (November 1984), 24–31.

Hall, S., 'The Culture Gap', *Marxism Today*, vol. 28.1 (January 1984), 18–24.

Hobsbawm, E. (ed.), *The Forward March of Labour Halted* (London, Verso, 1981).

Jessop, B., *The Capitalist State* (Oxford, Martin Robertson, 1982).

Johnson, R., McLennan, G., Schwarz, B. and Sutton, D. (eds.), *Making Histories: Studies in History-Writing and Politics* (London, Hutchinson, 1982).

Joshi, S., and Carter, B., 'The Role of Labour in a Racist Britain', *Race and Class*, vol. 15 (Winter 1984), 53–71.

Laclau, E., and Mouffe, C., *Hegemony and Socialist Strategy* (London, Verso, 1985).

Lawrence, E., 'Just Plain Common Sense: The "Roots" of Racism', *The Empire Strikes Back: Race and Racism in '70s Britain*, CCCS (London, Hutchinson, 1982), 95–142.

Miles, R., and Phizacklea, A., *White Man's Country: Racism in British Politics* (London, Pluto, 1984).

Phizacklea, A., and Miles, R., *Labour and Racism* (London, Routledge and Kegan Paul, 1980).

Poulantzas, N., *State, Power, Socialism* (London, Verso, 1980).

Rex, J., and Moore, R., *Race, Community and Conflict: A Study of Sparkbrook* (London, Oxford University Press, 1967).

Sivanandan, A., 'From Resistance to Rebellion: Asian and Afro-Caribbean Struggles in Britain' in *Race and Class*, vol. 23 (Autumn 81/Winter 82), 111–53.

Solomos, J., Findlay, B., Jones, S., and Gilroy, P., 'The Organic Crisis of British Capitalism and Race: The Experience of the Seventies', *The Empire Strikes Back: Race and Racism in '70s Britain*, CCCS (London, Hutchinson, 1982), 9–46.

Stedman Jones, G., 'Working Class Culture and Working Class Politics: Notes on the Remaking of a Working Class', *Languages of Class – Studies in English Working Class History 1832–1982* (Cambridge, Cambridge University Press, 1983).

Wright, E.O., *Class, Crisis and the State* (London, New Left Books, 1978).

Wright, E.O., *Class Structure and Income Determination* (New York, Academic Press, 1979).

Wright, E.O., 'Class Boundaries in Advanced Capitalist Societies', *New Left Review*, 98 (July/August 1976), 3–43.

Wright, E.O., 'Giddens' Critique of Marxism', *New Left Review*, 138 (March/April 1983), 11–37.

THE LABOUR PARTY

Abrams, M., Rose, R., Hinden, R., *Must Labour Lose?* (Harmondsworth, Penguin, 1960).

Benn, T., 'From Defeat to Victory', J. Curran (ed.), *The Future of the Left* (Cambridge, Polity Press, 1984), 148–58.

Bush, J., *Behind the Lines: East End Labour 1914–1919* (London, Merlin, 1984).

Coates, D., *The Labour Party and the Struggle for Socialism* (Cambridge, Cambridge University Press, 1975).

Coates, D., *Labour in Power? A Study of the Labour Government 1974–79 (London, Longman, 1980).*

Cook, C., and Taylor, I. (eds.), The Labour Party: An Introduction to its History, Structure and Politics (London, Longman, 1980).

Crewe, I., 'The Labour Party and the Electorate' in D. Kavanagh (ed.), *The Politics of the Labour Party* (London, Allen and Unwin, 1982), 9–50.

Crosland, C.A.R., *Can Labour Win?*, Fabian Tract 324 (London, Fabian Society, 1960).

Crosland, C.A.R., *The Future of Socialism* (London, Cape, 2nd edn. 1980).

Crossman, R., *The Diaries of a Cabinet Minister*, vol. 1 (London, Hamilton and Cape, 1975).

Curran, J. (ed.), *The Future of the Left* (Cambridge, Polity Press, 1984).

Dowse, R., *Left in the Centre: The Independent Labour Party 1893–1940* (London, Longman, 1966).

Drucker, H.M., *Doctrine and Ethos in the Labour Party* (London, Allen and Unwin, 1979).

Dunleavy, P., and Husbands, C., *British Democracy at the Crossroads* (London, Allen and Unwin, 1985).

Foot, M., *Aneurin Bevan* vols. i and ii (St Albans, Paladin, 1979).

Foote, G., *The Labour Party's Political Thought: A History* (London, Croom Helm, 1985).

Heath, A., Jowell, R., and Curtice, J., *How Britain Votes* (Oxford, Pergamon Press, 1985).

Hindess, B., *The Decline of Working Class Politics* (London, MacGibbon and Kee, 1971).

Hindess, B., 'Marxism and Parliamentary Democracy' A. Hunt (ed.), *Marxism and Democracy* (London, Lawrence and Wishart, 1980), 21–55.

Hindess, B., *Parliamentary Democracy and Socialist Politics* (London, Routledge and Kegan Paul, 1983).

Hinton, J., *Labour and Socialism: A History of the British Labour Movement 1867–1974* (Brighton, Wheatsheaf, 1983).

Jupp, J., *The Radical Left in Britain 1931–41* (London, Cass, 1982).

Kavanagh, D. (ed.), *The Politics of the Labour Party* (London, Allen and Unwin, 1982).

McKibbon, R., *The Evolution of the Labour Party 1910–1924* (Oxford, Oxford University Press, 1974).

Miliband, R., *Parliamentary Socialism: A Study in the Politics of Labour* (London, Merlin, 2nd edn. 1973).

Miliband, R., *Marxism and Politics* (Oxford, Oxford University Press, 1977).

Miliband, R., *Capitalist Democracy in Britain* (Oxford, Oxford University Press, 1982).

Pimlott, B., *Labour and the Left in the 1930s* (Cambridge, Cambridge University Press, 1977).

Sharpe, L.J., 'Labour and the Geography of Inequality: A Puzzle', D. Kavanagh (ed.), *The Politics of the Labour Party* (London, Allen and Unwin, 1982), 135–70.

Tatchell, P., *The Battle for Bermondsey* (London, Heretic Books, 1983).

Taylor, I., 'Ideology and Policy', C. Cook and I. Taylor (eds.), *The Labour Party: An Introduction to its History, Structure and Politics* (London, Longman, 1980) 1–32.

Thompson, P., *Socialists, Liberals and Labour: The Struggle for London 1885–1914* (London, Routledge and Kegan Paul, 1967).

Turner, J.E., *Doorstep Politics in London* (London, Macmillan, 1978).

Whitley, P., *The Labour Party in Crisis* (London, Methuen, 1983).

Wilson, H., *Selected Speeches* (Harmondsworth, Penguin, 1964).

Warde, E., *Consensus and Beyond: The Development of Labour Party Strategy since the Second World War* (Manchester, Manchester University Press, 1982).

Wyncoll, P., *The Nottingham Labour Movement 1880–1939* (London, Lawrence and Wishart, 1985).

LOCAL GOVERNMENT AND COLLECTIVE PROVISION

Alexander, A., *The Politics of Local Government* (London, Longman, 1982).

Bealey, F., Blondel, J., and McCann, W.P., *Constituency Politics* (London, Faber, 1965).

Birch, A.H., *Small Town Politics* (London, Oxford University Press, 1959).

Blunket, D. and Green, G., *Building from the Bottom: The Sheffield Experience*, Fabian Tract 491 (London, Fabian Society, 1983).

Blunkett, D. and Jackson, K., *Democracy in Crisis* (Hogarth Press, London, 1987).

Boddy, M. and Fudge, C. (eds.), *Local Socialism* (London, Macmillan, 1984).

Cawson, A., *Corporatism and Welfare: Social Policy and State Intervention in Britain* (London, Heinemann, 1982).

Cockburn, C., *The Local State* (London, Pluto, 1977). 57.

Davies, E., *The Evangelistic Bureaucrat* (London, Tavistock, 1972).

Dearlove, J., *The Politics of Policy in Local Government: The Making and Maintenance of Public Policy in the Royal Borough of Kensington and Chelsea* (Cambridge, Cambridge University Press, 1973).

Dearlove, J., *The Reorganisation of British Local Government* (Cambridge, Cambridge University Press, 1979).

Dunleavy, P., 'The Urban Basis of Political Alignment: Social Class, Domestic Property Ownership and State Intervention in Consumption Processes', *British Journal of Political Science*, vol. 9 (1979), 409–43.

Dunleavy, P., *The Politics of Mass Housing in Britain 1945–75: A Study of Corporate Power and Professional Influence in the Welfare State* (Oxford, Clarendon Press, 1981).

Dunleavy, P., 'The Limits to Local Government', M. Boddy and C. Fudge (eds.), *Local Socialism* (London, Macmillan, 1984), 49–52.

Forest, R., 'Residualisation and Council Housing: Aspects of the Changing Social Relations of Housing Tenure', *Journal of Social Policy* vol. 12, 4, 453–68.

Goss, S., 'Women's Initiatives in Local Government', M. Boddy and C. Fudge (eds.), *Local Socialism* (London, Macmillan, 1984), 109–33.

Gray, F., 'Consumption in Council House Management', S. Merrett (ed.), *State Housing in Britain* (London, Routledge and Kegan Paul, 1979), 196–232.

Griffith, J.A.G., *Central Departments and Local Authorities* (London, Allen and Unwin, 1966).

Gyford, J., *Local Politics in Britain* (London, Croom Helm, 1976).

Gyford, J. and James, M., *National Parties and Local Politics* (London, Allen and Unwin, 1983).

Gyford, J., *The Politics of Local Socialism* (London, Allen and Unwin, 1985).

Hampton, W., *Democracy and Community* (London, Oxford University Press, 1970).

Harloe, M. and Lebas, E., *City, Class and Capital* (London, Edward Arnold, 1981).

Harloe, M. (ed.), *New Perspectives in Urban Change and Conflict* (London, Heinemann Educational Books, 1981).

Hepworth, N.P., *The Finance of Local Government* (London, Allen and Unwin, 1976).

Hoggett, P. and Hambleton, R., *Decentralisation and Democracy* (Bristol, SAUS, 1987).

Jones, G.W., *Borough Politics* (London, Macmillan, 1969).

Judge, K., Smith, J. and Taylor-Gooby, P., 'Public Opinion and the Privatisation of Welfare: Some Theoretical Implications', *Journal of Social Policy*, vol. 12. (1983), 469–90.

Keith-Lucas, B., *The English Local Government Franchise: A Short History* (Oxford, Basil Blackwell, 1952).

Keith-Lucas, B. and Richards, P.G., *A History of Local Government in the 20th Century* (London, Allen and Unwin, 1978).

Lowe, S., *Urban Social Movements: The City After Castells* (London, Macmillan, 1986).

Merrett, S., *State Housing in Britain* (London, Routledge and Kegan Paul, 1979).

Midwinter, A., *The Politics of Local Spending* (Edinburgh, Mainstream, 1984).

Mishra, R., *The Welfare State in Crisis* (Brighton, Wheatsheaf, 1984).

Newton, K., *Second City Politics* (Oxford, Clarendon Press, 1976).

Offe, K., 'Crisis of Crisis Management: Elements of a Political Crisis Theory', *International Journal of Politics*, vol. 6. 930 (1976), 29–67.

Offe, K., 'Some Contradictions of the Modern Welfare State' in *Critical Social Policy*, vol. 2. 2 (Autumn 1982), 7–16.

Parkinson, M., *Liverpool on the Brink* (Policy Journals, 1985).

Parkinson, M., *Reshaping Local Government* (Oxford, Transaction Books, 1987).

Pemberton, A., 'Marxism and Social Policy: A Critique of the "Contradictions of Welfare"', *Journal of Social Policy* vol. 12.3 (July 1983), 289–308.

Redlich, J., and Hirst, F.W., *Local Government in England* (Macmillan, London, 1903).

Rhodes, G., *The Government of London: The Struggle for Reform* (London, Weidenfeld and Nicolson, 1970).

Rhodes, G. (ed.), *The New Government of London: The First Five Years* (London, LSE, 1972).

Rhodes, R.A.W., *Control and Power in Central–Local Relations* (Farnborough, Gower, 1981).

Rhodes, R.A.W., 'Power, Dependence, Theories of Central Relations: A Critical Assessment' in M. Goldsmith (ed.), *New Research in Central–Local Relations* (Farnborough, Gower, 1986).

Robson, W.A., *The Government and Misgovernment of London* (London, Allen and Unwin, 2nd edn. 1948).

Robson, W.A., *Local Government in Crisis* (London, Allen and Unwin, 1966).

Saunders, P., *Urban Politics* (Harmondsworth, Penguin, 1979).

Smallwood, F., *Greater London: The Politics of Metropolitan Reform* (New York, Bobbs-Merrill, 1965).

Sharpe, L.J. and Newton, K., *Does Politics Matter* (Oxford, Clarendon Press, 1984).

Stewart, J. *Local Government: The Conditions of Local Choice* (London, Allen and Unwin, 1983).

Taylor-Gooby, P., 'The New Right and Social Policy', *Critical Social Policy*, vol. 1.1 (Summer 1981), 18–31.

Young, K., *Local Politics and the Rise of the Party* (Leicester, Leicester University Press, 1975).

Index